The Art of Netw Architecture

MW00835590

Russ White, CCIE No. 2635

Denise Donohue, CCIE No. 9566

Cisco Press

800 East 96th Street

Indianapolis, Indiana 46240 USA

The Art of Network Architecture

Russ White, CCIE No. 2635
Denise Donohue, CCIE No. 9566

Copyright© 2014 Cisco Systems, Inc.

Published by:
Cisco Press
800 East 96th Street
Indianapolis, IN 46240 USA

Printed in the United States of America

First Printing April 2014

Library of Congress Control Number: 2014932356

ISBN-13: 978-1-58714-375-5

ISBN-10: 1-58714-375-5

Warning and Disclaimer

This book is designed to provide information about the architecture aspects of network design. Every effort has been made to make this book as complete and as accurate as possible, but no warranty or fitness is implied.

The information is provided on an "as is" basis. The authors, Cisco Press, and Cisco Systems, Inc. shall have neither liability nor responsibility to any person or entity with respect to any loss or damages arising from the information contained in this book or from the use of the discs or programs that may accompany it.

The opinions expressed in this book belong to the authors and are not necessarily those of Cisco Systems, Inc.

Trademark Acknowledgments

All terms mentioned in this book that are known to be trademarks or service marks have been appropriately capitalized. Cisco Press or Cisco Systems, Inc., cannot attest to the accuracy of this information. Use of a term in this book should not be regarded as affecting the validity of any trademark or service mark.

Special Sales

For information about buying this title in bulk quantities, or for special sales opportunities (which may include electronic versions; custom cover designs; and content particular to your business, training goals, marketing focus, or branding interests), please contact our corporate sales department at corpsales@pearsoned.com or (800) 382-3419.

For government sales inquiries, please contact governmentsales@pearsoned.com.

For questions about sales outside the U.S., please contact international@pearsoned.com.

Feedback Information

At Cisco Press, our goal is to create in-depth technical books of the highest quality and value. Each book is crafted with care and precision, undergoing rigorous development that involves the unique expertise of members from the professional technical community.

Readers' feedback is a natural continuation of this process. If you have any comments regarding how we could improve the quality of this book, or otherwise alter it to better suit your needs, you can contact us through email at feedback@ciscopress.com. Please make sure to include the book title and ISBN in your message.

We greatly appreciate your assistance.

Publisher: Paul Boger

Associate Publisher: Dave Dusthimer

Business Operation Manager, Cisco Press: Jan Cornelssen

Executive Editor: Brett Bartow

Managing Editor: Sandra Schroeder

Senior Development Editor: Christopher Cleveland

Senior Project Editor: Tonya Simpson

Copy Editor: Barbara Hacha

Technical Editors: Mark Cloud, Peter Welcher

Editorial Assistant: Vanessa Evans

Book Designer: Gary Adair

Cover Designer: Mark Shirar

Composition: Mary Sudul

Indexer: Erika Millen

Proofreader: Debbie Williams

Americas Headquarters	Asia Pacific Headquarters	Europe Headquarters
Cisco Systems, Inc.	Cisco Systems (USA) Pte. Ltd.	Cisco Systems International BV
San Jose, CA	Singapore	Amsterdam, The Netherlands

Cisco has more than 200 offices worldwide. Addresses, phone numbers, and fax numbers are listed on the Cisco Website at **www.cisco.com/go/offices**.

CCDE, CCENT, Cisco Eos, Cisco HealthPresence, the Cisco logo, Cisco Lumin, Cisco Nexus, Cisco StadiumVision, Cisco TelePresence, Cisco WebEx, DCE, and Welcome to the Human Network are trademarks; Changing the Way We Work, Live, Play, and Learn and Cisco Store are service marks; and Access Registrar, Aironet, AsyncOS, Bringing the Meeting To You, Catalyst, CCDA, CCDP, CCIE, CCIP, CCNA, CCNP, CCSP, CCVP, Cisco, the Cisco Certified Internetwork Expert logo, Cisco IOS, Cisco Press, Cisco Systems, Cisco Systems Capital, the Cisco Systems logo, Cisco Unity, Collaboration Without Limitation, EtherFast, EtherSwitch, Event Center, Fast Step, Follow Me Browsing, FormShare, GigaDrive, HomeLink, Internet Quotient, IOS, iPhone, iQuick Study, IronPort, the IronPort logo, LightStream, Linksys, MediaTone, MeetingPlace, MeetingPlace Chime Sound, MGX, Networkers, Networking Academy, Network Registrar, PCNow, PIX, PowerPanels, ProConnect, ScriptShare, SenderBase, SMARTnet, Spectrum Expert, StackWise, The Fastest Way to Increase Your Internet Quotient, TransPath, WebEx, and the WebEx logo are registered trademarks of Cisco Systems, Inc. and/or its affiliates in the United States and certain other countries.

All other trademarks mentioned in this document or website are the property of their respective owners. The use of the word partner does not imply a partnership relationship between Cisco and any other company. (0812R)

About the Authors

Russ White, CCIE No. 2635, is a principal engineer in the IPOS team at Ericsson. He has worked in routing protocols and routed network design for the past 15 years. Russ has spoken at Cisco Live, Interop, LACNOG, and other global industry venues. He is actively involved in the IETF and the ISOC, has co-authored more than 30 software patents in the area of network protocols, and has co-authored nine books in the area of network protocols, design, and architecture. He holds a Master of Information Technology in Network Design and Architecture from Capella University and a Master of Christian Ministry in Christian literature from Shepherds Theological Seminary.

Denise Donohue, CCIE No. 9566 (Routing and Switching), is a senior solutions architect with Chesapeake NetCraftsmen. Denise has worked with computer systems since the mid-1990s, focusing on network design since 2004. During that time she has designed for a wide range of networks, private and public, of all sizes, across most industries. Denise has also authored or co-authored many Cisco Press books covering data and voice networking technologies and spoken at Cisco Live and other industry events.

About the Technical Reviewers

Mark Cloud is a senior network engineer for The Walt Disney Company. As a member of the Enterprise Engineering Group, Mark carries broad responsibilities for the Disney Global Network with focus on the Core WAN, the routing plane, and address space management. Mark also has architectural oversight over DNS and DHCP services. In his long tenure at Disney and former subsidiary Vista-United Telecommunications, Mark has helped build and support everything from two-wire teletype feeds, multipoint analog data circuits, carrier transmission gear, early generation bridges and multiprotocol routers, to the current high-performance IP routing technologies linked by carrier MPLS and multi-gigabit WAN technologies that are in wide deployment today. Mark holds an Associate of Arts in Music from Polk Community College and a Bachelor of Science in Computer Information Services from Florida Southern College.

Dr. Peter J. Welcher is a principal consultant heading up the data center practice for Chesapeake NetCraftsmen, a Cisco Gold partner focused on providing high-end network, unified communications, and data-center consulting services. Pete is CCIE R&S No. 1773, has CCIP certification, and is a Cisco Champion. Over the years Pete has consulted on network architecture and design with many organizations, both large and small. He continues doing network architecture, design, and migration planning, both pre- and post-sales, as well as network assessments and other consulting tasks. He had a major role in developing version 2.0 of the Cisco courses for the CCDA and CCDP certifications and did tech review for the 2.1 Cisco Press book by John Tiso. Pete leads and coordinates a team doing infrastructure and data center consulting. Pete has taught Nexus classes via FireFlyEducate. He has presented on various topics at U.S. Cisco Live events since about 2005, and previously taught a number of the Cisco R&S courses. Pete blogs and tweets and has technically reviewed a number of Cisco Press books.

Dedications

Russ White: I would like to dedicate this book to my beautiful wife, my two beautiful daughters, to Dr. Doug Bookman, and the folks at Shepherds Theological Seminary. Finally, to God, who provides me with the energy and skills to write; may I use the skills He has given with wisdom and to His glory.

Denise Donohue: This book is dedicated to my husband, who carries on without me when I'm writing, to my dogs, Buddy and Raleigh, who keep me company during the long hours at the computer, and to Jesus Christ, who is the solid rock in this constantly changing sea.

Acknowledgments

Russ White: To Alvaro Retana, Don Slice, James Ng, Denise Fishburne, Danny McPherson, Donnie Savage, and all those I've worked with over the years at Cisco, Verisign, VCE, and Ericsson—thanks for taking the time and trouble to help me learn the many different aspects of network design and architecture. Without the help and guidance of mentors and sounding boards, I wouldn't have a clue about how to design a network.

To my children—thanks for the insanity I've inherited. A little insanity is useful when dealing with something as strange as network architecture.

To Denise Donohue—thanks for sticking with this project. Books are always a bigger project than they seem at the beginning and a smaller project than they seem at the end.

To Brett Bartow, Chris Cleveland, and the crew at Pearson—thanks for, once again, giving me an opportunity to take what I know, add more to it, and produce something that will, I hope, influence and build the world of network engineering for years to come. Your trust and work is always appreciated.

To Pete Welcher, Mark Cloud, and all the "unofficial" reviewers—thanks for putting the time and effort into reading this book and thinking about where things didn't make sense, where they do make sense, and what needed to be done to make it better. It's always a pleasure to work with each and every one of you.

Denise Donohue: To Brett Bartow, Chris Cleveland, and the staff at Pearson—you have been more than patient as we worked to fit in authoring, day jobs, and life. I appreciate it, and want to thank you.

To Russ—Thanks for the opportunity to work on this book. It has indeed been a journey.

To the reviewers—Your work has been crucial to creating an understandable and useful book.

To the people at all the networks I've worked with over the years—I've tried to distill the lessons learned (good and bad), the processes and rationales behind design decisions, and the results of our labors into something that will help others going through that same process. Any examples that sound familiar to you are strictly a coincidence, honest!

Contents at a Glance

Contents

Command Syntax Conventions

The conventions used to present command syntax in this book are the same conventions used in the IOS Command Reference. The Command Reference describes these conventions as follows:

- **Boldface** indicates commands and keywords that are entered literally as shown. In actual configuration examples and output (not general command syntax), boldface indicates commands that are manually input by the user (such as a **show** command).

- *Italic* indicates arguments for which you supply actual values.

- Vertical bars (|) separate alternative, mutually exclusive elements.

- Square brackets ([ ]) indicate an optional element.

- Braces ({ }) indicate a required choice.

- Braces within brackets ([{ }]) indicate a required choice within an optional element.

Introduction

After a number of outages that clearly indicated a complete network redesign was in order, the vice president of a large company demanded that every network designer on the Cisco Global Escalation Team gather in a single conference room and perform the necessary work. One of the designers responded with what is bound to be the classic response to anyone who wants to nail network design down to a science. "The only problem with this plan," he said, "is there will be one person drawing, and fifteen people erasing."

This story perfectly illustrates the problems we face in defining the idea of network architecture. If you take 16 people and confine them to a room with the assignment to "define network architecture," you will have one person writing and 15 erasing. Clearly, then, we must begin this book with some definitions.

What is network architecture? What's the difference between architecture and design? Why is it an art?

What Is Network Architecture?

If you examine any corporate organization chart, you're likely to see a number of positions labeled "Architect." The title of "Architect" includes people who design buildings, people who design applications, and people who design networks. What can these three different disciplines have in common that they should all bear the same title?

A simple point of commonality is they are all concerned with the combination of systems. A building consists of air conditioning, electrical, lighting, and various other services that must all interact in some way. An application is made up of many modules that must all interact, as well as any interaction with other applications, the hardware on which the application runs, and the network across which the application runs. A network is made up of layers of protocols, the applications that run on the network, and the network hardware.

But this definition, although appealing, doesn't withstand closer scrutiny, for it is too broad to be useful. The person driving a car must manage the interaction between the brakes and the engine, both of which are complex systems; is a driver an architect because of this? Clearly the answer is no.

What else do building architects, application architects, and network architects have in common?

Defining Architecture

First, there is interaction with flow. For those who deal with physical spaces, there is traffic flow and mechanical flow. How will people and equipment get from here to there? How will their needs be met? How can groups of people be given access to priority pathways for emergencies, or to promote the most efficient use of time and resources?

For those who deal with applications and networks, the questions are the same, but the units in question are different. How does information move from place to place and state to state? How will different sorts of information or data be given priority access? These interactions define the technical requirements of a network.

Second, there is interaction with time. For those who design buildings, it is crucial to know how this particular building will be used now and also how it might be used in the future. Will it be residential or commercial space? What are the possible future uses, and how do they impact the way the building needs to be built today? Will the building be expanded? Will it be broken into smaller units?

Network designers face this challenge as well. How can you design a network to roll with the business punches, to take changes in stride? Will the network need to be expanded, broken into multiple pieces, or otherwise radically changed over time? Can the network be designed to adapt to changes in technology requirements without building up ossified layers of equipment and protocols, like so many layers of paint or so many useless wires running nowhere?

Third, and finally, there is interaction with people. Although the concept of flow involves interaction with people in the design of buildings, there is much more than just flow. Buildings have interfaces, entry areas and exit areas, common spaces, and transportation hubs. Buildings also interact with people on other levels. What does a person feel when they walk through this space or approach the building from the outside? A building's design conveys more than utility; it conveys intangibles such as prosperity, humility, strength, or subtle charm.

It might seem to the casual observer that this is where buildings and networks part company, but the casual observer is wrong. In reality, networks also have common spaces, entry points, and transportation hubs. Networks impress on their customers—both internal and external—something about the businesses that build and use them. What impression does a company's network leave? It might show that the business is conservative in its approach to technology, or that it risks being bleeding edge. Is it concerned with practical matters, using whatever works so long as it works? Or does this company embrace technology leadership?

Network architecture, then, is as much about overlapping spaces as other forms of architecture. Networks must interact with flow, time, and people. It is at this intersection that the network architect works. Throughout this book, we examine the intersection of flow, time, and people across two broadly competing and more widely understood realms: business and technology.

Get Out of the Silo

One way to view network architecture is to look at each specific area of expertise, and each piece of the network, as a silo. Over here is a data center that seems to be the center of its own universe, with its own protocols, processes, and people. Over there is the wide-area network, carrying data from continent to continent. Each of these "places in

the network," seems to be a separate entity, and it's tempting to see them as little self-contained worlds that touch only at the edges—the "interconnects."

The world of network engineering is largely to blame for this perception of networks being places with interconnects; we ride the pendulum between centralization in the data center and decentralization through local processing. As centralization sets in, the data center takes central stage in whatever form it might be called. Centralization is the most logical idea, devices connected to the network will be thin, and the world will be happy. This almost never works as promised, so it is followed by a wave of decentralization.

Just as social structures go through pushes for centralization (no one has his or her own place to work, all spaces are open spaces) and decentralization (if you want productivity, give each person his or her own office), so, too, networks go through these phases. What's the solution to these swings?

Get out of the silo.

A network is not a single thing; it is made up of many smaller parts. A network is also not a lot of smaller parts with simple and easy-to-find interconnects. It is a whole system with complexity that rises above each individual piece. Part of the challenge of this book is to combine these two, to work in the intersection of the parts and the whole, and to understand how they relate to one another and to the businesses they support.

Why Is Network Architecture an Art?

Why is network architecture—the intersection of time, flow, and people—an art? This is the simpler question to answer, and the answer can be given in a single word: elegance.

Networks not only need to work well now, they must also provide a foundation for business and transform business, provide boundaries for information and people, and yet enable collaboration. To do all these things, network designs must go beyond mechanical algorithms, and even beyond the uncertain heuristic, into the world of abstract concept, mathematical theory, and raw power.

Interaction with people is the clearest point where network architecture becomes an art. What is the perception of the network within the company? What is the perception of the technology stance beyond the company? If competitors see your network design, will they wonder why they didn't think of it, or just wonder why it works at all? If a potential partner sees your network design, will that partner see the future or the past?

All these things contribute art to the world of network architecture.

A Look Ahead

This book is laid out in several large sections. The first two sections, Chapters 1 through 3, examine the interaction between business needs and network design, the type of business information a designer needs to consider, and how to collect that information. It looks at various business challenges and how network design helps address them. Then, Chapter 4 discusses different design models.

The third section, Chapters 4 through 10, discusses concepts such as modularity, resilience, security, and management. Here we cover various ways of conceiving of a network. One of the most important problem-solving skills an architect can develop is the ability to use frameworks, or conceptual models, to understand the way something works. Virtually everyone is familiar with the seven-layer model of networks; these chapters provide you with other models and frameworks that may prove as—or more—useful over time.

The fourth section, Chapters 11 through 14, dives deeper into the structure of a network by covering various topologies—going beyond the normal rings and meshes used in most networks. It looks at network virtualization and overlay networks, routing and the design implications of routing choices, and network complexity.

Finally, Chapters 15 through 18 bring together the concepts of business requirements, design framework, and network structure in considering several specific design challenges. This section addresses the network changes brought about by increasing user mobility, working with "the cloud," software-defined networking, and changes to data center structure and usage.

A Final Word

For those readers who are technical, this book might feel like it is too much about business and not enough about technology. For those who are approaching network architecture from a business perspective, the opposite is going to seem true—there's too much technology here and not enough business. In reality, there's probably too much of both (at least it seems so, judging by fingers numb from typing), or perhaps there's not enough of either. This is going to be the nature of a book that covers such a broad cross-section of ideas that are each very deep in their own right. We've done our best to cover every topic in the world of network architecture with a depth that will enable you to understand the outlines of the problem and to know the right questions to ask.

Remember the questions.

The questions are really the key to fitting new business problems, and new technologies, into the world of network architecture.

Chapter 1

Business and Technology

Most businesses rely on at least one network for their smooth, efficient functioning. A small company that takes credit cards relies on the network or Internet to get purchases approved and recorded. Even a cash-only company relies on the bank's network when it deposits its money. Networks have become essential parts of business infrastructure, critical to business operations. Who bridges the gap between business and technology? The same person who bridges the gap between a family's needs and the design of a new house—the architect. A *network* architect develops and implements technical solutions to business problems.

This reliance on the network makes the job of the network architect more difficult in some ways and easier in others. It is more difficult in part because technology is changing. We are in a time of fast development in networking equipment and technologies. Where do you jump into that stream? Choose the wrong point and you may end up limiting the business functions down the road. Requirements change, as new technologies bring about new ways of working, and it is difficult to design for both today's needs and tomorrow's. On the other hand, the job of a network architect is easier because creating a business-centric network provides some parameters to design within. One technology may suit the business requirements better than another, making the decision process more straightforward (and more business relevant). But regardless of whether it makes the architect's job easier or more difficult, increasing reliance on the network means that good network architecture is critical to business success.

In this chapter, we discuss what information you need to determine business requirements, and how to gather that information. In later chapters, we'll address how to use the information to tailor your network design to the business requirements.

Note   In this book, we use the terms "business," "enterprise," and "company" interchangeably; the concepts covered under these terms apply equally to small enterprises, large enterprises, educational, and public agencies. All these entities are in the business of providing something to someone and want their networks to support or improve their ability to do that.

Business Drives Technology

Before an architect designs a building, he or she needs to know something about how it will be used. Will it be a professional building or a home? If it's a home, what are the needs of the family that will live there? How many bedrooms, bathrooms, and common areas will they need? Are there any special requirements, such as handicap adjustments? Likewise, before you design a network you should learn about the business functions it will support. Networks don't exist in a vacuum; they exist to perform a service, connecting people and things together. This can be as mundane as checking your friend's online status or as sublime as doctors assisting a surgery on a child's cleft palate from the other side of the world. From an operational standpoint, a well-designed and well-run network has the capability to transform how an enterprise does business. It helps you function internally as well as reach customers—and be reached by them—quickly, efficiently, and optimally.

Architects rely on business to drive the network technology, choosing the technologies and design patterns that will best fit the business requirements. But saying, "Let business drive technology," is easy. Actually doing it is another problem entirely. Determining business requirements isn't always straightforward; people don't always know or say exactly what they want, and forecasting for the future is challenging if you are in a constantly changing industry. Many IT people shrink from the thought of becoming "business-y," but to create a network that functions as a business enabler rather than a cost center, you must start with the underlying business goals and build on that. You must be able to ask the right questions about business—and understand the answers well enough to translate them into design decisions. When you have a good understanding of the business environment, you are able to choose technologies that benefit the company and design networks that move it forward. Plus, you're much more likely to get a project funded if you can solidly align your design with business initiatives! So, the first step is to learn something about the business.

The Business Environment

To learn about a company, you need to look at both the company itself (the internal environment) and the market in which it operates (the external environment). Understanding the internal environment will give you the ability to determine what technologies will help the business thrive, and design the network to support those. Looking at the external environment, the industry in which the business operates, will allow you to make an educated guess about future changes and design the network to support those also. Understanding the competitive landscape and evaluating the company against others in

the field gives you a good idea of where the industry is headed and what capabilities the business will need in order to be competitive.

If you are involved in your company's management or business decision making, you probably already know most of the information you will need. You may want to scan this section to make sure you are taking everything into account. If you are a network engineer, consultant, or architect, the following sections will help you start the process of gathering and understanding business requirements.

The Big Picture

A good place to start gathering business intelligence is with a high-level overview of the company, its goals, issues, and future direction. If you're designing for your employer or a long-time customer, you probably already have a good idea of what the company is about; otherwise, you will need to do some research. Given that architecture happens at the intersection of business and technology, you're going to need information from both sides of the house to really understand the challenges ahead.

Begin with basic information about the networking environment. How big is the company—how many users are connected to the network, how many sites, and where are they located? Answering these questions will give you a basic overview of what the network looks like right now. A corporate website might give you basic information about company locations and number of employees, but you will have to find out how large the network is from internal, rather than external, sources.

To learn about enterprise goals and future plans, you will probably need to look outside of IT. All too often, the IT staff learns about a business initiative only when they're asked to make last-minute changes to the network! Find out the corporate goals and business strategies. Look for vision statements. Learn where the company is investing its resources—its money, people, time, and technologies—because that shows what is important to them. Look for information on business initiatives planned or in progress, and ask about the drivers for those initiatives.

Some good sources for this information are the following:

- **Upper management and executives:** They are the ones who determine the company's goals and create strategies and initiatives to meet them. Although this is a great place to start, we understand that, depending on your role within the organization, it might be difficult to identify the right person and have a business-related conversation with them.

- **Line of business manager:** Managers responsible for a specific corporate business unit may be more accessible. Their departments consume IT resources as they work to achieve the company's initiatives and are frequently very aware of where IT changes could help them.

- **Corporate website(s):** Vision and goals statements are frequently on the website.

- **Press releases and articles:** Many times, initiatives, acquisitions, mergers, or divestments are announced publicly before they are widely known internally. I once told an IT manager about an article quoting the company CTO concerning an enterprise-wide video initiative. This was a done deal in the CTO's mind, but a complete surprise to the IT manager. If you are involved in network design, keep on top of what your company (or your client) says publicly.

- **Third-party analysts:** Websites and papers from groups that evaluate and report on companies can add valuable insights.

After you know the basics, gain an understanding of the future. For the internal environment, much of this is going to relate to what people expect from the technologies they interact with to do their jobs. People are able to do so much from their home computers, smartphones, and tablets. Employees expect that a corporate network will be even faster, more powerful, with more capabilities. It can be a rude awakening when faced with a company that hasn't kept pace, and whose network reflects outdated processes and technologies. It can even cost you employees as more people expect and place a high value on having the technical tools to do their jobs easily and well.

For the external environment, turn your focus to customer expectations. It is likely that the way you interact with your customers has changed in recent years in response to changes in technology and expectations. For instance, how many times have you not bought something because the website was so slow or poorly designed? Many studies have shown that even small increases in website delay result in a significant loss of sales because customers have come to expect quick service. If you learn how and where changing expectations affect the company, your network design can provide the capability to meet those expectations.

The Competition

The competitive landscape has changed for most companies in the past 10 to 15 years; gone are the days when they were competing in only a narrow geographic range. If your local store doesn't have what you want, you can go online and order it without much regard for where it's coming from. If a service doesn't require someone's physical presence, it can be provided by a competitor anywhere in the world (given the right network setup, of course). Because business is so global, it can be affected by global events, such as an earthquake or volcano halfway around the world. The ability to move with changes in the market is now a matter of gathering, processing, and understanding market data, then making changes to business plans and products very quickly. Every company is now an information company, no matter what other service it might offer, or what product it might make. When you understand the competitive forces facing a business, you can build agility into the network to minimize the effects of events outside the business's control.

Use the same sources as before, but ask different questions.

- Who are the company's biggest competitors?

- How has the competitive landscape changed in the past several years?

- Which new companies have entered the field and which have dropped out?

- What has your business done in response to those changes?

- How and where does the company interact with the information it needs to survive?

After you have this information, do some research on the competition. Find out how they are performing—are they growing, shrinking, or pretty stable? Are they profitable or struggling? If possible, find out something about the technologies used by competitors. Understanding your competitors helps you to understand what the future may hold for your company. It will also give you a basis for explaining how your design will help the business compete.

The Business Side of the Network

Notice that we have not yet mentioned anything about assessing the company's existing network from a technology perspective. Learning about the enterprise itself gives you a standard against which to measure the overall design. Until you know what the network should be doing, you don't know how well it's meeting that goal.

Technologies and Applications

Take a look at the technologies that contribute to business success and determine what other capabilities or technologies are needed or planned. Look at the applications being used. For instance, how does the company communicate? Does it rely on email, voice, or video? Are virtual desktops used? Are there a lot of remote users accessing the network? What applications are most critical for the business to do its job well? Are these technologies filling the enterprise's needs now, or do they need to expand or add capabilities? You may find that you need to recommend different technologies, which may lead to different business processes, which will, in turn, put different demands on the network and on your design.

Note   The term "applications" is used here and throughout the book in a broad sense to encompass those network-wide high-level applications that support the technologies in use.

For each application you find, ask questions such as the following to understand the requirements it places on the network.

- How well is the application working today? Are there any issues with slowness, or are there other things that might prevent the application from running optimally?

- How much data does it produce, and what type of data is it?

- Where does the data need to go? How fast does it need to get there? How important is consistency in the delivery of data?

- Does the application's traffic need to be separated from other data, or can it be mixed?

- Where in the life cycle is the application? Is it just installed, in midlife, or in the process of being replaced?

- What of the future requirements for those applications? How long will they be in use?

These types of questions allow an architect to determine just how far the network should be driven to support each application. The answers may lead to technical recommendations for changes in things such as quality of service, speeds and feeds, network topology, and virtualization. An important application that will soon be replaced might not merit a large scale redesign, whereas an important application that is just being deployed likely would.

Network Evaluation

You will want to evaluate the current state of the network. Depending on how familiar you are already with the environment, this might be as exhaustive as a complete assessment, or it might simply entail sitting back and taking a bird's-eye view of the network. You may already have a good idea of which portions of the network will need changing; if so, concentrate on those. But don't forget to gather information about all parts of the network that might be affected by a changing design or a new application.

In your evaluation, be sure to include three things:

- Profile of the current network

- Profile of the current support staff

- Profile of the current network management, monitoring, and support methods

It obviously makes sense to look at the network, but you might be wondering why you should bother to examine support staff and the network monitoring. The answer is that these may have an impact on the new network design. You may need to tailor network design to the company's ability to support it. You may need to recommend changes or additions to the current staff, or training for them. More than likely you will need to recommend changes or additions to the network management tools or processes. People have been trying to perfect network management for as long as there have been networks, yet there is almost always room for improvement.

The Network's Customers

The interface between the network and people is as important as the interface between any specific application and people. It's part of the time, flow, and people triad that's so important to going beyond design into the realm of architecture.

The "customers" of the network include employee end users (internal users) as well as customers of the business itself (external users). There are several things you need to learn about the network's customers in general. First, find out who they are (in general terms, not names and addresses!). Are they centrally located or widespread? How does the business interact with them, and how would it *like* to interact with them? How does information flow between users and systems? How hard is it for them to use the network? It's always easier to toss problems like this into someone else's court: "Data access is the responsibility of the applications folks"—but architects shouldn't participate in such games. Instead, your design should be conscious of users' willingness to interact with technology and should build around their expectations and desires.

Internal Users

When describing the internal company users, you need to consider both user endpoints and the people themselves. The front line for IT within an organization is the devices users interact with to reach the data they need to do their jobs. Desktops have different requirements than tablets do, and the location of the endpoints (static, mobile, or both) will determine the network design needed to support them. When learning about user endpoints, ask questions such as these:

- What computing environment are the users accustomed to? How well is this environment serving them and the business?

- Is there a need for real computing power at the user's end of the network, or would tablets or thin clients suffice? An increasing number of companies are moving to thin clients due to the easier management and increased security that they provide, but this means they'll need a network that can deliver the type of service these clients require.

- Are there proprietary endpoints, and are endpoints static or mobile? For example, hospitals have computers with proprietary applications on carts that might roam throughout the entire hospital. They must always be able to reach their servers and data while maintaining the security of patient information. Retailers might have static proprietary endpoints running proprietary applications, or mobile tablets with a point-of-sale application. All these require different types of network support and perhaps different network security solutions.

- Is there any compliance checking needed for endpoints to ensure they meet company policies?

Wise network architects never forget the "people" element of network design. Making changes to a network, or introducing new technologies, involves some nontechnical risks. New technologies bring a change in established processes, which may entail a change in behavior for employees and customers. A different network design might require the IT staff to learn new skills or support it differently. Change can be scary, and the prospect of scary change can derail a project, so address this early and often. Learn the current way things are done, and discuss with users how things will change. Include training for

IT staff and users in your plan. Help everyone affected understand how the advantages to them and to the business will make the risk worthwhile.

To this end, it helps to have both a technical and a nontechnical profile of the users themselves. Some of the questions the architect can ask in this space include the following:

- Are the people who use this network interested in change, or resistant? If a new system is rolled out, will they take to it quickly or take months (or years) to develop an interest?

- Who are the influential users in this company, and who are the power users? These are the people that can tell you what changes are really needed. And these are the people you will want to include in a pilot of any new network technologies.

- How do users typically manage their data? Do most users take responsibility for their own data? You may need to design in some sort of network-based backup for users who do not protect or back up their data themselves.

- Do the users travel extensively or often work from home? How important is it to replicate the "in office" work environment while users are away from their office?

- How do people within the company communicate with each other and with external partners? How well is this working for them?

External Users

The next thing you need to learn about is the company's external users, those who access enterprise resources from outside the corporate network. There are typically two types of external users: business partners and everyone else. Many companies have a business relationship with partner organizations and share a network component with them. Partner users might access applications and data held within the company, and vice versa. For example, an HVAC maintenance supplier might need to securely reach device management servers, or a food services supplier might need to check inventory. Access is sometimes given to specific servers on the inside of the network, but more frequently to a DMZ device with controlled access to the inside of the network. A network architect would evaluate partners' connectivity needs in order to choose the appropriate type and bandwidth, and to build in the appropriate security.

"Everyone else" includes those who access company resources but don't maintain a constant connection with them. They may have only an occasional business relationship with the company, such as people buying from an online reseller. Or they may be long-term customers who regularly access company data. The important thing to learn in this case is what types of users they are, how the company wants to communicate with them, and what it wants their experience to be. For instance, a high-end investment firm would likely want to maintain a high level of personal touch with its customers, so you would probably include video conferencing and a lot of personalization of customer experience into the design. Calls into a contact center would be quickly routed to an expert (or the correct auto attendant, at least). In contrast, when you or I interact with our bank, we

probably go through a standard web portal, or our calls are queued until an agent is free. Different types of customers require different types of services from the network, and thus different network designs.

Guest Users

Guest users compose a third category that falls between internal and external users. Guests usually connect to the network, but their access to enterprise resources is either controlled or denied altogether. A contractor working onsite may be allowed to log in to certain portions of the network, and may be allowed to perform only specific procedures or access specific resources. Their laptops or tablets may need to be checked for compliance with corporate policies before being granted access. Users who are true guests are typically sent directly to the Internet. If you're designing for guest users, you need to know what the company policy is toward contractors and guests. Will it be enough to use access control lists (ACL) to protect the corporate network, or will some type of virtual separation (such as Virtual Routing and Forwarding [VRF]) or a Guest VLAN be needed? A more scalable, dynamic security structure will be able to identify users and place them in groups with the correct access level.

This might seem like a lot of information to gather and, in truth, it may not all be needed at once. The amount and type of technical and business data required will depend on why you need it. What is enough for a specific project would differ from what is needed to set the technology direction for the entire company. In the long run, keeping abreast of the overall business and network environment will give you the knowledge to handle both specific initiatives and the ongoing interaction between business and technology-focused staff.

Technology Drives Business

We just spent the first part of this chapter making the point that business should drive design. Virtually every network designer in the world knows this concept. What separates the good from the great is turning the question around.

> *How does design drive the business?*

The triad of time, flow, and people make it obvious that architects should be asking this question. Not only does the flow of information impact the way the network needs to work, the way the network actually works impacts the way information is able to flow. Over time, the network's abilities and limitations affect what the company is able to do on that network. How people are able to interact with and leverage the network affects their performance, and thus the company's. So, what question can we ask here?

> *If I choose this technology, or if I use this design paradigm, what impact will it have on the business in the future?*

Quick, choose a new network WAN. If you answered "an L3VPN service," you're on the same page as a large majority of network designers (and service provider salesmen). It's cheap and it's (relatively) easy, sure, but what are the future effects of leasing a WAN

based on an MPLS service from a provider? If you can't think of any, then you need to think harder. What if the business wants to provide a virtual topology for four or five business units? What is the added complexity of providing such services over a service that's already a virtual overlay on top of a service provider's network? Will it drive up the ultimate cost? What about the service level to the business?

How about this: name a simple way to save money on network operations. If you said "outsource operations," you're on the same page as some companies. But again, you need to ask what constraints outsourcing might impose on the way the business operates. Specifically, consider the time element in network architecture. What happens, for instance, if the company decides to enter a new line of business? How quickly can you negotiate a new contract with the outsourcer, spin up the network changes, put them through an acceptance test, and get them into production? A crucial point you must remember when outsourcing is that you're assuming your business goals will match those of the outsourcer, particularly in terms of new services. An architect should not only think about these questions, but press for acceptable answers.

Is standardizing the end systems with which users can attach to the network a net positive, or a net negative? It certainly simplifies administration in many ways, but what are the negative effects? Assuming all hosts (or any other class of device) are the same can actually make it more difficult to replace these devices when the need arises. This assumption can also lead to a narrowed view of network security, leaving dangerous holes that simply aren't visible to network managers.

Thus, in every situation, the architect needs to go beyond asking how to design the network to fit the business. It's just as important to ask how the network could constrain the business, or how the presuppositions built into technical choices made today can backfire into bad business choices in the future.

Chapters 2 and 3 discuss how to apply the business information gathered in this chapter. They look at the common problems of designing for an ever-changing network and using network architecture to improve business operations. Further chapters of the book go in depth into the models and frameworks for a business-driven design.

Designing for Change

Chapter 1 discussed some of the business knowledge you need when designing a network. This chapter examines how to apply that knowledge in creating the network blueprint.

We all understand that typically families grow and shrink as children are born, mature, and leave home—but you can't assume that every family will follow the same pattern. Some will have different needs. Children could return home, perhaps bringing their own children in tow; aging parents may need a place to live for the final years of their lives; death or divorce may shrink the family; or, as in older times, the family may spread out into several houses on one large piece of property. If, like most of us, you live in a house that was designed for a limited number of family possibilities, you might find yourself needing to make structural changes to your home, or to move to a larger house, a larger piece of property, or even move to a smaller house or a smaller piece of property.

The life cycle of a company's network is similar in many ways. Although we all hope our companies will succeed and grow, the reality is this isn't always what happens in real life. Those that do grow might experience organic growth from within or might expand the business through mergers and acquisitions. Those that decline might experience an organic decrease in network use, or the company might divest itself of portions of the business. The pendulum of network centralization versus decentralization also leads to structural network changes, as does the swing between insourcing and outsourcing. Although you can't foresee or design for every possibility, you can strive to create a design that meets the current needs, yet is flexible enough to accommodate changes down the road.

Three tools are your friends when designing and managing a network in the process of change:

- Network management
- Modularity
- Simplicity

Other chapters in this book will discuss each of these three tools in depth; this chapter examines common business-related causes for changes in network design and outlines ways to address them.

Organic Growth and Decline

Organic growth or decline comes from a company's normal business activities, rather than through acquisitions or divestments. The organic growth or decline of a business could be analogous to a family's increase in grocery bills as their children grow older and eat more. Unless you pay close attention to your budget, this increase can be difficult to notice and plan for accurately, because it is gradual. It might seem like your grocery bills have doubled overnight. Similarly, as businesses add users or applications over time, the load on the network increases gradually. Unless you are watching carefully, it can seem like the network needs have changed overnight.

Changes in usage patterns can also cause organic change in network requirements. For instance, you might have deployed a wireless network solely for guest use, and then find that your employees are using it for their personal devices. Many companies are giving their employees laptops rather than desktop computers, and then find that employees don't bother connecting them to the wired LAN. Wireless printers have left the home and are becoming popular in the enterprise. This leads to growth in wireless network usage. In another example, increased employee mobility might lead to more remote users connecting via VPN, which could overload your Internet connection and also your VPN termination device. Both of these patterns could lead to a decline in usage of your wired network infrastructure as fewer devices are connecting to the wired LAN.

Good network monitoring and management can alert you to organic growth or decline and allow you to proactively adjust your design. You need to have good baseline measurements for each portion of your network and comparative measurements over time.

Another type of network growth or decline occurs as sites are added or removed from the network. This is much easier to see because the network team is (hopefully!) involved when an office is added or shut down. The effect on your overall network may be a little less apparent, however. For example, suppose you have the network shown in Figure 2-1. Your company is growing, you're adding sites, and things are going along fine, when one day a link goes down. And routing never converges.

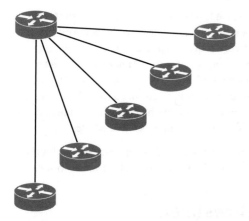

Figure 2-1 *Organic Network Growth*

This might seem like a problem with the hub router being undersized to handle the load, but it is actually a design problem. If the organic growth had been measured and planned for proactively, the network might not have failed. Network monitoring that included routing counters such as Shortest Path First (SPF) runtimes could have warned you that routing was approaching a critical limit, thus giving you time to make changes in the network.

Modularity is an important tool when you are experiencing network growth or decline. A modular design breaks the network into pieces that can easily be added or removed as requirements change. It aids in proactive planning by setting limits on module size, based on testing, best practices, and documentation. Then, with good network monitoring and measurement, the need for new modules can be predicted and planned. In the case of this example, when the topology approached a predetermined size, the company could make an intentional decision about how to respond—perhaps to build a second module such as in Figure 2-2, or increase the size of the hub router.

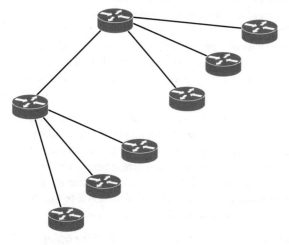

Figure 2-2 *Modular Design*

Design simplicity is another important tool. Some level of complexity is a given in networks of any size, but the more logical simplicity you can build into the network design, the better you can respond to changes in network requirements. Think of the 2:00 a.m. test—if you were awakened in the middle of the night because of a network problem and had to figure out the traffic flows in your network while you were half asleep, could you do it? During times of organic growth or decline, you might need to add or remove portions of your infrastructure. A logically simple design will help you better understand and account for the effects these changes will have on the network as a whole.

Modularity and the trade-off between network simplicity and complexity are such critical design concepts that we have devoted separate chapters to them later in this book.

Mergers, Acquisitions, and Divestments

Mergers, acquisitions, and divestments can be very disruptive to the network. When two companies merge, or when one company acquires another, their IT infrastructure must be joined in some way. Sometimes each original company maintains a portion of its network, with an area joining it to the larger company, and sometimes one company is brought completely into the fold of the other company. During divestment, a company sells or closes down a portion of its business, or spins it off into its own entity. This requires separating a part of the network and accounting for any services it may have provided to the parent company.

Mergers and acquisitions by definition involve the joining of two companies, and thus two different IT infrastructures—LAN, WAN, communications, data centers—which often reflect two different design philosophies. Frequently, there are different routing protocols, with the attendant decisions to be made about migrating to a new protocol or route redistribution. You will likely need to work out a myriad of differences, such as spending priorities, degrees of redundancy, equipment vendors, change control, and technology deployment processes. IP addressing issues can complicate network mergers. You might find IP address overlap, or just a difference in addressing philosophies, such as one company that always uses a /24 mask and another that tailors the mask to the subnet size. Readdressing entire sections of a network becomes complex and time consuming. In a best-case scenario, both networks are well documented and have good, up-to-date management data. The authors have never actually experienced this best-case scenario, though.

Good management provides information about the current state of the networks to be merged, so that proper planning can be done. Checking the documentation and filling in the gaps are among the first things that need to be done. Be prepared to conduct a network assessment if needed. Then compare your findings to current best practices and design standards to determine where changes need to be made. Don't minimize the personnel issues that a merger or acquisition brings, because there is also a need to join two different IT groups that each has a stake in its own network.

An acquisition typically involves bringing the new company in line with the existing standards and practices of the acquiring company. In a merger, you will hopefully be able

to draw from the best portions of both companies' networks to create joint standards and design practices. You might find that each network has some strong points and some weaker points. Both networks must be in line with company standards, and in a merger that might require negotiation of what those standards will be, with a creation of a new set of standards for the merged company. Find out the business requirements for the merged network. Let the requirements inform the decisions about how each portion of the network will continue to operate and what services or servers will be pulled into the larger company.

Modular design is a great help, especially during divestment, because separating a module from the rest of the network is much easier than redesigning the entire network. Modularization allows the network to be broken apart and reformed with new locations or regions, and so on. In a merger or acquisition, where one portion of the network needs to be brought in line with standard best practices, modular design reduces the amount of new design work necessary. The standards are already in place, and the effort then becomes one of bringing the new network in line with those standards. The goal is to use the same design everywhere—a "cookie cutter" approach—so there is no need to spend a lot of time and effort on one-off design problems. Additionally, modular design aids in the budget planning for network mergers and divestments—because you have a pretty good idea what the network will look like, you can determine fairly accurate budgetary costs for current and future functions.

Simplicity of design aids in mergers and acquisitions by reducing the amount of time it takes for IT staff to fully understand all components of the network. This understanding will help necessary changes to the network go more smoothly with fewer problems. It helps in designing those changes to the network so that they provide as much benefit and create as little downtime as possible. During divestments, simplicity makes removing pieces of the network much easier. It also makes troubleshooting easier by allowing a faster understanding of how the network is set up.

Centralizing Versus Decentralizing

The centralizing/decentralizing game has always been a series of pendulum swings. For a while, all servers and services were hosted in the data center; then they were all moved out to individual sites, and currently they are being brought back into data centers again. The increased bandwidth of Internet and WAN links allow the progression to extend even further to include outsourced, cloud, and hosted solutions. Changes in the location of network services have tremendous implications for network and data center design.

When servers and services are centralized, it becomes critically important that all users are able to reliably reach their data centers. This means that company locations require connections of sufficient bandwidth and reliability that users are able to perform their functions. These might be direct connections, WAN connections, or tunnels over the Internet, depending on the business requirements. Critical sites will require redundant connections; other sites may need just a primary link and a lower speed backup link. The LAN design becomes focused primarily on optimizing user traffic to and from the WAN

edge. Two exceptions to this are IP voice traffic and wireless control. You are likely to see voice traffic flows between users within the LAN, although the voice control is still typically centralized. As wireless deployments become denser, the trend is shifting away from centralized controllers to either wireless controllers on individual access switches or site-based controllers.

Tremendous advances are being made in data center design. New switches are being developed that are faster and tailored to data center needs. New technologies are being developed to deal with an unprecedented, ever-increasing amount of data and number of servers. Data center design is a topic that is critical enough to have a chapter of its own in this book—Chapter 18, "Data Center Design." For the purposes of this chapter, we would like you to understand the importance of designing your data center with as much flexibility as possible, so that it is capable of robustly supporting your business for the future. A modular design that is simple to understand and implement will help you as changes develop in data center design.

Deciding to use hosted, cloud-based, or outsourced applications, services, or data center infrastructure will change the WAN and/or Internet requirements for each of your locations. Instead of user traffic being directed to the data centers, more user traffic will be directed to external locations. Whereas hosting sites and outsourced services may have a connection into your WAN, cloud-based solutions are usually reached over the Internet. If you centralize Internet access, WAN traffic may not change much, but Internet traffic will increase. Enough cloud usage may lead to the return of local Internet access at each site. If you're outsourcing some of your applications, servers, and storage as a backup or Disaster Recovery (DR) to your production data centers, there must be a good connection between the production and the outsourced data centers to support timely data replication. Outsourced services such as network monitoring usually require a VPN to the monitoring company from every site being monitored.

Services that provide monitoring and management can be a big help in keeping your network stable and reliable, especially for small to medium companies without 24-hour IT staff. Cloud-based applications can help make your users more productive by providing anywhere/anytime access to those applications without tying up company resources to manage and maintain that constant uptime. Co-located (co-lo) or multitenant data centers have many qualities that are attractive to businesses as well. The vendors in essence divide the cost of setting up, equipping, and running multiple data centers among all their customers. This lets each individual company trade the upfront capital expenditures to build high-speed, redundant data centers, and the operating expenses to operate and maintain them, for the recurring expense of leasing those services. One big caveat around outsourcing any functionality is that this does not remove your responsibility for the security of your data and applications. Carry out your due diligence when selecting a co-lo or services provider. Find out how they protect your data at rest and in motion, what hardening they have in place, and what their track record is for response to attacks.

Good network management data can provide the measurements required to accurately judge the cost of making a change in network services or network operations. It can help you compare your current performance against the projected future performance

after the change. As you centralize servers and services or move them to the cloud, network management data can also give you a good idea of the bandwidth and other access parameters needed to optimize results. Monitoring after a network change can alert you to any needed future adjustments.

Simplicity in network design reduces the time required to move, add, or change connections and equipment. It also reduces the background time required for staff to understand and consider network policies and security when making a change to services.

For in-depth discussions of the topics covered in this chapter, see the following chapters of this book:

- Chapter 6, "Principles of Modularity"

- Chapter 7, "Applying Modularity"

- Chapter 10, "Measure Twice"

- Chapter 14, "Considering Complexity"

- Chapter 18, "Data Center Design"

Improving Business Operations

Effective network architects must be more than technical—they must have a foot in the business world also. Chapter 1 reviewed some of the business knowledge required when designing a network. This chapter examines at a high level how you can use that knowledge to create a custom network design that helps support or even improve the way the company does business. It discusses three common areas where network design and business operations intersect and impact each other:

- Workflow

- BYOD

- Business continuity

Understanding the data flows and business processes used within these three areas of your business will allow you to create a good technical solution to support the company, and also to explain that solution in terms of how it answers business needs and enables the business to improve.

Subsequent chapters in the book build on this high-level overview to provide detail on network technologies and design choices.

Workflow

One of the main criteria people use in evaluating a house is traffic flow. In designing a house, architects have to consider how it will be used, which determines how traffic will flow, which in turn should influence the design decision. For instance, a house used for frequent entertaining would need good, open paths between public areas and between the kitchen and public areas. On the other hand, a young family might want quick access between the kitchen and the children's play area. The flow within the kitchen can be just as important as the flow between the kitchen and other rooms—the path between the refrigerator, stove, and sink is described as a "magic triangle," which should be no more

than a few steps along each side. The right house design can make its occupants' lives easier and improve communication among the occupants.

Similarly, network design should take into account how traffic needs to flow within the company—who talks to whom? What applications are in use? Where is quick access needed? The right design can make business processes easier and improve communication within the business. For this reason, you need to have at least a high-level understanding of your business processes and workflows before beginning the network design. Additionally, it will help to know whether any changes in process are planned or being considered.

Take, for example, the case of a retail company with many fairly small stores. Sales information is uploaded to a couple of data centers, and stock information is downloaded from these same data centers. On the surface you might think that a hub-and-spoke WAN would serve this company well, with hubs located at the data centers and perhaps the company headquarters. If the status quo is fine, the surface might be an appropriate place to stay. But further investigation might reveal the potential for an improvement in processes, leading to a change in workflow and thus a different network design. Consider the case of a company that sells some specialty items. It is expensive to train and place experts on every item in every local store. However, if staff could quickly locate someone with the needed expertise and get them on the phone with a customer, sales would likely improve. Adding video would let the expert demonstrate how to use the items, giving terrific customer service and resulting in even higher sales. With these changes, the expert staff can be physically located wherever is best—perhaps at higher-volume stores, at a call center, or even at home. These changed information flow requirements would probably drive the network design from hub and spoke to full mesh connectivity, with support for QoS for voice and video. By using technology to drive efficiency, IT has also gone from supporting the current business processes to enabling improvements in the business, which would allow the company to stay one step ahead of the competition and increase its market share.

Matching Data Flow and Network Design

As you can see, matching your network design to the flow of data is not just a matter of "paving where the grass is worn out." The goal is to create a network that is customized to support and optimize your business processes now and also into the foreseeable future. This can also help you control network growth and costs by providing a blueprint to follow. One place to start your flow analysis is by examining the consumption of data within the company. Who uses what data? Where is that data located? How is it obtained? Information from the network management software can help you uncover traffic patterns (assuming that software, and information, exists) but don't just stop there. Look at how existing data flows fit with best practices and any standards the business has established. Check for outliers—such as a big flow to one legacy server in a remote site that should have been decommissioned or moved to a data center long ago. What you learn about current data flows can be merged with the current business process information to help determine any needed changes in flow patterns or network design.

Data flows can be broken into three general categories:

- Person to person
- Person to machine
- Machine to machine

We'll examine each of these, and their network design implications, in the following sections.

Person-to-Person Communication

This is usually real-time or near real-time communication, such as phone calls, interactive video, or instant messaging. Voice and video are sensitive to latency and drops and thus require QoS on the network; instant messaging is less so. Voice and instant messaging are low-bandwidth applications, whereas video is higher bandwidth and typically bursty. Video may need multicast to be configured.

The people communicating could be dispersed throughout the network, so full-mesh WAN connectivity is needed to facilitate this. For best performance, the WAN solution also needs to support QoS. Don't forget about the control traffic that facilitates this communication—be sure to provide bandwidth and appropriate QoS for that traffic. Call/ messaging management servers need to be highly available, redundant, and reachable by every user. You may want to provide local backup call-control solutions for remote offices in case the WAN link goes down. Management applications that monitor voice and video quality will help you proactively respond to degradation in network service for these data flows.

Person-to-Machine Communication

This category includes users accessing centralized data and applications, such as pulling data from, or saving data to, company servers or storage devices. Data flow for person-to-machine communication is typically hub and spoke, with data centers as the hubs. Spokes (users) may be at company sites, partner sites, or coming in over the Internet. Data centers may be company owned and managed or hosted in the cloud. In the case of web servers especially, users may not even be affiliated with the company.

One example of person-to-machine communication is a virtual desktop infrastructure (VDI) such as VMware's View or Citrix's XenDesktop. These provide an image or set of applications that exist only on company servers and must be downloaded through a LAN or VPN connection. When using VDI, network bandwidth along with storage and capacity must all be sized appropriately. VDI can be either server-based or client-based. If the image stays on the server, users cannot work if the image is inaccessible, so both good network connectivity and server redundancy are critical. Latency must be low enough to give users the most "desktop-like" experience possible. The amount of traffic varies depending on what users are doing on their VDI clients. If the image is downloaded to the client device, users can work offline, but the initial download is fairly large.

You may want to implement WAN optimization to reduce the bandwidth load for both types of VDI.

Not all person-to-machine communication is as time critical as server-based VDI. If users can't upload a file, back up their computers, or download a virus patch, they can usually retry later. But if an ecommerce website is unavailable, it can cost the company money. Or a critical file that can't be downloaded can interfere with business function. Know your application needs and traffic-flow patterns, and tailor your design to support them.

A highly available, resilient data center with fast internal communication is, of course, important for all types of user-to-machine communication. Chapter 18, "Data Center Design," goes into further depth but, at a high level, Internet bandwidth and link redundancy into the data center is important for VPN, web, and remote VDI users. Within the data center, build in security between users and servers, and between front-end DMZ servers and back-end database or other servers. Data center security is a balance between policy and throughput; avoid creating bottlenecks at your policy points—use virtual security or policy devices, use data screening techniques that can be done at line speed, or at least be aware of the actual measured throughput of any security devices you use in the data center.

Machine-to-Machine Communication

Machine-to-machine data flows are growing rapidly within most businesses. Within this category you typically think of the traditional data backup between computers/servers and storage devices, as well as data replication between storage systems. Network engineers used to be able to ignore storage traffic—that "other" team ran fiber channel from each server to their own fiber switch that connected to the storage and never touched the "real" network. Those days are gone. The popularity of Fibre Channel over Ethernet (FCoE) and iSCSI means that storage traffic is running on your network, over your switches. Replication traffic between data centers traverses your network, along with virtual servers moving between physical servers and between data centers. Server, storage, application, and network teams all need to learn a little bit about each other's worlds and work together on data center design.

Speaking of data replication and backup, it's important to understand the amount of data that will travel between users, servers, and storage, and the times of day this data will be sent. When planning the links between data centers, and between offices and data centers, take into account the volume of data and the way storage data will be replicated. For instance, data that is backed up asynchronously, such as at night, will take high sustained bandwidth during the backup period. Data that is synchronized in real time will need less bandwidth, but that bandwidth must be constantly available and guaranteed.

Another, even faster growing, type of machine-to-machine communication is between other kinds of networked devices—sensors whose job it is to gather information. That information is then transmitted to or read by other devices that use the data to make decisions or issue instructions to other machines.

One example of this is an airport that uses RFID-embedded baggage tags linked to your flight and destination information. RFID readers tell the automated system to route your luggage onto the correct conveyor belts as it goes through security checking and ultimately on to the loading area for your airplane. This minimizes human error in potentially misrouting a suitcase. It also provides tracking data for bags as they pass each RFID reader, helping to minimize loss.

Another example comes from the medical field. Patients may use monitors in the hospital or even at home for critical information such as their heart rate, blood pressure, or blood sugar. These monitors then report the results back to an application that records them in the patient's electronic medical record and that can alert the patient's caregiver for values outside of normal ranges.

Sensor traffic is usually low bandwidth and small packets. It could come from either fixed or mobile locations, but usually is bound for static sites. It may seem as though data traffic patterns are fairly straightforward—just from sensor or device to data center. But this is another place where it is important to understand the process. The data may travel from sensor to collector to data center, but it may then be acted on by a server in the data center that sends out an alert to someone remote, perhaps as a text or email. That data may also trigger an instruction back to the host device, perhaps something like a medical refrigerator that needs to adjust its temperature. Make sure you understand all the various traffic flows so that your design supports them.

Bringing It All Together

Most networks include all three types of data flows, which add to the complexity of the network design. Most companies find that they need full-mesh WAN connectivity between sites with employees at them, to allow for person-to-person communication. They frequently choose an MPLS or Ethernet WAN, or dynamic Internet tunnels for this. Some companies route interdata center traffic through their WAN; others implement dedicated high-bandwidth links between data centers to accommodate backup and replication traffic. If your company has unmanned locations that primarily monitor and report on the operation of onsite equipment, you may need only small bandwidth links. The decision about whether to make these point-to-point links or rings connecting into the data centers or aggregation sites, or part of the corporate multiaccess WAN, frequently comes down to cost.

Using the services of a cloud provider may change where your data travels, but it does not change the basic premise of "know your flows." How will you access those cloud services? You might choose a connection from your WAN, dedicated links perhaps from your data centers, a VPN over the Internet, or just a secure browser session over the Internet, depending on your needs. For example, a cloud-based application that users access at work may lead you to extend the company WAN to a provider site or set up a "split tunnel" arrangement where a single link from each office gives access to both the WAN and the Internet. Or you may choose to rely on your existing corporate Internet connection, depending on the criticality of the application and the amount of anticipated traffic. On the other hand, using a cloud provider to back up your data would call for

a more secure and higher-bandwidth connection. In that case, you may opt for either a WAN connection to the provider or a VPN over the Internet.

A good understanding of your traffic flows and how they work together with your business processes will help you make the best design decisions.

BYOD

Bring Your Own Device (BYOD) has become a catchphrase that includes so much more than its original meaning. It was originally driven by user desire to use their smartphones, tablets, or personal laptops at work—or at least to access some company applications or data, such as email, on those devices. But it has evolved to more of a "Choose Your Own Device" movement that implies the capability to be mobile both within the enterprise network and outside it. Users want to access company resources with the most appropriate device at the time. Companies, on the other hand, want to control and protect access to resources. Loss of company and customer data are major concerns for those considering BYOD, and maintaining data security is a major success criterion for a BYOD implementation. As with most things, there is a trade-off.

The business case for BYOD is mixed. Employee-owned devices can actually wind up costing more when you consider no longer being able to buy equipment and cellular plans at bulk prices (assuming the company reimburses employees for at least some of the device costs), the likely need to upgrade the corporate wireless network, and the additional management and security resources that will be required. On the other hand, there are benefits in terms of increased productivity, increased worker satisfaction, reduced help desk support, and the ability to work remotely in case of an emergency. In fact, multiple surveys tell us that for a majority of companies, the main driver for BYOD is not cost reduction, but employee satisfaction. Employee mobility and productivity are also important drivers.

At this point, it's pretty futile to try to prevent the use of personal devices completely, unless you require a very high level of security and have a closed network. So from a design standpoint, the main questions to ask are: Which aspects of BYOD will provide the most benefit? How does that, then, impact my network design?

BYOD Options

How people implement the different aspects of BYOD varies greatly. Almost everyone expects to at least get work email on his or her smartphone. Beyond that, at its most basic, companies may provide Internet access for guests or allow company employees to get on the guest network with their personal devices. This has become almost an expected level of access; it can greatly increase customer and employee satisfaction and can even be used for business purposes. Consider a hospital patient, the parents of a new baby, or a sick child, and think how Internet access could make their time in the hospital much more pleasant, plus increase satisfaction scores for the hospital itself. Stores that offer Internet access not only provide a way for you to get more information on their

products, they can use location information to track the displays you view or the departments in which you spend time, and then tailor offers or coupons based on your interests.

This raises a couple of network design issues:

- **Separation of Internet and internal traffic:** The most basic, if most expensive, way to do this is to have a guest SSID that sends traffic to a guest VLAN that is routed to a separate Internet connection. Sometimes a Virtual Routing and Forwarding (VRF) instance is used to separate guest traffic. A slightly more involved solution requires login to a guest portal, which then allows that device to access the guest SSID. One advantage of this solution is that you can require guests to agree to an acceptable use policy that limits the company's legal liability in case of a misbehaving user. Most companies don't need a separate guest Internet connection or physical infrastructure. Most business requirements can be met by routing guest traffic to a separate firewall interface—with or without VRFs—and then disallowing that traffic to "hairpin" back into your internal network. This lets you aggregate Internet bandwidth for economies of scale and administration, plus save the cost of a dedicated LAN infrastructure.

- **Network bandwidth:** With an increase in devices on your network comes an increase in demands on network bandwidth. Typically, both guest and internal traffic use the same wireless network. Even if guest and internal traffic are in separate VLANs or VRFs, they travel through a shared LAN to reach the Internet edge. Be sure to plan for the additional bandwidth. Quality of Service (QoS) can be used to control guest bandwidth and ensure enough for internal traffic.

The next level of BYOD is to separate guest traffic but also provide some level of access to company resources for authorized users. That access could range from just email or the ability to print, to full functionality as if you were using a corporate-owned device on the LAN. This is the point where legal, security, and access control issues typically raise their head. Nobody wants a virus-infected laptop connecting to the network. The same with jailbroken phones or devices that might be infected with malware. No users want their smartphones or tablets seized as evidence in a legal case because they contain company files, or completely erased when they leave the company. Data loss prevention becomes a real issue, because email that might contain sensitive information now sits on a device that can be easily lost or stolen. But how do you control that? And how are you going to authenticate users, then make sure they can access only the company resources they should? Some frequently used solutions include the following:

- **Authentication:** This is typically against a centralized database such as Active Directory (AD) to identify users and place them in groups. Access to resources can be controlled on a per-group basis. One implication of this is that you need to make sure the authentication database is highly available, reliably reachable, and accurate.

- **Tracking:** After users are authenticated and placed in a group, how do you track their traffic to make sure they're able to reach the appropriate resources and are blocked from inappropriate resources? One option is to place them in VLANs by group, and then use access lists to filter by address. A more scalable option is to use

software that can tag traffic by security group and network equipment that can read and filter on those tags.

- **Mobile Device Managers (MDM):** Whereas authentication and tracking concentrate on users, MDMs provide the tools to find out information about the mobile devices themselves—phones and tablets. For instance, you can learn if a phone has been jailbroken, if a device has a password or PIN code, and what OS version it has. Some authentication solutions can interact with MDMs to prevent a device from accessing company resources unless it meets standards set in the MDM. For instance, you may want to require a PIN code on a smartphone before allowing it to access email. MDMs can also remotely find, access, configure, and erase devices.

- **Posture Assessment:** To help secure the network, companies may set policies outlining minimum levels of settings, such as antivirus or OS patch level. This may entail a scan of the computer's registry when it tries to get on the network, or a small client that's installed on the machine and tracks posture status. Enforcing very rigid posture requirements can become difficult and time consuming in a large network. Track posture without enforcing it for a while until you get most people into compliance—it will make your life much easier.

Note Authentication, tracking, mobile device management, and posture assessment are functional areas that may be combined in the same software solution.

- **Virtualization:** One way to prevent company information from being obtained from a stolen laptop or mobile device is keep it off the device altogether. A virtual desktop infrastructure (VDI) is one way to do this. Because applications and data are never on the device itself, a lost or stolen laptop or mobile device presents less of a security risk, and terminated employees can be prevented from downloading data before they leave. This also allows IT to control the desktop image and applications used. A similar solution is an SSL VPN that uses a temporary memory space that is then erased when the VPN terminates. Some MDMs can create a separate container on mobile devices for email or other corporate data. That container can then be wiped if necessary without erasing all the device apps and content.

All these solutions present specific challenges to a network designer. Because they rely on users being able to reach security-related servers, these must be always reachable and sized to handle the load. The LAN and WAN networks must support the bandwidth and QoS needed. Virtual desktops place an additional load on your data center network, servers, and storage, as well as network requirements for latency and bandwidth. Scalability is also a concern; devices proliferate, and your solutions must be scalable to handle the increasing load without becoming a management nightmare. Pay attention to "bump in the wire" devices such as IPS or web anti-malware equipment that tend to be ignored until you have to troubleshoot a traffic flow through them. Manageable versions that give you useful data such as throughput, CPU, memory use, and dropped packets will help verify that they are able to handle the load.

BYOD Design Considerations

No matter where you fall on the BYOD/CYOD/Mobility spectrum, you will need to address a few problems common to all solutions. The first is IP addressing. Think of all the wireless enabled devices in your network, each one looking for an IP address. Although limiting your DHCP scope is a way to limit the number of guest devices that can connect, it is likely to increase support calls and decrease user satisfaction when people are not able to connect. Make sure you plan adequately sized DHCP scopes, and allow for the additional traffic traveling to and from the DHCP servers. Also make sure your servers are sized correctly and placed in optimal locations.

VLAN planning goes along with planning your IP addressing. Will you have separate guest VLANs per Layer 3 boundaries, just as you have separate user VLANs, or will you set up one guest VLAN that spans the entire network? The authors hope you choose the former! VRF planning is similar to this. A VRF provides separation at Layer 3 similar to the way a VLAN provides separation at Layer 2. Guest users are still associated with a VLAN at the point where they enter the network, so VLAN planning must still be done. After that, the first Layer 3 device places them in a VRF, and their traffic is carried through the network in that VRF until they hit the Internet edge.

For devices on the LAN, wireless design must be considered. When people walk in the door, their devices look for a wireless network and try to get an IP address. Fortunately, people don't usually stay by the door, or those would be the most overloaded access points. This does, however, point out the need for a well-thought-out wireless design that looks at usage patterns as well as walls and microwave ovens. This lesson was reinforced recently while troubleshooting a problem with wireless IP phones in a hospital surgical suite. Voice quality was poor, packets were dropped, and sometimes phones had problems connecting, but only near the entrance to the operating room area. It turned out that operating room staff were stowing their smartphones and other personal devices there during surgeries and overloading the access point located at the entrance to the suite. Again, know your flows and processes.

With BYOD, it is no longer just a one-to-one ratio for users and networked devices. Assume at least three devices per user when doing your wireless capacity planning.

The fact that mobile devices are *mobile* means that you have to consider that users will want to connect remotely to enterprise resources. Chapter 15, "Network in Motion," considers the network design implications of supporting remote users. From a BYOD perspective, the issues of security, user and device authentication, and data access control apply whether you are on a LAN or coming across a WAN.

BYOD can also be part of your disaster recovery/business continuity plan; if so, it becomes critical to design a secure, highly available BYOD solution (see the later section, "Business Continuity," for more on this topic).

BYOD Policy

Probably the biggest consideration in implementing BYOD has nothing to do with the network; it's the "Layer 8" issue of deciding what policies will be used—who and what will be allowed on the network, what company resources will be accessible, and by whom. Do not underestimate the importance of this step or the length of time it can take to make these decisions. These policies determine what your BYOD design must look like. They determine how flexible your business will be with personal and wireless devices. They determine how many user complaints the Help Desk has to deal with! This is not something to be taken lightly and is not a decision to be made completely by the IT department. Because potentially everyone in the company could be affected, it is important to involve other groups within the company and to get management buy-in for the final set of policies.

A good BYOD policy details both company rights to monitor and manage corporate data on mobile devices and employee rights to privacy for their personal data on mobile devices. Some difficult decisions are required in several areas, such as the following:

- Minimum security baseline that any device accessing the network must meet.

- Identifying which company-owned and user-owned devices will be allowed on the network.

- Identifying user groups and determining the access each needs; this is typically the toughest decision to make and one that will definitely require management involvement.

- Protection from data loss. Will you erase an entire lost smartphone, or will you segment company data in some way? Bear in mind that it may not be so easy to separate personal and business information. For instance, considering photographs as "personal" would leave open the possibility of losing corporate data because people have pictures of whiteboard drawings on their device. This is another tough decision.

- How will you "onboard" users and devices?

- Regulatory compliance. Are you subject to any regulations that would influence your BYOD strategy?

- Expense reimbursement or other stipend for personal device use.

This policy should be written, and then signed by every employee who accesses corporate resources with a mobile device, whether company provided or not. If you are an employee, you will want to read it carefully and make sure you understand what your rights and obligations are before signing.

The BYOD policy will guide your network design. It determines what kind of security controls to put in place and who needs to reach them, the wireless design, and how much additional traffic to plan for on the WAN and LAN. It's a wise—and rare—company that figures out the policies first, designs the network to support them second, and only then rolls out BYOD.

Business Continuity

In the past several years, terrorist attacks, weather events, political upheavals, and natural disasters have shown us the fragility of our daily systems and pointed out the need for contingency planning. Different businesses depend more or less on their IT infrastructure, but most would be adversely affected in some way by a network, server, or ISP outage. How much money your particular business would lose depends on many factors—the type of business, the type of outage, the time of day, and the length of downtime. Even short outages can cause major losses from factors, such as the following:

- Revenue from lost sales

- Loss of customers to competitor

- Damages from lawsuits due to late deliveries, medical injuries, or SLA payments

- Damage to company reputation

- Lost employee productivity due to people unable to work

- Lost employee productivity due to people having to spend time diagnosing and fixing the problem (and perhaps lost money from paying overtime)

Business Continuity Versus Disaster Recovery

There are a lot of definitions and understandings of disaster recovery (DR) and business continuity (BC), but what we will use for the purposes of this book are these: Business continuity involves proactively planning and building a system that will allow your business to continue to operate the way you want it to if some event compromises your systems, data, or part of your ability to function. This may mean that you have redundancy or resiliency already in place for critical systems or functions, and failover happens quickly. Disaster recovery is more reactive and might involve bringing up a secondary server, or loading back up data, or relocating staff, for instance, and could take days or weeks. DR may be a portion of your BC strategy, especially for less-critical systems and functions. It may also be all that some businesses need, depending on how long an outage they are able to sustain.

Business Continuity in Real Life

Stories abound of business failure because of technology failures. In one situation, a company had two data centers within a couple of miles of each other. A hurricane hit the city, and both data centers were taken offline. One was severely damaged by the storm. The other was located on a high floor in the building, so it escaped with little damage, but the fuel tanks for the generators were in the basement, and those fuel tanks floated away. The company was able to get that data center functioning again when fuel was available a few days later, but had to operate for months on just one data center until power and WAN links were fully restored. In another instance, two senior engineers sat idle while outsourced contractors attempted to bring up an IPsec tunnel to restore operations worth millions of dollars a minute. Why weren't the senior engineers engaged? Because the terms of the outsourcing contract forbade anyone but an employee of the outsourcer to touch device configurations. And let's not even think about the impact of a network outage in a medical facility, or at a construction site where a failure could cost lives rather than money.

With all the apocryphal stories that abound, why don't managers and network engineers pay more attention to failure modes and business continuity? Why aren't geodiversity and diversity of power, telecom, and road grids top-of-mind subjects? There seem to be a number of reasons.

Many engineers just don't think it could happen "here." There is little sense of the urgency or importance of this system from a business perspective, so there is little planning around failures. Or perhaps IT staff are too busy with the day-to-day tasks to have time to worry about how a failure will impact the network, and hence the business. Much of the time it's a lack of understanding and appreciation of the complexity and interdependence of the IT systems we build and maintain. Our ability to abstract, although required to help us focus on solving one specific problem at one specific point in time, is also our enemy when it comes to failures and failure modes. We need to seek out the interconnections between systems and try to understand them so we can really understand all the different areas that would be impacted by an outage.

Business Continuity Planning

More and more businesses are creating a business continuity management plan to help guide them in building the components needed to minimize loss during an unplanned outage and provide guidelines for staff to follow when one happens. When business continuity is mentioned, IT people frequently think of their own network going down, but what about the network of a major supplier? Or a business partner that has an outage in one of its processes? A full BC plan covers all the facets that you need to consider in order to restore processes and functions, such as staffing, application access, network access, data integrity, and communications. For manufacturing and sales companies, it will need to include the physical facilities, product inventory, and machinery required.

Some typical components of a BC plan include the following:

- **Risk Assessment:** What events might affect your company? How much of an outage would each of these cause? Which ones are most likely to happen and thus should

have mitigation plans, and which can you fairly safely ignore? You can't plan for every contingency. Try to plan for the most likely ones, if possible in a way that also covers you for less likely ones. The final decision about which risks are highest priority to mitigate should come from the company management, taking into account business as well as technical factors.

- **Business Impact Analysis:** What would an outage cost? How long could you sustain an outage? Remember to include both partial and full outages—the loss of an application, loss of staff, loss of some data—not just the loss of an entire data center or office site. This plan does not have to be a huge document (although it could be for some companies). Its purpose is to give the company a basis for prioritizing and focusing its BC plans and designs.

- **Continuity Requirements:** Based on the Risk Assessment and the Business Impact Analysis, decide what systems you need to have working, and when. On the networking front, the BC spectrum ranges from multiple fully redundant active sites to offsite backup data you can restore onto a cold standby system. Your continuity requirements will help you determine where along this spectrum your company falls and help you decide how best to fulfill the requirements.

- **Business Continuity Plan:** This provides guidelines on how your company will manage a disaster. Each company's plan will be different and will be more or less complex as needed. It typically includes topics such as the failover, redundancy, and contingency mechanisms for critical functions, how management and staff will communicate in an emergency, which personnel will continue to work, and how, and how processes will be restored.

Security is crucial during major disasters to safeguard business data. This goes beyond the data and network access security we typically think of to include physical device security. If a building is destroyed and your switches and servers are strewn across a field, how will you secure physical access to them and the data they hold? Or if an area is quarantined, who is authorized to enter your building and retrieve or secure your equipment? These are decisions better considered in advance because the necessary decision makers may not be available following a disaster. If you are using a cloud provider, find out its policies concerning physical security of equipment containing your data.

Because this book covers *network* architecture, the rest of this section will concentrate on how network design can help your business continue in the face of a disaster.

Business Continuity Design Considerations

Probably the best way to ensure the continuity of your business is to avoid preventable problems. Look at the most likely events in your Risk Assessment—are there network design changes that will help mitigate some of those risks? Perhaps you could create geo-diverse data centers, add some redundancy, strategically distribute spares, provide hot or cold standbys, or set up remote working. Good network management will help you here in two ways. It will provide a baseline for how the network operates normally and alert

you as problems develop, allowing you to take remedial action faster and possibly prevent a large outage.

Good network management and an understanding of how your business processes work will also help you with making the decision of when to call a network "down" and initiate your contingency plans. This often isn't easy to measure or understand. Is the failure of a single application enough to call the entire network "down"? Or is the failure of a single section of the network enough to call the network "down"? Strive to build a resilient network that adapts to changing conditions rapidly with minimal impact on the services running over the network. A resilient network can adapt to hard failures, such as network or service outages, as well as soft failures. A soft failure can be harder to define and detect because the network might be operational, but be

- Not usable to solve business problems

- Not running optimally

- Running in a "fragile state," with little capability to cope with changes beyond the current ones.

Business requirements will set the standards for which applications, sites, and portions of the network are critical. The question of how to make your network more resilient so that your data and applications are always available to your users is addressed in detail in subsequent chapters of this book.

A lot of business continuity planning focuses around data centers. Will you have multiple active, redundant data centers, or will you have a primary site and one or more backup sites? Or if you have some critical applications that must be always up, you might choose to have active/active data centers for those applications in combination with a primary/backup design for less-critical applications. Another option is to use online services that provide completely cloud-based applications accessible over the Internet, or host your servers and storage. Location of the data centers is another point of discussion. You want them far enough away from each other that they aren't likely to be affected by the same events, but close enough that latency for data replication isn't too high. Again, you cannot plan for every scenario, so plan for the most likely ones.

Don't forget about staffing. If your staff is affected by the same natural disaster that brought down the data center, for instance, they are likely not going to be able to travel to a backup location. They might need to help their own families or be evacuated. Staff that are onsite at a data center or office during an emergency may not be able to leave; how will you feed and clothe them? An existing BYOD system can help with business continuity if it allows staff to work remotely. To make this work, VPN termination points must be up and available, the servers or data needed must be up and available, and network and Internet connections must be present to make these available to remote users. Keep in mind, however, that your staff may not have electricity or Internet access to work remotely.

Staffing also plays a factor in designing your network for business continuity. When choosing a design, make things simple enough that they can be understood by a broad

range of engineers, because your primary staff may not be available, or you may have to call in outside help. There are three main components involved in recovering from a network failure, and they all depend on staff knowledge for their success:

■ **Detection:** How long does it take to detect a failure condition? This is impacted by the level of monitoring and management you have deployed, and by how complete a picture you have of the ideal system state. Rapid response will be improved if your engineers understand the software and are comfortable working with it.

■ **Troubleshooting:** How long does it take to chase the problem to the root cause? This is highly dependent on the skill of the person doing the troubleshooting. The complexity of the network design also impacts it, as do your monitoring and management platforms and the knowledge of the ideal system state.

■ **Repair:** How long does it take to repair the problem after it's discovered? This again is highly dependent on the skill of the person accomplishing the repair, and his or her knowledge of the ideal system state.

Hopefully, your company will never face a major disaster or failure. However, every complex system is likely to experience some level of degradation or failure during its lifetime. Advance planning will help minimize the impact to your business and speed recovery of your system's functionality.

Summary

The creation of a network that functions as a strategic part of the business, rather than just a cost center, starts with a good understanding of business requirements and processes. This leads to an examination and understanding of data flows involved in those processes. With that knowledge, you are able to create high-level LAN, WAN, and data center designs that support and enable the business. From this knowledge also flows lower-level decisions, such as whether to use single or dual supervisors in a specific switch.

This chapter looked at three areas where business requirements and network design commonly intersect: workflow and processes, BYOD, and business continuity. The main takeaways from all these examples are to know your data flows and the business functions and processes they support. Then use that knowledge to inform your network design decisions.

Models

Models have always served a place in conceptualizing and understanding ideas and spaces. In fact, for many years the U.S. Patent Office required that every patent filing required a physical model implementing the idea. This would not only allow the patent examiner to fully understand the idea in an intuitive way, it would also allow easy comparison of new ideas to old by comparing the models. In the world of networking, models serve much the same purpose—to illustrate an idea in a way that makes it intuitive, or easy to grasp.

If you're thinking about the seven-layer International Standards Organization (ISO) model of computer networks, you're on the right track. But unless you've explored other possible models of network architecture, you're working with a rather constrained view of how models can improve your understanding of networking technology and networks.

There are, in reality, different types of models used in the world of computer networks, including models of how the various protocols interact to transport data across a network, models that examine how protocols and network devices interact, and models that interact with design and architecture.

This chapter begins with models describing how protocols interact to transport data across a network, including the well-known ISO seven-layer model,[1] the lesser-known four-layer Department of Defense (DoD) model, and the little known iterative model. Working from the theoretical to the more practical, we present a hybrid model that provides a conceptual overview of not only protocol interaction, but also the operation of forwarding devices. Using the concepts of control and data planes, the concepts of reactive and proactive network elements are explored.

After this, we move into models used in network architecture and design. Specifically, we'll address the waterfall model of traffic flow and routing, and contrast this with

---

1. "ISO/IEC 7498-1:1994 - Information Technology—Open Systems Interconnection—Basic Reference Model: The Basic Model."

treating the network as a set of flows. In the area of network design, we'll examine Places in the Network (PIN). Another model for understanding network design—hierarchy—is covered in Chapter 6, "Principles of Modularity," and Chapter 7, "Applying Modularity."

The Seven-Layer Model

Virtually anyone who has ever been through a networking class or studied for a network engineering certification is familiar with using the seven-layer model to describe the way networks work. Connectionless Networking Protocol (CLNP) and a routing protocol, Intermediate System to Intermediate System (IS-IS), were designed by the ISO to meet the requirements given within the seven-layer model. These protocols are still in wide use, particularly IS-IS, which has been modified to support routing in IP networks. Figure 4-1 illustrates the seven-layer model.

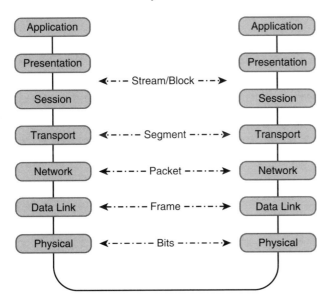

Figure 4-1 *Seven-Layer Model*

The genius of modeling a network in this way is that it makes the interactions between the various pieces much easier to see and understand. Each pair of layers, moving vertically through the model, interacts through an application programming interface (API). So to connect to a particular physical port, a piece of code at the data link layer would connect to the socket for that port. This allows the interaction between the various layers to be abstracted and standardized. A piece of software at the network layer doesn't need to know how to deal with various sorts of physical interfaces, only how to get data to the data link layer software on the same system.

Each layer has a specific set of functions to perform:

■ The physical layer (Layer 1) is responsible for getting the 0s and 1s modulated, or serialized, onto the physical link. Each link type has a different format for signaling

a 0 or 1; the physical layer is responsible for translating 0s and 1s into these physical signals.

- The data link layer is responsible for making certain that transmitted information is sent to the right computer on the other side of the link. Each device has a different data link (Layer 2) address that can be used to send traffic to that specific device. The data link layer assumes each frame within a flow of information is separate from all other packets within that same flow and only provides communication for devices that are connected through a single physical link.

- The network layer is responsible for transporting data between systems that are not connected through a single physical link. The network layer, then, provides network-wide (or Layer 3) addresses, rather than link local addresses, and also provides some means for discovering the set of devices and links that must be crossed to reach these destinations.

- The transport layer (Layer 4) is responsible for the transparent transfer of data between different devices. Transport layer protocols can be either be "reliable," which means the transport layer will retransmit data lost at some lower layer, or "unreliable," which means that data lost at lower layers must be retransmitted by some higher-layer application.

- The session layer (Layer 5) doesn't really transport data, but manages the connections between applications running on two different computers. The session layer makes certain that the type of data, the form of the data, and the reliability of the data stream are all exposed and accounted for.

- The presentation layer (Layer 6) formats data in a way that the application running on the two devices can understand and process. Encryption, flow control, and any other manipulation of data required to provide an interface between the application and the network happen here. Applications interact with the presentation layer through sockets.

- The application layer (Layer 7) provides the interface between the user and the application, which in turn interacts with the network through the presentation layer.

Each layer in the model provides the information the layer below it is carrying; for instance, Layer 3 provides the bits Layer 2 encapsulates and transmits using Layer 1. This leads to the following observation: not only can the interaction between the layers be described in precise terms within the seven-layer model, the interaction between parallel layers on multiple computers can be described precisely. The physical layer on the first device can be said to communicate with the physical layer on the second device, the data link layer on the first device with the data link layer on the second device, and so on. Just as interactions between two layers on a device are handled through sockets, interactions between parallel layers on different devices are handled through network protocols:

- Ethernet describes the signaling of 0s and 1s onto a physical piece of wire, a format for starting and stopping a frame of data, and a means of addressing a single device

among all the devices connected to a single wire. Ethernet, then, falls within both Layer 1 and Layer 2 in the OSI model.

■ IP describes the formatting of data into packets, and the addressing and other means necessary to send packets across multiple Layer 2 links to reach a device that is several hops away. IP, then, falls within Layer 3 of the OSI model.

■ TCP describes session setup and maintenance, data retransmission, and interaction with applications. TCP, then, falls within the transport and session layers of the OSI model.

This was illustrated in Figure 4-1, where each "layer-wise" interaction is labeled using the name used to describe the blocks of information transferred. For instance, segments are transferred from the transport layer on one device to another, while packets are transferred from the network layer on one device to another.

Problems with the Seven-Layer Model

Although the OSI model represented a huge leap forward in modeling and understanding the operation of networked systems, it doesn't truly fit the protocol suite most commonly used today—TCP/IP. Two glaring examples are routing protocols and IPsec.

Routing protocols in the OSI model run directly on the data link layer; however, OSPF, EIGRP, and BGP, three of the most commonly used routing protocols in TCP/IP networks, run above the data link layer. OSPF and EIGRP run directly on top of IP, and BGP runs on top of TCP. How can a protocol that fits into the purpose ascribed to the network layer run on top of the network layer, or even on top of the transport and session layers?

IPsec is another difficult case, because it's designed to manage the privacy of a connection—a function specifically given to the session layer. And yet TCP, which is at the transport and session layers, runs on top of IPsec. How can IPsec, which handles the presentation of data, really be said to run at the network layer?

These mismatches might cause you to wonder what the relationship between the OSI model and TCP/IP really is—the surprising answer is the OSI model and TCP/IP were developed independently. The IP suite of protocols was developed around another model, the four-layer DoD model.

The Four-Layer Model

One of the reasons we have so much difficulty fitting TCP/IP to the seven-layer model is that TCP/IP was developed with a different model of network communications in mind. Instead of a seven-layer model, TCP/IP was designed around a four-layer model, roughly described in RFC 1122 and illustrated in Figure 4-2.

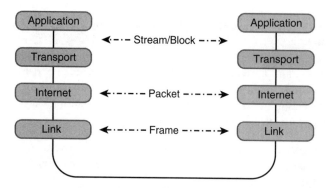

Figure 4-2 *Four-Layer Model*

In this model

- The link layer is roughly responsible for the same functions as the physical and data link layers in the OSI model—controlling the use of physical links, link-local addressing, and carrying frames as individual bits across an individual physical link.

- The Internet layer is roughly responsible for the same things as the network layer in the OSI model—providing addressing and reachability across multiple physical links and providing a single packet format and interface regardless of the actual physical link type.

- The transport layer is responsible for building and maintaining sessions between communicating devices and providing a common transparent data transmission mechanism for streams or blocks of data. Flow control and reliable transport may also be implemented in this layer, as in the case of TCP.

- The application layer is the interface between the user and the network resources, or specific applications that use and provide data to other devices attached to the network.

In this model, Ethernet fits wholly within the link layer; IP and all routing protocols fit in the Internet layer; and TCP and UDP fit within the transport layer. Because of this neatness, this is a cleaner model for understanding TCP/IP as it is deployed today, although it doesn't provide the detailed structure of splitting up the various levels of signaling that might be useful in a more research-oriented environment.

Iterative Layering Model

The seven- and four-layer models rely on the concept that as we move up the stack from the physical to the application, each layer adds some specific function not provided by the layer below. If you examine the actual function of each layer, however, you'll find many similarities between them. For instance, the Ethernet data link layer provides transport and multiplexing across a single link, while IP provides transport and multiplexing across a multihop path.

> **Note**   For a fuller development of this model of network operation, see John Day's *Patterns in Network Architecture.*[2]

This leads to the following observation: There are really only four functions that any data carrying protocol can serve: transport, multiplexing, error correction, and flow control. There are two natural groupings within these four functions: transport and multiplexing, error and flow control. So most protocols fall into doing one of two things:

- The protocol provides transport, including some form of translation from one data format to another, and multiplexing, the ability of the protocol to keep data from different hosts and applications separate.

- The protocol provides error control, either through the capability to correct small errors or to retransmit lost or corrupted data, and flow control, which prevents undue data loss because of a mismatch between the network's capability to deliver data and the application's capability to generate data.

From this perspective, Ethernet provides transport services and flow control, so it is a mixed bag concentrated on a single link, port to port (or tunnel endpoint to tunnel endpoint) within a network. IP is a multihop protocol (a protocol that spans more than one physical link) providing transport services, whereas TCP is a multihop protocol that uses IP's transport mechanisms and provides error correction and flow control. Figure 4-3 illustrates the iterative model.

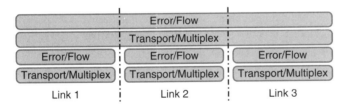

Figure 4-3   *Iterative Model of Network Protocols*

Each layer of the model has one of the same two functions, just at a different scope. This model hasn't caught on widely in network protocol work, but it provides a much simpler view of network protocol dynamics and operations than either the seven- or four-layer models, and it adds the concept of "scope", which is of vital importance in considering network operation. The scope of information and interaction is the foundation of network stability and resilience.

As an example of how using the iterative model can provide a better feel for specific protocols, let's consider the case of EIGRP. Within the OSI model, does EIGRP operate at Layer 3, 4, or even 7? Because EIGRP uses IP as a transport, it doesn't really fit at Layer 3—but it provides the information necessary to make Layer 3 routing happen, so it's

---

2. Day, *Patterns in Network Architecture: A Return to Fundamentals*. Indianapolis: Prentice Hall, 2008.

traditionally considered a Layer 3 protocol. There is no "end-to-end" error correction or flow control in EIGRP, just hop-by-hop, so it's difficult to place it at Layer 4, either.

The four-layer DoD model, described earlier, resolves the problem by placing all routing within the network layer. But doesn't EIGRP act like an application, riding on top of IP? Simply putting a routing protocol into the network layer doesn't make it a network layer protocol.

The iterative model resolves this problem by classifying protocols by their function in terms of data transport, rather than in terms of their application. From the perspective of the iterative model, EIGRP relies on IP for transport—IP fulfills the role of the first, or lower, protocol, within each layer in the model. EIGRP itself provides flow control and error correction through its own transport mechanism, so EIGRP neatly fits within the space of the upper, or second, protocol found at each layer. That EIGRP "tops" the layer as an application providing metadata to the networking system isn't an issue; it simply runs in parallel with other applications. Applications that need end-to-end functionality can build in another layer on top of IP (TCP and UDP) to supply those functions, or they might not—because EIGRP performs only hop-by-hop transport, it doesn't need the end-to-end functionality of any additional layers.

The iterative model, then, adds value in not trying to force artificial layers into the networking stack; rather, it classifies by observing similarity of purpose, which helps to apply common solutions to common problems.

Connection-Oriented and Connectionless

The iterative model also brings the concepts of connection-oriented and connectionless network protocols out into the light of day again.

Connection-oriented protocols set up an end-to-end connection, including all the state to transfer meaningful data, before sending the first bit of data. "State" could include such things as quality of service requirements, the path the traffic will take through the network, the specific applications that will send and receive the data, the rate at which data can be sent, and other information. After the connection is set up, data can be transferred with very little overhead.

Connectionless services, on the other hand, combine the data required to transmit data with the data itself, carrying both in a single packet (or protocol data unit). Connectionless protocols spread the state required to carry data through the network to every possible device that might need that data, whereas connection-oriented models constrain state to only devices that need to know about a specific flow of packets. As a result, single device or link failures in a connectionless network can be healed by moving the traffic onto another possible path, rather than redoing all the work needed to build the state to continue carrying traffic from source to destination.

Most modern networks are built with connectionless transport models combined with connection-oriented quality of service, error control, and flow control models. This combination isn't always ideal—for instance, quality of service (QoS) is normally configured

along specific paths to match specific flows that should be following those paths. This treatment of QoS as more connection oriented than the actual traffic flows being managed causes strong disconnects between the ideal state of a network and various possible failure modes.

A Hybrid Model

The models discussed so far describe traffic flow and protocol interaction, particularly shaped around end host to end host, or application to application, communications. Keeping interfaces between layers clean, and thinking about what each protocol in each layer should do, provides a solid foundation for developing well-behaved network applications and protocols.

Although these models are helpful in understanding protocol operation, they aren't generally useful in network design and architecture. How does understanding that TCP presents data, Ethernet carries it across single links, and IP carries it across multihop links help us with network design and architecture?

What we need is a model of how network protocols interact with network forwarding hardware and software—routers and switches. The model illustrated in Figure 4-4 begins with the four-layer model and expands it where necessary to create a useful model for understanding network protocols and interfaces in the context of network architecture. It has functional modules rather than layers, and the arrows show how modules communicate with each other.

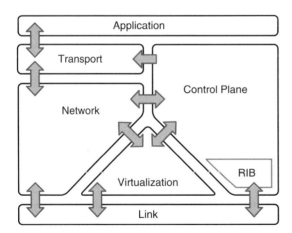

Figure 4-4 *Hybrid Network Operation Model*

This model looks much more confusing than the previous ones, but don't let it scare you. Rather than focusing on the flow of information between two applications, the hybrid model focuses on the relationships between each of the moving parts (including hardware) and protocols that make a network work, concentrating on the forwarding devices that make up the majority of the equipment deployed in real networks.

As with the four-layer model, the link, network, and transport modules provide physical connectivity, end-to-end connectivity, and session services. These three modules are provided, for instance, by Ethernet, IP, and TCP or UDP, respectively.

The virtualization module is new and provides virtualization services that interact with both the control plane and the network layer. Virtualization services don't fit in just one place on the diagram because they can run over link (such as MPLS and 802.1Q), network (such as GRE and IPsec tunnels), or transport (such as TCP-based tunneling mechanisms) protocols. The placement of the virtualization module in the diagram, then, is a compromise that illustrates where they are most commonly found in the network.

The control plane is new as well, and is described in more detail in the following section.

The Control Plane

The control plane includes any protocol that provides the information needed to move traffic from one device to another through the network. To put it in simple terms, the control plane answers three questions:

- What am I trying to reach?
- Where is it?
- How do I get there?

What Am I Trying to Reach?

The first of these three questions is the simplest: What am I trying to reach? Am I trying to retrieve a web page, an application, or a piece of data? Am I trying to write data to some service, such as file storage, a database, or a printer? Services are the focus at this level, rather than hosts. I don't really care which server I connect to, so long as I connect to a server that has the information (or service) I want to reach.

The most widely deployed control plane protocol that interacts with this question is the Domain Name System (DNS). DNS interacts with the location of services in many ways, such as

- Through load sharing between multiple instances of the same service. When a DNS server receives a query for a particular server or service, it might return an answer based on current load, geographic location, or any number of other factors.

- The concept of subdomains, which are effectively services available at a particular domain. For instance, mail.somedomain.com will generally indicate a mail service located within a particular organization's network, and www.somedomain.com will generally indicate an HTTP service within that same organization's service.

The DNS service also acts as a way to find out *where* a service is located based on knowing *what* the service is—or rather, DNS provides service to location mapping.

Where Is It?

The DNS takes a name and provides an address—and just like in the real world, an address tells you where something is. But we need to be careful at this point to differentiate between "where it is" in a physical sense, and "where it is" in a logical sense. Although a service must, ultimately, live on a physical server, located in a physical rack, in a physical data center, it can be logically attached to a network just about anywhere. Figure 4-5 illustrates the difference between these concepts.

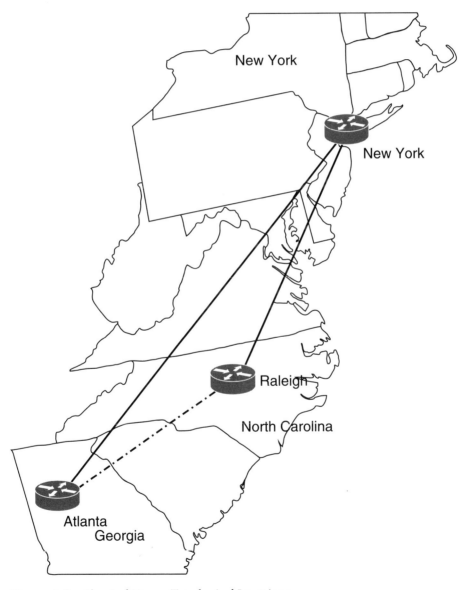

Figure 4-5   *Physical Versus Topological Locations*

In Figure 4-5, Atlanta and Raleigh are both closer to each other than they are to New York City physically, but there is no network link directly between Atlanta and Raleigh—so from the network topology's perspective, Atlanta is actually closer to New York City than it is to Raleigh.

Why is this so important? Because it impacts addressing, information hiding, traffic flow, and almost everything else about network design. The first abstraction a network engineer must make is between the physical and the logical.

This abstraction between the physical and the logical is crucial because it clearly shows the point behind IP addresses in the first place—an IP address does not label a specific computer or device, it labels a specific location in the network. If you move a house from one place to another, the house's address changes; it would be insane to move a house from 120 Elm Street to a location between 110 South Street and 112 South Street, and yet leave its address as 120 Elm Street. Enough moving, and the entire postal system would collapse in a heap.

To overcome this problem, layers of indirection must be put into the network so a device can be mapped to a location. "Indirection" inserts a relay point between hosts that are communicating. A host sending data communicates with the relay, or indirection, point, which knows how to reach the receiving host. This is the concept behind mobile IP, for instance, with the home agent being the indirection point. One of the worst habits of network engineering is treating the location as an identifier, which eventually causes massive scale problems, and then inserting a new layer of indirection to solve the massive scale problem created through poor discipline in the first place.

How Do I Get There?

After you have an address, you need to know how to reach that address. The control plane employs routing protocols to solve this problem. Routing protocols map the best path through a set of physical links and devices to reach any topological location or any device. Routing has been modeled in a number of ways through the years; each of these models is useful in its own way:

- **Routing as an application running on top of the network:** In this model, routing is a distributed application that interconnects the various devices that make up a network. For instance, routing protocols are seen as part of the application layer within the DoD and ISO network models. Because routing protocols rely on the host-to-host transport mechanisms provided by network protocols, this makes sense only from the perspective of these models.

- **Routing as a widely distributed real-time database:** This model treats the routing table (or the protocol tables) as the primary end of routing, and the protocols themselves as a language or system used to produce those tables. The emphasis here is on the concept of real time, because the routing database must reflect the state of the real topology within seconds (and increasingly milliseconds) of changes in that topology. For instance, OSPF and IS-IS model routing within a single flooding domain as a set of a synchronized databases. A set of on-the-wire protocols are

specified to keep this distributed database synchronized in near real time, along with a set of operations every node on the network must perform on these synchronized databases. OSPF, specifically, is described as a set of state machines around a distributed database.

■ **Routing as a widely distributed policy database:** This model not only treats routing as a distributed database, but as a distributed database containing policy—one link is preferred over another link because of costs or because it better supports a specific application, and so on. This layers policy on top of the distributed database view, adding complexity. For instance, the process of carrying BGP information through a network is described as a set of interactions with policies local to each device and autonomous system through which the routing information passes.

■ **Routing as a set of algorithms running on a centralized set of controllers:** This is the model of bandwidth brokers, centralized traffic engineering, and Software Defined Networks (SDN), which will be covered in greater depth in Chapter 17, "Software-Defined Networks."

We won't spend a lot of time in this book explaining routing; instead, we refer to the many fine books published through Cisco Press that explain the operation and deployment of various routing protocols.

Other Network Metadata

A network not only needs names, addresses, and road maps to operate, it also needs information about the current state of devices and links, policies that are outside the routing database and quality of service. This piece of the control plane puzzle is provided through protocols such as SNMP, RSVP, ICMP, NetFlow, and many others. Each of these protocols is designed to run on top of the network itself and provide information about the network.

Control Plane Relationships

The control plane consists of a number of different classes of protocols and services, including routing, quality of service, and measurement. Network engineers tend to think of the control plane as being restricted to the automated process (such as routing protocols) that provide the metadata—the information about the network—that makes the network itself "go." However, the control plane, in theory at least, reaches into manual configurations provided by network operators, routing protocols, quality of service information, and network management. It's not easy to draw a definitive line around what is part of the control plane and what isn't; for this discussion, we'll draw the line rather broadly. Each of these different relationships is discussed in the following sections.

Routing

To determine where a packet has been in the Internet, all you have to do is look at the autonomous system path of the route that brought the packet to the local router, right? Although this way of thinking is widespread, it's wrong.

Packet-based networks are designed to allow traffic to continue flowing even when there are disruptions in the topology—the control plane discovers the change in the underlying network, reacts to it, and moves flows from one path to another. There is not, in reality, a single control plane in most networks. Any given router might be running multiple routing protocols, and there's always static routing, policy-based routing, traffic engineering, tunneling, and any number of other mechanisms that can direct traffic down a given path.

This loose coupling of the data plane and the control plane is a difficult concept, and not grasping it leads to all sorts of mistaken thinking about network engineering in general, such as the idea that you can determine how a packet arrived at the local router by simply looking at the autonomous system path in a BGP update. The control plane, in essence, is not a single "thing," but a collection of different protocols and mechanisms, each of which can direct a packet down a different path moment by moment. Further, the control plane in a packet-switched network is designed so that every router and every switch makes a decision about which path it thinks is best to reach any given destination independent of any other device in the network.

To illustrate this concept, let's use Figure 4-6.

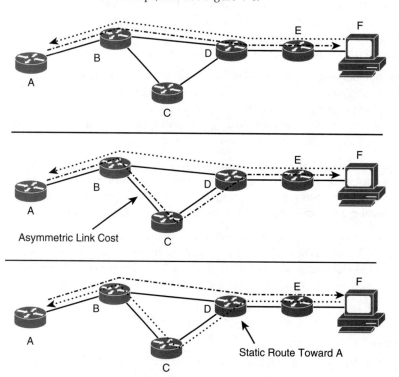

Figure 4-6 *Examples of Path Modifications in Routing*

Three networks are depicted in Figure 4-6; let's examine each one in turn. The top network illustrates what most engineers think about when they look at the routing table at Router A. Traffic from the host on the far right travels along the same path as traffic sent

to Host F, so the routing information shown in the routing table at Router A accurately describes the path any particular traffic has taken from the host to the local router.

The middle illustration shows a situation that's far more common than most engineers imagine, asymmetric routes. Here, the traffic from the host on the far right travels along the path (E,D,B,A), even though the local routing table shows the best path as being (A,B,C,D,E). Looking at the routing table at Router A, you would assume the traffic travels the same path in both directions, but because of asymmetric costs across the (B,C) link, the traffic actually passes along two different paths.

The bottom illustration shows the same network with a bit of manually configured policy; a static route has been configured at Router D. The result is that examining the routing table at either Routers A or E will provide a false view of the path traffic takes between Host F and Router A.

Other examples of the control plane at any particular device in the network not actually showing the path any particular traffic has traveled to reach a specific destination include packets routed around a failure during the time of network convergence, traffic that is tunneled or traffic engineered through tunneling techniques, and any situation where there are two routing protocols interacting with one another in the same network. RFC5123, *Considerations in Validating the Path in BGP*, provides a more detailed set of examples drawn from experience with interdomain routing.

Another interaction between the control plane and lower layers of the network stack is the use of the lower layers as a transport for the control plane itself. Routing protocols use transport, network, and link services to transport the metadata that keeps the network running; for instance, BGP runs over TCP (a transport protocol), OSPF runs over IP (a network protocol), and IS-IS runs directly over link layer services.

Routing protocols don't pull link (or interface) state directly from the link layer in IOS (nor most other implementations); routing doesn't interact with physical interfaces at this level. Instead, routing protocols read link status from the network layer, specifically by receiving updates about the state of connected routes through the routing table.

Virtualization's interface with routing is the same as the remainder of the network—routing protocols provide reachability information through the tunnels. A control plane process must be used to separate or segment traffic at the point where the virtual topology separates from the physical topology in order to pull the correct traffic into the virtual topology.

Quality of Service

The control plane's interface to network and link services includes the distribution and implementation (including manual configuration!) of quality of service (QoS), which is designed to control the order in which packets are transmitted on either the outbound or inbound side of each device in the path. QoS also interacts with traffic engineering mechanisms and virtualization services to channel traffic of various types along specific paths through the network to support policies such as better bandwidth usage, or the lowest possible delay and jitter through the network.

For instance, Resource Reservation Protocol (RSVP) reserves bandwidth along a given path in a network, and MPLS/TE modifies the path traffic takes through a network to ensure link utilization is optimized for all applications. As noted previously in the "Iterative Layering Model" section, QoS is one of the outliers in the general design of connection-oriented services running over connectionless transport protocols. This is easily seen in the operation of protocols such as RSVP, which introduce state end-to-end in a specific path before the first packet is transmitted along the path.

Network Measurement and Management

Measurement is critical to operating a network. Network engineers need to know what the normal state of the network is and how the network is changing over time. Measuring the state of a network involves control plane protocols such as NetFlow and SNMP that run on top of network and transport protocols.

Chapter 10, "Measure Twice," covers network measurement and management in more detail.

Interaction Between Control Planes

The hybrid model also provides a solid basis on which to understand the relationship between multiple control planes running on the same network. Figure 4-7 illustrates the interaction between different routing protocols.

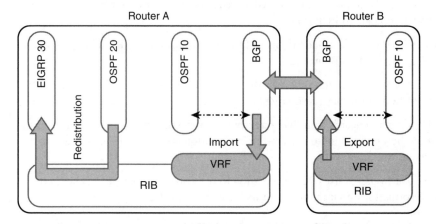

Figure 4-7 *Redistribution and Import/Export*

The first interface between routing protocols shown in Figure 4-7 is redistribution. It's common to think of redistribution as the insertion of routes learned by one protocol into another protocol—in the figure, reachability information learned by OSPF 20 is injected into EIGRP 30. But although this is the way redistribution is configured, this isn't the way redistribution actually works.

In reality:

- OSPF 20 installs routing information it has learned into the Routing Information Base (RIB).

- EIGRP 30 is notified when OSPF 20 installs a new route into the RIB, and pulls this route out of the RIB, assigning some locally derived metric and other information to the route in the EIGRP topology table.

In other words, all redistributed routing information is redistributed through the RIB, rather than protocol to protocol.

The second interface shown in Figure 4-7 is the import/export interface. This interface is specific to BGP and is used only for carrying OSPF and EIGRP routing information across an L3VPN service. Even though import/export is configured using redistribution commands in Cisco IOS Software (within the address family configuration), it really isn't redistribution at all. How does this interface operate?

- OSPF 10, at Router B, installs a prefix into a Virtual Routing and Forwarding (VRF) table, which is a RIB with forwarding information restricted to a specific virtual interface (or virtual topology).

- BGP is notified of this prefix installation.

- BGP communicates directly with OSPF to obtain any information about this prefix OSPF would like to insert into the BGP extended communities—this information is completely opaque to BGP itself.

- BGP carries the route, including this additional information OSPF has handed off, across the network to Router A.

- The BGP process at Router A installs the route into the correct VRF, causing OSPF to be notified of this new destination.

- OSPF 10 communicates with BGP directly to retrieve the information attached to the route by OSPF 10 in Router B—this information is still completely opaque to BGP itself.

- OSPF 10 at Router A uses this information to reconstruct the proper metrics and other information about the route for its local link state database.

In no case is internal routing information, such as metrics or policy markers, transferred from one routing protocol to another. The only information redistributed between two different routing protocols is the destination and the next hop. In the case of the import/export interface, two OSPF processes are using BGP as a signaling channel to communicate; the routing information transferred between the OSPF and BGP processes (that BGP actually uses) is still only the reachable destination and the next hop.

Furthermore, routes are transferred only if the route is being used to forward packets on the local device. The second-best route to a destination in OSPF 20 at Router A isn't ever

redistributed to EIGRP 30. Backup routes, such as Loop Free Alternates (LFA) and EIGRP Feasible Successors, are never redistributed from one routing protocol to another.

Why do we go to so much trouble to provide this type of separation between different routing processes?

Because the capability of a routing protocol to determine loop-free routes is based on internally consistent state. Injecting random state into a routing protocol can (and sometimes does) cause major network failures.

> **Note** It might be interesting to consider, for a moment, the difference between internal and external routing information. Because routing protocols draw their information from the local RIB, and more specifically from what we might consider the "connected process," on the router, what is—really—the difference between internal routes and redistributed routes? The real difference is not in the origin of the routing information, but in the type of metric itself. If the metric of the route is "native" to the protocol, the route is an internal route. If the metric is "not native" to the protocol, the route is an external route. The process of redistribution, then, tells the routing process, "this metric isn't like your internal metrics, so treat it differently." The process of distribution tells the routing process, "this metric is like your internal metrics, so treat this route as an internal route." The case of redistributed connected routes and distributed connected routes (connected routes distributed through a network statement in Cisco IOS Software), is illustrative—there's no real difference in the actual metrics involved; it's just an administrative (or policy) decision at the point of origination. The administrative nature of metric types is seen even more clearly in BGP, which almost always draws its routing information from a local IGP routing process. Should the metrics be considered internal or external? It depends on the configuration.

Reactive and Proactive

We've moved from models of network protocol operation to a model that sits on the edge between network protocols and network operation at the level where it impacts design. Before moving into pure design models, it's important to discuss one aspect of network operation that interacts with both the control and data planes in more detail— the concepts of *reactiveness* and *proactiveness*.

The concept of a reactive control plane is simple to understand in theory: *the control plane finds the information required to forward a particular packet only when there is an actual packet to be forwarded*. In a proactive control plane, information about every reachable destination is always available at every device that might be on a path toward that destination.

Reactive data planes are a bit more complex to understand, but they essentially always involve a cache of forwarding information of some type. This cache is updated only when there is a packet presented to the control plane that needs to be forwarded. Proactive data planes are built just like proactive control planes (and require a proactive control

plane to build); data plane forwarding tables are built based on information about the state of the network, rather than on traffic flows.

Combining these two concepts, we find there are four models of interaction between control and data planes:

- *A proactive control plane with a proactive data plane*, where every reachable destination within the network is known by every node in the network (note that aggregated routing information still fits this definition) through a routing protocol (or other control plane), and this reachability information is installed in the local forwarding table of every device in the network. An example of this is a network running OSPF to provide routing information combined with a fully populated forwarding table through Cisco Express Forwarding (CEF).

- *A proactive control plane with a reactive data plane*, where every reachable destination within the network is known by every node in the network through a routing protocol (or other control plane), but forwarding information is installed only when a packet needs to be forwarded to a specific destination. An example of this is a network running OSPF to provide routing information combined with a cached forwarding table, such as Cisco's fast cache. If a packet to a particular destination is received for which there is no forwarding information, the forwarding process queries the control plane, which knows all reachable destinations, for that information. The forwarding process will cache information learned from the control plane for some period of time; some caching systems attempt to intelligently decide when forwarding information is no longer needed by examining local traffic patterns.

- *A reactive control plane with a reactive data plane*, where information about every reachable destination is available on some node someplace in the network, but not on any particular node in the network. When a packet is received for which there is no forwarding information, the forwarding process will query the control plane for information about this destination. The control plane, in turn, queries the other nodes on the network to discover the location of the destination, and then does whatever processing is necessary to find the best path to that destination. The information discovered through this process is often cached in both the data and control planes until these processes determine it is no longer needed. An example of this type of implementation is the Locator Identifier Separation Protocol (LISP), where the information required to forward packets is discovered only as packets arrive at some network edge.

- *A topology only control plane with a reactive data plane*, a variation on a reactive control plane with a reactive data plane. In this type of design, the control plane is only responsible for building a single loop-free topology that connects all reachable destinations, rather than finding the best path to every reachable destination from every network device. Reachability information is discovered by examining actual traffic flows on the network itself and is cached by the data plane's forwarding processes until it is deemed out of date or otherwise not needed. Spanning tree is an example of this type of operation.

Why should a protocol designer or implementer choose one model over another? Why should you, as a network architect, be concerned about which model a specific protocol uses?

Reactive systems can introduce unpredictable and difficult to manage delay and jitter into the network. Although faster reaction times, and more intelligent caching rules, can reduce the impact of the reaction time in the network, the reaction time will always remain—and because applications don't know about this reaction time, it's difficult for them to manage and account for it. Should the first packet's round-trip time be taken as normal for the connection to a particular destination, or is it just an artifact of a reactive control plane? From the application's perspective, there's no way to know.

Reactive systems can, however, reduce the amount of state in any given network device— so long as the reactive control or data plane is properly designed and managed. Reactive state is almost always kept at the host reachability level, rather than the aggregated level. Reactive forwarding devices often must buffer the first few packets in a flow so traffic isn't dropped while a path to the destination is being discovered through the control plane. These two factors combined often counteract any savings the control plane realizes by keeping less state information at each device.

The Waterfall Model

The waterfall model isn't a model of network operation, but rather a model of traffic flows. This model is based on the basic insight that all routing and switching protocols essentially build a tree sourced at the destination and spreading out to each available source. Figure 4-8 shows the waterfall model.

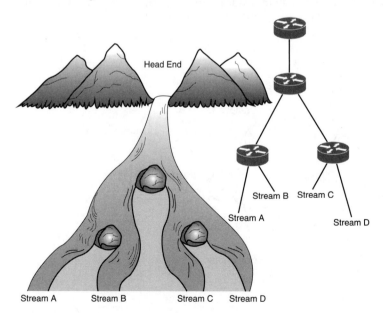

Figure 4-8 *Waterfall Model*

The waterfall model shows how data flow splits in a network at every router (Layer 3 junction), so that a single stream becomes a series of streams. Although the data flow is upside down (data actually flows in the opposite direction of the water flow, so it's more like a salmon leaping up the waterfall towards the head of the falls), the imagery is useful. After any network data stream has split, there is no way to rejoin the streams back into a single stream of data without risking loops in the network topology. To understand how this relates to modeling a network, consider the difference between spanning tree and routing operation in a waterfall model.

Spanning tree builds one large tree that is shared by every source and destination pair. This single tree means that all traffic must "leap up the waterfall" to the head end, where it can then follow the flow of water back toward its real destination. With OSPF, for instance, not only is every router the head end of a waterfall (a spanning tree), every destination is the head end of a waterfall.

The most efficient path through the network is always going to be against the flow of the water in this model. Any network in which data must switch directions in relation to the current represents suboptimal traffic flow. The higher the number of destinations that must switch directions relative to the direction of the current, the more inefficient the network is.

This effect will be discussed in terms of network stretch in Chapter 6, "Principles of Modularity."

Places in the Network

Places In the Network (PINs) are a way to divide a network along functional, rather than topological, links. Figure 4-9 illustrates a PINs view of a network.

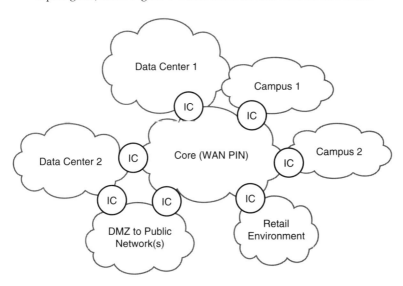

Figure 4-9   *PINs View of a Network*

Each functional section of the network is separated into a different component, such as the two data centers, two campuses, and so on. Splitting the network up in this way emphasizes the function of each piece of the network. Different design paradigms can be used in each section to match the specific purpose of the PIN being designed. For instance, a large scale hub-and-spoke topology might dominate the retail environment, and the first data center might be designed as a full mesh of tunnels, and the second as a Clos design. Clos network design is discussed in Chapter 11, "The Floor Plan."

Security, management mechanisms, and other aspects of each PIN can also be different; Data Center 1 might have an open security policy within the data center itself, and strong restrictions on outside access, while Data Center 2 might have no entrance policies, but strong per server/application security mechanisms. Every PIN is completely opaque to every other PIN in the network. Data Center 1 is simply a traffic sink for Data Center 2, and the WAN PIN is simply a transport mechanism to reach the other PINs in the network.

Connecting these different PINs is a series of interconnects, shown as the small circles labeled IC in Figure 4-9. Some PINs might connect directly to each other as well as to the Core WAN PIN, as illustrated with the DMZ and Data Center 2 PINs. Others might connect only to the Core. Each PIN's internal structure is completely different from every other PIN's. For instance, Data Center 1 might have core, distribution, and access layers, and Data Center 2 might have only core and aggregation layers. These layers are completely independent of the overall network design.

PINs are useful for understanding a network design from an operational perspective, because they provide a strong functional view based on business use for each PIN. This allows each business problem to be approached independently, which can often clarify the problems involved. Vendor sales folks tend to work within PINs almost exclusively because it helps to narrow the solution to a particular environment, helping to drive requirements.

PINs are also useful for network planning; data center equipment, for instance, can be handled on a different replacement schedule than the remaining equipment in the network. Prioritized business needs fall naturally into the various PINs, making cost management easier and more effective.

As a network design paradigm, however, PINs fail on several counts. First, PINs treat the network as a series of interconnected black boxes that have little relationship to one another. This encourages thinking in bits and pieces, rather than treating the network as an end-to-end system. As an example, consider the case of QoS controls; if each PIN handles quality of service independently, with various mechanisms simply interfaced at the interconnect points, the ability of a network engineer to understand the actual QoS implemented for a particular stream end-to-end is severely compromised.

Second, PINs encourage spaghetti topologies and fragmented policy implementation. Overall traffic planning is not normally a consideration in PINs, and overall scalability is assumed from splitting functionality into multiple pieces. This clearly doesn't work—too many interconnects between PINs that don't run through the WAN PIN will destroy any

ability to hide information along module boundaries. If each PIN is managed with an independent security policy to best support the purpose of the PIN itself, building an overall security policy that can be applied to any location in the network becomes almost impossible.

An illustration may help to drive these points home.

Suppose you decide to build a new house. You proceed to a local builder's office and select from among all the available living room designs one that you think will fit your needs. From another stack of designs, you select a kitchen that will best fit your needs and budget. Next, you select three bedrooms from the stack of available bedroom designs and select some bathroom designs from the stack of bathroom designs.

You then take all these different designs, pile them on the builder's desk, and say, "Now build me a hallway that will connect all these pieces, and I'll have a nice house."

PINs fail as a network design paradigm for all the same reasons building a house room by room, with an interconnection hallway, fails. They may help the architect understand the way a network is laid out, and connect the network to the business in a more apparent way, but they aren't a solid network design tool.

Summary

This chapter has covered a dizzying array of models, from the esoteric to the well-known. What's the point of all this modeling?

Each model provides a view into the mind of protocol designers, network equipment designers, and network designers through the years of networking as a profession. Each one brings some new information to the table and hence is worth digging in to and understanding on its own. As a whole, finding, learning, and understanding every model on its own terms provides a deeper understanding of network design and operation from a number of different perspectives.

Underlying Support

No matter how far up the networking stack you might roam, you'll always come back down to speeds and feeds—as rule 9 in RFC1925 states, "For all resources, whatever it is, you need more." But how does the physical layer, with all those bits and bytes and headers and trailers and stuff, relate to network architecture?

The first part of this chapter discusses the crucial questions every network designer needs to be able to answer about every link type (virtual or real), and why each of these questions matters. The second section provides an overview of the Spanning Tree Protocol (STP) and the points you need to remember to design for STP. The third section covers Transparent Interconnection of Lots of Links (TRILL) as a standards-based example of the various data center fabrics that are now available.

Questions You Should Ask

Have you ever sat and had a long discussion with a network link? If you haven't, you really should sometime—the physical links that run rack to rack, building to building, and city to city are the real workhorses of the networking industry. Okay, so maybe you can't talk to a physical link, but if you could, what would you ask?

Here are the absolutely crucial questions to understand before using a particular link type.

What Happens When the Link Fails?

The first question an engineer might ask about a link is, "How does this work?" Is the signaling optical, or electronic? What sort of modulation is used? What's the maximum length of a single run? Is the link multiplexed or not? All these questions are interesting, but they aren't the first question a network designer should ask. So what is the first question a network designer should ask?

What happens when the link fails?

This might seem a little pessimistic, but it's important because link failure is where network design really interacts with the physical characteristics of the link itself. Link failures cause loss of service, jitter, and changes in end-to-end delay for applications running on top of the network.

To put the problem another way: a network's performance is closely tied to the speed at which the control plane reacts to changes in network topology. It's very difficult to react to a change the control plane doesn't know about, so it's crucial to consider how long it takes to discover a failure across this type of link.

The classic example of a link type with no real down notification is a switched Ethernet segment—all reachability to every device across the segment could be lost, but as long as there is a carrier between the router interface and the switch, the link will be shown as operational in the local routing table. Multicast only failures, unidirectional failures, and other failure types can also post serious challenges to the capability to deliver traffic across a link while allowing the link to appear operational from the routing protocol's perspective.

What options does the designer have in those situations where the network must converge more quickly than the physical link will detect a failure and notify the routing protocol? An alternative polling mechanism such as fast hellos at the protocol level or Bidirectional Forwarding Detection (BFD) can be used to detect link failures quickly where needed. Reachability to external devices can be tracked using solutions such as IP Service Level Agreement (IP SLA); however, it's important to remember that polling mechanisms are always slower than event-driven mechanisms, and require a lot more processing and work to provide good failure detection while minimizing false positives and other problems.

What Types of Virtualization Can Be Run Over This Link?

Virtualization through tunneling is a common feature of most network technologies in current architectures; this means it's very important to think about what types of tunnels a particular link can support. For instance, if you are running a set of circuits across an L3VPN provided using MPLS, the only way to run MPLS on top of the service is to run some other tunneling protocol (such as Multipoint Generic Routing Encapsulation [MGRE]) on top of the IP service, then configure MPLS forwarding on top of the second tunneling protocol. This could be a problem if you're planning to use an MPLS Layer 2 service to provide data center interconnect over the L3VPN service. You may wind up with less useable bandwidth than you thought.

For instance, Maximum Transmission Unit (MTU) is a major consideration when determining whether to run a virtual link across any given transport. An L2TPv3 link running over an L3VPN provided on top of an MPLS service has a local header for each link, an MPLS header, an IP header, an L2TPv3 header, another IP header, and finally any other transport headers on top of that. It's possible to eat up the entire MTU of some link types with headers.

You can also run into performance and throughput issues if the tunnel processing is done in software rather than hardware. It is difficult to get accurate data from most vendors, so be sure to do your own testing before making production decisions.

Another aspect of virtualization to consider is fate sharing; anytime you run multiple virtual links over a single physical link, the virtual links will share the fate of the physical link. If 100 VLANs are carried over a single Ethernet segment using trunking or 802.1Q, then all 100 virtual links fail when the single Ethernet segment fails. Fate sharing is a major problem when a virtual link and its backup are both carried across a single physical link—a single failure can take out all available paths, a fact that can be easily hidden on network diagrams.

How Does the Link Support Quality of Service?

Quality of service (QoS) support will generally fall into three broad areas:

- The ability to mark packets on each link type based on the priority or class of service a particular stream or application expects

- The ability of each interface implementation along the path to read, understand, and act on these packet markings

- The types of queues and rate limiting mechanisms available on the interfaces along a particular path, as well as the parameters and adjustments the operator can make to these queues and rate limiters

Marking Packets

How many bits are available for marking packets on this link type? The number of bits available determines the number of queues any interface along the path is going to be able to act on. If there are only 3 bits to use for marking the class of service, then there will only be 8 possible classes (0–7) with which you can mark the traffic. Some link types will have no bits available to mark traffic; for instance, an Ethernet link without trunking enabled. In this case QoS will have to rely on a higher-level protocol for marking, such as the TOS bits in IP.

Remember that when you rely on a higher-level transport protocol to mark packets for specific quality of service handling, there is often no way to translate those markings into actual differences in the way traffic is handled when being forwarded through the network. Layer 2 devices, such as switches, may not pay attention to QoS or Type of Service (ToS) markings in the IP packet header if these headers are not examined during packet forwarding operation. Other switches can, and will, look at higher-layer marking such as DSCP if they are configured to do so.

Queues and Rate Limiters

It's also important to understand the types of queues and rate limiters available across a particular transport system. When and where can traffic be rate limited or shaped? Based

on what information—the type of service bits in the packet headers, the protocol type, or other factors? How does shaping work along this circuit, and what impact will shaping (which necessarily involves queuing packets for some period of time) have on critical business applications?

Another queuing consideration is related to the type of interface a link uses. For switches, the number of queues available, the existence of a priority queue, and the number of drop thresholds within each queue all vary depending on the type of device and the module within the device. It's important to check this when deciding what equipment will fit your network design.

Also note where queuing takes place in a device, or rather what types of quality of service controls are implemented at various points in the processing of a packet in any given device. Queuing is normally implemented after switching, in between the switching process and the output interface. Queuing might also be implemented across the fabric or BUS that connects line cards. Rate limiting might take place on the outbound interface, the inbound interface, or both—it's very important to understand which when you're considering how to manage the amount of traffic accepted into the network from any given edge device.

Speeds and Feeds Versus Quality of Service

Talk to any network engineer long enough about quality of service, and you're likely to hear something like this: "Quality of service is only necessary when there are bandwidth constraints; if you have enough bandwidth, you don't need QoS." There is some truth in this statement. If there were always enough bandwidth to transmit every packet offered to the network, there would be less need to control how traffic is transmitted. However, you might still have the problem of a large packet delaying the transmittal of a small packet, and thus introducing jitter into a real-time traffic stream. Additionally, people often forget that even the most granular link usage statistics are but an average. You can have microbursts of data that cause critical packets to be dropped but never show up in your network management reports. So no matter how big your pipe is, or how lightly used you think it is, it might save the day to have at least some basic QoS implemented.

On the other hand, the cost of links sometimes drive network engineers to use highly tuned QoS systems to reduce bandwidth usage to the minimum possible. In this valiant effort, traffic is classified into as many different buckets as possible, with strict rules on how packets from different classes of service should be serialized onto the wire. "Maybe we can wring just one more flow out of this link, if only we can figure out how to..."

So how do we balance between the two? When do we upgrade our links, and when do we introduce finer-grained QoS to resolve problems with a particular application? The key to this problem lies in naming and understanding both sides of the equation.

What is the cost of increasingly complex QoS? The first cost is in the time required to set up and run the QoS system, including managing the unexpected flows and situations that will arise in any complex system. Keep in mind that you want to standardize your QOS settings as much as possible across the entire enterprise. That means you'll need to

design for applications and traffic flow throughout your entire network. And any QOS changes will need to be deployed throughout your entire network. The second cost is in the time required to troubleshoot the QoS system when it fails, or when the network itself fails. To make this problem worse, most QoS problems show up as difficult to diagnose application performance problems. The third cost is in the time and processing required for routers and switches to build and manage large numbers of queues, and in the diminishing returns of slicing traffic into smaller and smaller queues, each of which will necessarily receive an ever smaller piece of the available bandwidth.

The cost of adding higher bandwidth connections includes, of course, the cost of the link itself. For a WAN link this might be a real drawback. On both LAN and WAN connections there may be additional interfaces required or even an upgrade to your network equipment. Configuration changes will be needed.

Good QoS design is not a trivial exercise. There have been entire books written on quality of service, such as *End-to-End QoS*, Second Edition, by Tim Szigeti, and we refer you to them for complete understanding of QoS. From a network design standpoint, it boils down to understanding your business and understanding the needs of your business applications, then designing a network that can support the QoS requirements.

Spanning Tree

The Spanning Tree Protocol (STP) is one of the simplest control planes available, and also probably one of the most widely deployed. Three specific points are important for the network designers to consider in using STP:

■ STP builds a single tree of the entire topology, rather than per destination/device. This implies that the topology must match the tree STP will build, or only those parts of the physical topology that match a spanning tree will be used by the protocol. Figure 5-1 provides an example.

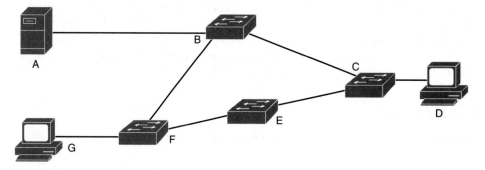

Figure 5-1 *Spanning Tree Inefficiency*

While this topology is a loop, STP needs to build a single tree that can be used to forward traffic. Assuming Switch C is chosen as the root of the spanning tree, the link between Switches B and F will be blocked, so traffic from Server A to Host G is

switched along the path [B,C,E,F]. This is clearly a much longer path than the optimal, which is [B,F].

- All reachability (for both network nodes and end hosts) is learned in the data plane, rather than being carried through the network in the control plane. In the network in Figure 5-1, the spanning tree across the network is built node-to-node to include the links [B,C], [C,E], and [E,F]. This tree is enforced by shutting off all traffic along the [B,F] link, rather than actually building a local forwarding table based on reachability information learned from the control plane.

  The implication for design is that mobility and loop-freeness are built on the back of data plane timers, rather than control plane convergence speed. To increase the speed of convergence in an STP network, the protocol is removed from edge links (such as [A,B]) by techniques such as the Cisco PortFast, timers are adjusted to produce faster detection of link and node failures, and faster link layer failure detection mechanisms are deployed, such as Ethernet OAM.

- There are no loop breaking mechanisms in most data link layer protocol specifications, such as a time-to-live counter in the header; if a loop occurs, packets will loop until the control plane breaks the loop. If the looping packet interferes with the control plane's capability to break the loop, it could be impossible to break the loop, causing a permanent failure condition (until a network operator intervenes and manually breaks the loop).

Some large scale data center networks have moved away from using STP by designing their physical topologies in the form of a spanning tree, and then using MAC address filtering or multiple spanning tree domains to prevent packet loops. One example of such designs is covered in Chapter 12, "Building the Second Floor."

TRILL

Transparent Interconnection of Lots of Links (TRILL) was originally conceived with a simple idea: what happens if we replace STP with a link state protocol? A common misconception engineers often form from this simple basis is that TRILL routes Layer 2 frames much like any traditional routing protocol routes Layer 3 (IP) packets—but this isn't really the idea behind TRILL, nor the way TRILL actually operates.

TRILL Operation

Figure 5-2 is used as a reference for explaining TRILL operation.

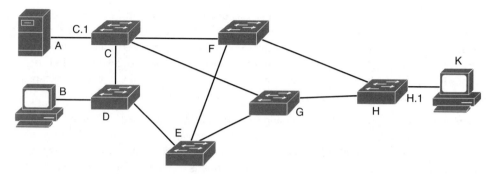

Figure 5-2   *Example Network for TRILL Operation*

TRILL operation proceeds in three steps.

In the first step, a set of shortest path trees are built node to node (not edge to edge, as in routing), across all the switches in the network. IS-IS is used to find neighbors, advertise node-to-node links, and build the trees that provide connectivity across the switches. In this example, H would build a tree that includes reachability to the following:

- Switch F along the path [H,F]

- Switch C along the path [H,F,C]

- Switch G along the path [H,G]

- Switch E along the path [H,G,E]

- Switch D along the path [H,G,E,D]

After this set of shortest path trees is built through the network, *the second step,* learning reachability, can begin. Unlike routing (and like STP), reachability is learned through the data plane. If Server A forwards a packet toward Host K, Switch C now learns that Server A is reachable through interface C.1. Assuming Switch C doesn't have any forwarding information for Host K, it will place this packet onto a multicast tree that reaches every other edge node in the TRILL domain. The packet isn't transmitted "natively," but is encapsulated in a TRILL header (like Q-in-Q) that contains additional information, such as a TTL and information about the source switch in the TRILL domain. In this case, the header would contain Switch C's *nickname,* which is simply a unique identifier on the TRILL domain that can be used to forward packets directly to Switch C.

On receiving this packet from this multicast tree, each edge node will examine the TRILL header and inner (original) packet and learn that Server A is reachable through Switch C. Again, assuming Switches D and H have no prior knowledge of Host K, they will both unwrap the TRILL encapsulation and flood this packet to an unknown destination onto their attached segments. Note that the "core switches," or switches that are not on the edge, do not examine these packets, nor learn the MAC addresses carried in them. In this way, TRILL protects the core switches from learning the entire table of reachable Layer 2 addresses in the network.

In the third step, normal switching begins. Assume Host K responds; we can trace this response back through the process of being forwarded to Server A. When Host K transmits a packet to Server A, Switch H receives this packet at interface H.1 and examines its local forwarding table for information about the destination address. Switch H finds it does have a forwarding entry; Server A is reachable through Switch C. Switch H encapsulates the original packet into a TRILL header and forwards the packet to Switch F.

Switch F examines the TRILL header and finds the packet is destined to Switch C, so it simply forwards the packet on toward the correct destination. When Switch C receives the packet, it looks at the TRILL header and the source address, and learns that Host K is reachable through Switch H. After this information is entered into its local forwarding table, Switch C removes the outer TRILL header and forwards the packet onto the correct local link based on the forwarding information built previously—forwarding information discovered when the first packet from Server A was transmitted.

TRILL in the Design Landscape

What are the practical implications of TRILL operation? The most obvious is that TRILL allows every link in the TRILL domain to be used, rather than just those links that fall along a single spanning tree for the entire physical topology. This makes for more efficient link utilization. TRILL's use of a link state protocol to discover topology also implies that all the positive and negative aspects of a distributed link state control plane are brought into play in the TRILL domain.

Microloops are bound to be a part of any TRILL domain while it's converging, just as they are in IS-IS and OSPF networks supporting IPv4 and IPv6. Techniques used to provide fast reroute in link state based IP networks should also be applicable to TRILL domain, as well (although there are no standards in this space, nor has any vender expressed plans to implement fast reroute in TRILL based fabrics). Note the TRILL header does include a TTL to prevent either microloops or more permanent forwarding loops from looping individual packets until the control plane or manual intervention breaks the loop.

Although TRILL uses a link state protocol to discover the network topology, it does not use the link state protocol to discover reachability. This means that like STP, TRILL is reliant on data plane timers to discover when a device has moved from one place in the network to another; the current forwarding table information must time out in all nodes before devices can be assured their traffic is delivered to the correct end host in a TRILL network.

TRILL is also capable of providing control plane operations for large multitenant data centers supporting millions of virtual networks through various extensions and modifications to the base protocol.

TRILL and the Fabrics

TRILL and its close cousin, IEEE 802.1aq (Shortest Path Bridging), are both the foundation for a number of vendor fabric offerings, including Cisco's *FabricPath*. These offerings generally operate in a way that is similar enough to TRILL to be treated as a TRILL domain from a design perspective.

One major difference between these offerings and TRILL's basic operation is that it's possible to include reachability information in the IS-IS process that provides topology information for the TRILL domain. In the case of the example given in Figure 5-2, Switch C, on discovering that Server A is locally attached, can send an IS-IS update including this bit of reachability information, so the first packet directed at Server A doesn't need to be multicast through the TRILL domain.

> **Note**   Juniper's *Q Fabric* is based on an MPLS overlay fabric (much like a Layer 2 VPN provided by a service provider), using BGP and route reflectors. *Q Fabric* isn't based on TRILL, though it can still be treated as a single fast flat Layer 2 domain with optimal routing for the purposes of network design.

Final Thoughts on the Physical Layer

The primary place where the network designer is going to interact with Layer 2 control planes is in contained environments, such as a data center or campus network. Although these designs are an important component of the overall network, it's important to keep their contained nature in mind; the data center is not the network, it is a single Layer 2 failure domain within a larger Layer 3 routed network design.

Within the network at large, the primary considerations for a designer to consider when interacting with the physical infrastructure revolve around how it interacts with the routed control plane, quality of service, and virtualization. So as long as you can answer questions on these three areas about any physical link, you should be able to successfully design around the strengths and weaknesses of every available link type.

Principles of Modularity

Modularity is one of those "tried and true" concepts in network design that very few people ever think about. Networks are modularized, well, because it has always been done that way. Everyone knows that too big is bad, right? But how big is too big?

The biggest problem with answering this question is that not only is it dependent on what you're trying to do, but also on what materials you're working with and what year you live in.

What year you live in? Suppose you went back to the turn of the 12th century and asked, "How big of a house do I need?" Given the materials they had to work with, the expense of the labor required to build and manage a large physical space, and the need to fit large numbers of people inside difficult to build and maintain city walls, the answer would be quite small compared to our modern standards. Moving to the turn of the 19th century, the answer would be much larger—in fact, it might even be larger than what we're accustomed to today, in terms of sheer physical space (especially including outbuildings). The need to house large families along with the people needed to run a large farm, separating the kitchen from the main living area, and other factors would contribute to a "just right" living space being rather large.

What we often fail to recognize is that, similarly, the answer to the question, "how big of a network is just right," cycles through the years. Networking technologies are designed that will allow the size of a single domain within the network to grow large. Network engineers take this new technology as a way to build scale-free single domain networks, so they build huge domains. These huge domains fail for various reasons, injecting a little humility into the lives of network designers, the scale of a single domain contracts a little, and we relearn the lessons of modularity all over again using different terms and ideas. Then someone thinks of a new way to make huge flat domains, and we start all over again at the beginning.

Wouldn't it be better if we just learned the theory behind modularization, including the purpose, methods, and trade-offs, and then intelligently applied them so that we

could right size every module in a network from the beginning? Why not look at the technology we have available, make an intelligent guess as to how large it can go, and then modularize above that size?

This chapter starts with the question *why modularize?* In this section, we'll put all the reasons you've ever heard, and some you might not have heard before, in one place. After this we'll discuss how to modularize, and then consider the trade-offs between modularization and network efficiency.

Why Modularize?

There are, in essence, only two reasons to modularize networks:

- To reduce the amount of data any particular network device must deal with when describing the topology and calculating the best path to any given destination

- To reduce the amount of information the humans working on the network must deal with when designing, deploying, managing, and troubleshooting the network

The following sections discuss these two concepts, including several areas of thought that branch off from each of them. Following these two discussions, there is an entire section on the Mean Time Between Failures (MTBF)/Mean Time to Repair (MTTR) curve. This is one of those foundational concepts in network design that you will meet time and time again; we'll run into it again when discussing resilience, for instance (see Chapter 10, "Measure Twice," for a complete discussion on MTBF and MTTR).

Machine Level Information Overload

Why shouldn't we rebuild the Internet, or every large network, as one large flat switched domain? Couldn't we find a way to build equipment that can handle one entry in the forwarding table per reachable host, or use caching to hold only the small part of the table any particular device needs at any given moment in time?

The simple answer is that if you build a single large switched domain as large as the Internet, you'd find yourself with no way to reduce the amount of information contained in any single device's control plane. Not only would every single device need to know how to reach every other device, each device would also need to know each and every time the state of any other device on the network changes. As an example, assume you built a network with 100,000 hosts attached, and where every forwarding device in the network knows about every host. If each device changes state once every 24 hours (once a day), there would still be one state change per second in the entire network—and well over 100,000 devices would need to be notified of this change in near real time to maintain forwarding. This amount of state, and this rate of change, simply isn't possible to maintain in the real world. What you'd have is a case of information overload at the machine level.

Machine Level Information Overload Defined

Information overload can be split into three independent problems:

- Processing and memory utilization

- Rate of state change

- Positive feedback loops

Processing and memory utilization is the simplest of these problems to understand—larger routing tables take up more physical memory and require more CPU cycles to process.

Rate of state change is slightly more complex because of the added time factor. Every time the network topology changes, the control plane must recalculate the best path to some number of impacted destinations. The quicker the topology changes, the more often these best paths must be calculated. If the rate of change is faster than the control plane can calculate (or propagate) new best paths, the network will never converge. The global Internet is an example of a running network that never truly converges because the rate of topology change is so fast (due in part to the sheer number of devices interacting) that the control plane (BGP, in this case) cannot keep pace.

What Is Network Convergence?

We often speak of network convergence in the network design field, but we rarely define it in technical terms. What does convergence mean?

If we treat the control plane as a distributed database, then the network is converged when every router (or device with a copy of the database) has the same view of the network's state, or a consistent set of best paths through the network. This doesn't mean that every device has the same database, only that the forwarding table on every router is consistent, there are no loops in the control plane, and there is no further information to be transmitted or processed.

This is a superset of a link state's protocol insistence that every router in a given flooding domain should have a consistent database, or that the link state databases of every device within a single flooding domain should be identical.

Convergence is different from consistent database replication in two ways. First, the database of every device in a network need not be identical for every device to have a consistent view of the network's topology. Devices in a network with aggregated information can have a consistent view of the network without having identical databases. Second, just having a matching database isn't enough; the database must be processed on each device, and forwarding information that produces a consistent view throughout the network must be installed on every device.

Positive feedback loops are the most complex of these three information overload problems because we must add the concept of rate of change with the rate of information flow. Figure 6-1 illustrates a positive feedback loop.

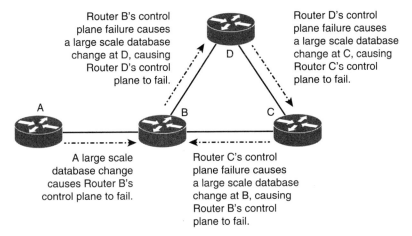

Router B's control
plane failure causes
a large scale database
change at D, causing
Router D's control
plane to fail.

Router D's control
plane failure causes
a large scale database
change at C, causing
Router C's control
plane to fail.

A large scale
database change
causes Router B's
control plane to fail.

Router C's control
plane failure causes
a large scale database
change at B, causing
Router B's control
plane to fail.

Figure 6-1   *Positive Feedback Loop*

The example of a positive feedback loop in Figure 6-1 begins with some large scale change at Router A, causing Router A to send a large update toward Router B. This large scale control plane update is too large for Router B's control plane to process in a reasonable amount of time (either due to lack of memory or processing power). Even while this update is being processed by Router B, it is forwarded (reflooded) to Router C, which also cannot process the information in a reasonable amount of time. While Router C is processing this information, it is passed to Router D.

At Router D, the information overload is large enough that it causes the peering relationship between Routers C and D to reset. This causes an apparent change in the network topology, and Router D sends a large update to Router B with information about this topology change—which begins the cycle once again. Positive feedback loops can be stable (they do not spread throughout the control plane) or self-reinforcing in a way that causes the entire network control plane to fail.

Note   A stable positive feedback loop can be either a good or a bad thing—depending on the intention of the designer. For instance, in an electronic circuit that creates a continuous frequency signal, a positive feedback loop can be used to maintain a consistent output. On the other hand, a stable positive feedback loop that keeps a routing loop in place isn't a good thing. Stable positive feedback loops are normally not a good thing in computer networks.

Reducing Machine Information Level Overload

Given that "too much information" is a problem, what is the solution? The primary tool the network architect uses to overcome machine level information overload is *information hiding*.

Information hiding reduces the routing table size by either combining multiple destinations into a single destination (aggregation, covered in more detail in Chapter 7, "Applying Modularity") or separating destinations into sub topologies (virtualization, covered in more detail in Chapter 12, "Building the Second Floor").

Information hiding reduces the rate of state change in the same way—by hiding reachability information through aggregation or virtualization. Hiding reachability information hides changes in state, as Figure 6-2 shows.

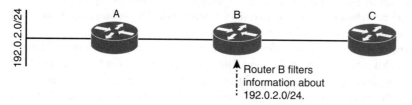

Figure 6-2   *Example of Information Hiding and Rate of State Change Reduction*

Because Router B is hiding information about 192.0.2.0/24 through a route filter, Router C never receives any state about this destination—so it doesn't have to do any recalculations if the reachability of that network changes.

Information hiding, finally, reduces the possibility of positive feedback loops by reducing or removing control plane updates due to state change from the network. Returning to Figure 6-1, if Router B filters, hides, or otherwise blocks the updated information from Router A, the information would not be passed on to Router C, then to Router D, to cause the neighbor adjacency failure between Routers C and D, which causes a second change at Router B.

Failure Domains and Modularity

Put in the simplest terms possible, a failure domain is the *set of devices that must recalculate their control plane information in the case of a topology change.* As an example, in Figure 6-2, Routers A and B are in the same failure domain because they share a common view of the network. Router C, however, is in a separate failure domain, at least in regard to 192.0.2.0/24.

What's the difference between a network module and a failure domain? One is a demarcation of policy or intent, whereas the other is a demarcation in the flow of control plane information. A module is a clearly definable area of the network topology.

The edges of network modules and the edges of failure domains coincide; where we find one, we often find the other. This is because policy implementation almost

always involves information hiding. This isn't always true, but it's true often enough that throughout this section we use the terms *failure domain* and *network module* interchangeably.

Remember, however, that failure domains and policy edges are not always in the same place in the network; although it's convenient to think of them in the same way, they are really different things with different purposes.

As an example, consider the network in Figure 6-3.

In this example, the reachability within each data center is aggregated at the edge routers B and C. Aggregating so the data center routes are not transmitted into the network core is a policy, but it also creates a failure domain boundary, so routers B and C are the edge of both a module—a specific place in the network, the data center, with specific policies and reachability information—and the edge of a failure domain. However, because there is a Layer 2 tunnel stretched between the two data center fabrics, these two data centers represent a single failure domain. Information about a single link failure at A must be transmitted all the way to router D in order to keep the control plane synchronized. These two data centers, although they are in the same failure domain, would not be considered the same module; each data center may have different policy of service, different link bandwidth, and other policies. In this example, then, the failure domain edge aligns with the module edge in one case, and not in the other case.

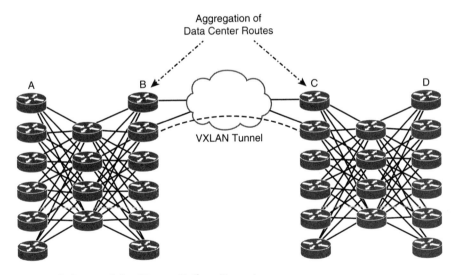

Figure 6-3 *Modules Versus Failure Domains*

Separating Complexity from Complexity

Where should you hide information in a network? The first general rule is to separate complexity from complexity. For instance, in the network shown in Figure 6-4, it's possible to hide information at Routers A and B toward Router C, or at Router C toward Router D. Which would be more optimal?

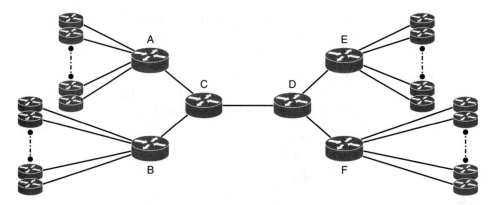

Figure 6-4 *Optimal Information Hiding Points*

In this example, the difference between these two choices might seem to be minor, but let's examine the two possibilities in more detail. From Router D's perspective, the only difference between the two options is that it receives information about two more routers (Routers A and B), and two more links ([A,C] and [B,C])—this isn't that much information. From Router A's perspective, however, the difference is between learning about every router, link, and destination reachable through Router B, including all state changes for those network elements, or only learning a single destination (in the optimal case), or destinations without links and routers (in the least optimal case) from B.

Clearly, hiding information at Routers A and B reduces the total information carried across all routers more than hiding information at Routers C and D. You will always find that hiding information at the point where any two complex topologies meet will provide the largest reduction in network-wide table sizes. This simple rule, however, must be balanced against the suboptimal routing that is always caused by removing state in the control plane, a topic discussed in the section "Modularization and Optimization," later in the chapter.

Note   Another way of looking at this is to compartmentalize complexity—to separate complex bits of the topology from the rest of the network through a module edge or making it into a separate failure domain. Either way, the point is to make certain that complex topologies don't interact in the control plane, either directly or through some simpler part of the network.

Human Level Information Overload

There is a second piece to the information overload problem, as well—the ability of network operators to quickly understand, modify, and troubleshoot the network. Because this is clearly more of a business-related problem, impacting operational rather than capital costs, this side of information hiding rises above strict design and into the purview of the network architect. There are two aspects to this side of information hiding: the ability

of the network designer to clearly assign functionality, and repeatable configurations. Each of these two aspects is discussed in the following sections.

Clearly Assigned Functionality

Imagine setting up the filters for the network in Figure 6-5 so that Host A can reach Servers M, N, and C, while Host K can reach Servers F, M, and N.

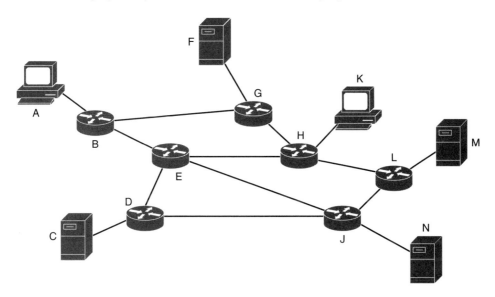

Figure 6-5   *Difficult Policy Problem*

There are a number of ways to solve this problem, including the following:

- Set up filters using the correct source and destination addresses at Routers B and H to enforce this policy.

- Set up filters using the correct source and destination addresses at Routers D, G, J, and L to enforce this policy.

- Create two VLAN overlays on the network, each containing the set of servers that Hosts A and K are allowed to reach.

All these solutions are going to be difficult to maintain over time. For instance, if Host A moves so it is no longer connected to Router B, but rather to Router H, then the filters associated with Host A must move with the host. If any of the servers move, the filters enforcing these policies need to be checked for correctness, as well. If the policies change, the network administrator must find every point at which each policy is enforced, and make the correct modifications there as well—the more widely these policies are dispersed in the network, the more difficult this will be.

How could we make this problem easier to solve? By gathering each device in the network together by purpose or policy, so policies can be implemented along the edges

leading to these groups of devices. This strategy of pulling devices with common policy requirements into a single module accomplishes the following:

- Reduces the number of policy chokepoints in the network to the minimum possible, so network operators need to look in fewer places to understand end-to-end policy for a particular flow or set of hosts

- Makes it possible to state a specific purpose for each module in the network, which allows the policies into and out of that module to be more easily defined and verified

- Allows the gathering of policy problems into common sets

This gathering of policy into specific points of the network is one of the ways modularization helps network operators focus on one problem at a time.

Repeatable Configurations

Gathering policy up along the edges between modules attacks the problem of operational complexity in a second way, as well. Each network device along the edge of a particular module should have a similar configuration, at least in terms of policy; hence they have repeatable configurations. Parameters such as IP address ranges may change, but the bulk of the configuration will remain the same.

In the same way, once policy is removed from the network devices internal to a module, those configurations are simplified as well. With careful management, the configuration of every router and/or switch internal to a network module should be very similar.

Mean Time to Repair and Modularization

The Mean Time to Repair (MTTR) is the time it takes between a problem arising in the network and the network returning to fully operational state. This time can be broken down into two pieces:

- The time it takes for the network to resume forwarding traffic between all reachable destinations

- The time it takes to restore the network to its original design and operation

The first definition relates to machine-level information overload; the less information there is in the control plane, the faster the network is going to converge. The second relates to operator information overload; the more consistent configurations are, and the easier it is to understand what the network should look like, the faster operators are going to be able to track down and find any network problems. The relationship between MTTR and modularization can be charted as shown in Figure 6-6.

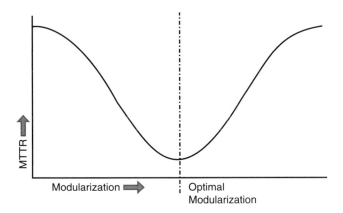

Figure 6-6   *MTTR Versus Modularization*

As we move from a single flat failure domain into a more modularized design, the time it takes to find and repair problems in the network decreases rapidly, driving the MTTR down. However, there is a point at which additional modularity starts increasing MTTR, where breaking the network into smaller domains actually causes the network to become more complex. To understand this phenomenon, consider the case of a network where every network device, such as a router or switch, has become its own failure domain (think of a network configured completely with static routes and no dynamic routing protocol). It's easy to see that there is no difference between this case and the case of a single large flat failure domain.

How do you find the right point along the MTTR curve? The answer is always going to be, "it depends," but let's try to develop some general rules.

First and foremost, the right size for any given failure domain is never going to be the entire network (unless the network is really and truly very small). Almost any size network can, and should, be broken into more than one failure domain.

Second, the right size for a given failure domain is always going to depend on advances in control plane protocols, advances in processing power, and other factors. There were long and hard arguments over the optimal size of an OSPF area within the network world for years. How many LSAs could a single router handle? How fast would SPF run across a database of a given size? After years of work optimizing the way OSPF runs, and increases in processing power in the average router, this argument has generally been overcome by events.

Over time, as technology improves, the optimal size for a single failure domain will increase. Over time, as networks increase in size, the optimal number of failure domains within a single network will tend to remain constant. These two trends tend to offset one another, so that most networks end up with about the same number of failure domains throughout their life, even as they grow and expand to meet the ever increasing demands of the business.

So how big is too big? Start with the basic rules we've already talked about, building modules around policy requirements and separating complexity from complexity. After

you get the lines drawn around these two things, and you've added natural boundaries based on business units, geographic locations, and other factors, you have a solid starting point for determining where failure domain boundaries should go.

From this point, consider which services need to be more isolated than others, simply so they will have a better survivability rate, and look to measure the network's performance to determine if there are any failure domains that are too large.

How Do You Modularize?

We know we want to build modules, we want to hide information, and we want to control the size of the failure domains we build in our networks. But given all of this, how do we go about modularizing a network? The primary means we have to implement policy and restrict the size of a failure domain is by hiding information. There are two ways to hide information in the control plane, and there are two types of information to hide.

Topology and Reachability

Whether you are hiding information horizontally or vertically, there are two types of information you can hide: topology and reachability. Figure 6-7 illustrates the difference.

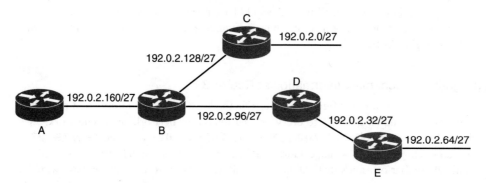

Figure 6-7 *Hiding Topology Versus Reachability*

Assume this network is running a link state protocol; in normal operation, Router A has the following information in its table:

- Router E is connected to Router D, 192.0.2.64/27, and 192.0.2.32/27.

- Router D is connected to Router E, 192.0.2.32/27, and 192.0.2.96/27.

- Router C is connected to Router B, 192.0.2.0/27, and 192.0.2.128/27.

- Router B is connected to Router A, Router C, 192.0.2.160/27, 192.0.2.128/27, and 192.0.2.96/27.

- Router A is connected to Router B and 192.0.2.160/27.

Let's examine three possible ways of hiding information in this network, along with their results.

Aggregating Topology Information at Router B

What if Router B is configured to hide all the topology information it knows about from Router A? Router A's database would contain the following:

- Router B is connected to Router A, 192.0.2.160/27, 192.0.2.128/27, 192.0.2.96/27, 192.0.2.0/27, 192.0.2.32/27, and 192.0.2.64/27.

- Router A is connected to Router B and 192.0.2.160/27.

Notice that the connections between each pair of routers to the right of Router B are no longer listed in the database; every destination (including the links between the routers) is still reachable, but Router A no longer knows the specific paths available to reach each one. Instead, Router A knows only that every destination is reachable through Router B and assumes Router B knows the more specific information required to reach them. Another way to look at this hiding of the topology is that Router A now believes every one of the destinations reachable to the right of Router B is directly connected to Router B itself, rather than through some multihop path that passes through Router B.

This is precisely the database Router A would have if this network were running a distance-vector protocol, or if Router B is configured as a flooding domain boundary in either OSPF or IS-IS.

Aggregating Reachability Information at Router B

What if Router B were configured to advertise the least amount of information possible while maintaining reachability to every destination on the network? In this network, all the addresses reachable via 192.0.2.0/27, 192.0.2.32/27, 192.0.2.64/27, and 192.0.2.96/27 could be represented by a single address, 192.0.2.0/25. If Router B advertises just the minimal number of routes that still preserves all reachability, Router A's database would contain the following:

- Router B is connected to Router A, 192.0.2.160/27, 192.0.2.128/27, and 192.0.2.0/25.

- Router A is connected to Router B and 192.0.2.160/27.

Notice that the topology information behind Router B is hidden as well as the more specific destination information; OSPF and IS-IS both allow route aggregation only at flooding domain borders, so there is no way to configure route aggregation in link state protocols without topology aggregation occurring as well.

This is precisely the database Router A would have if route summarization were configured at Router B in OSPF or IS-IS (route summarization can be configured only at borders between different flooding domains), or if aggregation were configured at Router B in a distance-vector protocol.

Filtering Routing Information at Router B

Finally, it is possible to hide information by filtering routing information at various edges in the network. Router B could be configured to filter all the transit links out of the network; the resulting database at Router A would be as follows:

- Router B is connected to Router A, 192.0.2.160/27,192.0.2.0/27, and 192.0.2.64/27.

- Router A is connected to Router B and 192.0.2.160/27.

Again, information about the topology to the right of Router B is not included in Router A's database. This is because OSPF and IS-IS only allow routing information to be filtered at the same place topology information is aggregated—at a flooding domain boundary.

To provide a more specific example of these two within OSPF, consider the various forms of information hiding OSPF provides at an Area Border Router (ABR):

- A summary LSA (type 3) contains all the reachability information, but summarizes the topology to make all the destinations within the area appear to be connected to the ABR itself.

- A summary LSA (type 3) with route summarization configured contains only partial reachability information (some destinations have been hidden within the single summary route), and these summary destinations appear to be attached directly to the ABR, hiding topology information.

- A type 3 filter removes some reachability information, hiding reachability while also hiding the topology information by making all the routes remaining in the type 3 appear to be attached to the ABR.

- An area border LSA (type 4) exposes the actual attachment point within an area of a specific external route. Here the topology information within an area is exposed to those routers outside the area, reversing the effect of a summary LSA (type 3).

Splitting Failure Domains Horizontally and Vertically

The first, and most commonly recognized, way to hide information in a network is through hierarchy. You can think of this as hiding information horizontally through the network. The second way to hide information in a network is a mechanism that isn't normally thought of as information hiding at all—virtualization. You can think of virtualization as hiding information along vertical layers within a network. Figure 6-8 shows the relationship between virtualization and hierarchy in network architecture.

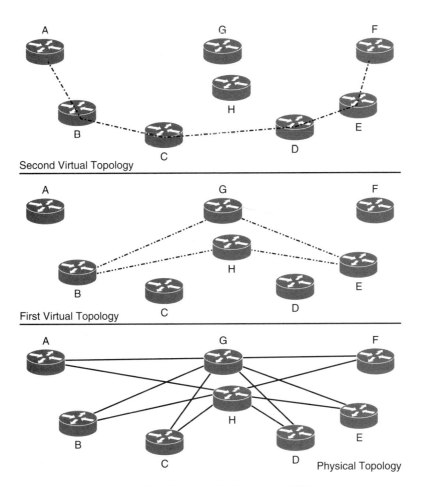

Figure 6-8   *Horizontal and Vertical Information Hiding*

Figure 6-8 shows three networks; the bottom network is the physical topology of a small network. The network administrator can decide to hide information about Routers D, E, and F from Routers A, B, and C, either through route filters or routing aggregation, at Routers G and H. This introduces a hierarchy into the network that hides information horizontally across the network, or within a single topology.

In the first virtual (or overlay) topology, the network administrator has used some method to create a virtual network from a part of the physical topology. This second topology has a separate control plane that only knows about the four routers within the topology; the other routers and links are hidden from this second control plane. Although the overall control plane in this network may be more complex, this second control plane is simpler than the control plane in the physical topology because information has been hidden.

In the second virtual (or overlay) topology, the network administrator has built tunnels along the path, [A,B,C,D,E,F]. This topology also must have a control plane (to draw

traffic along the tunnel path). This second control plane will not have any information about Routers G and H, for instance, although traffic must physically pass through those routers as it traverses the tunnels. Again, although the overall network may be more complex, this second control plane is much simpler than the control plane in the physical topology because of information hiding.

Virtualization and hierarchy are both methods of hiding information in order to solve for specific problems, and they are both forms of modularization. What form of problem might require virtualization? Carrying the traffic of multiple organizations that do not want to (or cannot) interconnect on the same physical infrastructure is a common use case. Carrying traffic that must be securely transported alongside traffic that doesn't need to be secured on a single physical infrastructure is another.

Modularization and Optimization

If modularization brings so many benefits to network architecture, why shouldn't every network be modularized at every point possible? Isn't more aggregation always better than less aggregation? Network design is, as all things, a matter of choosing trade-offs—there is no such thing as a free lunch! One of the trade-offs we deal with all the time is state versus stretch.

Stretch, quite simply, is the difference between the optimum path through the network (for any pair of hosts) and the actual path through the network. For instance, if the shortest actual path available is 2 hops, but traffic is flowing along a 3 hop path, the stretch is 1. Why should we ever have stretch in a network? It seems like you'd just never, ever, want stretch, because stretch always represents suboptimal use of available resources.

But you always end up with stretch, because one of the other fundamental concepts of network design is the use of information hiding to break up failure domains. Hierarchical network design, in fact, is the intentional use of aggregation to reduce the state information—the routing table size, in most cases—in the control plane, so that changes in one area of the network don't cause changes in the routing table halfway around the world. How does this relate to stretch?

Anytime you hide state you increase stretch.

This might not be obvious in all networks—specifically, anytime 100% of your traffic flows north/south, decreasing state will not impact stretch. But if you have a combination of north/south and east/west traffic, then aggregation—reducing state—will always cause traffic to take a suboptimal path through the network—thus increasing stretch.

Spanning tree is a perfect example of running to one extreme of the state/stretch trade-off. Spanning tree reduces the state by forcing all traffic along a single tree in the network and blocking links that don't belong to that tree. Control plane state is absolutely minimized at the cost of increasing the stretch through the network to the maximum possible—to the point that we often design network topologies around the elimination of links not used on the single tree. TRILL and other fabric solutions break the single tree by injecting more state into the network. Another example is virtualization—splitting

traffic off into a separate virtual topology removes the state information for large numbers of destinations reachable through the physical network topology, at the cost of setting the stretch for those destinations to infinite (they become unreachable).

So the reason you can't hide information all the time is because doing so decreases the overall efficiency of the network by increasing stretch.

Summary

Information hiding is one of the most critical tools network designers and architects have in their tool set; developing a thorough understanding of these tools, then, is crucial in becoming a successful architect. One way to see this is to note how often these topics crop up in every other area of network design. In Chapter 8, "Weathering Storms," you're going to see how breaking failure domains apart impacts the ability of a network to survive failures of all kinds. In Chapter 9, "Securing the Premises," failure and module boundaries form the firewalls through which attackers must pass to succeed in damaging the network. In Chapter 12, "Building the Second Floor," vertical modularization through virtual overlays and tunneling comes to the fore. In Chapter 14, "Considering Complexity," we spend time looking at the interaction between modularity, policy, and optimization. In virtually every area of network design, we're going to encounter information hiding.

Applying Modularity

Knowing and applying the principles of modular design are two different sorts of problems. But there are entire books just on practical modular design in large scale networks. What more can one single chapter add to the ink already spilled on this topic? The answer: a focus on *why* we use specific design patterns to implement modularity, rather than *how* to use modular design. Why should we use hierarchical design, specifically, to create a modular network design? Why should we use overlay networks to create virtualization, and what are the results of virtualization as a mechanism to provide modularity?

We'll begin with hierarchical design, considering what it is (and what it is not), and why hierarchical design works the way it does. Then we'll delve into some general rules for building effective hierarchical designs, and some typical hierarchical design patterns. In the second section of this chapter, we'll consider what virtualization is, why we virtualize, and some common problems and results of virtualization.

What Is Hierarchical Design?

Hierarchical designs consist of three network layers: the core, the distribution, and the access, with narrowly defined purposes within each layer and along each layer edge.

Right? Wrong.

Essentially, this definition takes one specific hierarchical design as the definition for all hierarchical design—we should never mistake one specific pattern for the whole design idea. What's a better definition?

> A hub-and-spoke design pattern combined with an architecture methodology used to guide the placement and organizations of modular boundaries in a network.

There are two specific components to this definition we need to discuss—the idea of a hub and spoke design pattern and this concept of an architecture methodology. What do these two mean?

A Hub-and-Spoke Design Pattern

Figure 7-1 illustrates a hub-and-spoke design pattern.

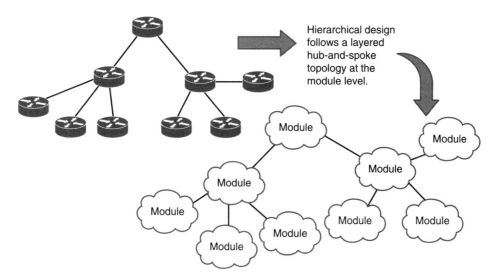

Figure 7-1   *Hub and Spoke Hierarchical Design Pattern*

Why should hierarchical design follow a hub-and-spoke pattern at the module level? Why not a ring of modules, instead? Aren't ring topologies well known and understood in the network design world? Layered hub-and-spoke topologies are more widely used because they provide much better convergence than ring topologies.

What about building a full mesh of modules? Although a full mesh design might work well for a network with a small set of modules, full mesh designs do not have stellar scaling characteristics, because they require an additional (and increasingly larger) set of ports and links for each module added to the network. Further, full mesh designs don't lend themselves to efficient policy implementation; each link between every pair of modules must have policy configured and managed, a job that can become burdensome as the network grows.

A partial, rather than full, mesh of modules might resolve the simple link count scaling issues of a full mesh design, but this leaves the difficulty of policy management along a mishmash of connections in place.

There is a solid reason the tried-and-true hierarchical design has been the backbone of so many successful network designs over the years—it works well.

See Chapter 12, "Building the Second Floor," for more information on the performance and convergence characteristics of various network topologies.

An Architectural Methodology

Hierarchical network design reaches beyond hub-and-spoke topologies at the module level and provides rules, or general methods of design, that provide for the best overall network design. This section discusses each of these methods or rules—but remember these are generally accepted rules, not hard and fast laws. Part of the art of architecture is knowing when to break the rules.

Assign Each Module One Function

The first general rule in hierarchical network design is to assign each module a single function. What is a "function," in networking terms?

- **User Connection:** A form of traffic admission control, this is most often an edge function in the network. Here, traffic offered to the network by connected devices is checked for policy errors (is this user supposed to be sending traffic to that service?), marked for quality of service processing, managed in terms of flow rate, and otherwise prodded to ensure the traffic is handled properly throughout the network.

- **Service Connection:** Another form of traffic admission control, which is most often an edge function as well. Here the edge function can be double sided; however, not only must the network decide what traffic should be accepted from connected devices, but it must also decide what traffic should be forwarded toward the services. Stateful packet filters, policy implementations, and other security functions are common along service connection edges.

- **Traffic Aggregation:** Usually occurs at the edge of a module or a subtopology within a network module. Traffic aggregation is where smaller links are combined into bigger ones, such as the point where a higher-speed local area network meets a lower-speed (or more heavily used) wide area link. In a world full of high speed links, aggregation can be an important consideration almost any place in the network. Traffic can be shaped and processed based on the QoS markings given to packets at the network edge to provide effective aggregation services.

- **Traffic Forwarding:** Specifically between modules or over longer geographic distances, this is a function that's important enough to split off into a separate module; generally this function is assigned to core modules, whether local, regional, or global.

- **Control Plane Aggregation:** This should happen only at module edges. Aggregating control plane information separates failure domains and provides an implementation point for control plane policy.

It might not, in reality, be possible to assign each module in the network one function—a single module might need to support both traffic aggregation at several points, and user or service connection along the module edge. Reducing the number of functions assigned

to any particular module, however, will simplify the configuration of devices within the module as well as along the module's edge.

How does assigning specific functionality to each module simplify network design? It's all in the magic of the Rule of Unintended Consequences. If you mix aggregation of routing information with data plane filtering at the same place in the network, you must deal with not only the two separate policy structures, but also the interaction between the two different policy structures. As policies become more complex, the interaction between the policy spaces also ramps up in complexity.

At some point, for instance, changing a filtering policy at the control plane can interact with filtering policy in the data plane in unexpected ways—and unexpected results are not what you want to see when you're trying to get a new service implemented during a short downtime interval, or when you're trying to troubleshoot a broken service at two in the morning. Predictability is the key to solid network operation; predictability and highly interactive policies implemented in a large number of places throughout a network are mutually exclusive in the real world.

All Modules at a Given Level Should Share Common Functionality

The second general rule in the hierarchical method is to design the network modules so every module at a given layer—or a given distance from the network core—has a roughly parallel function. Figure 7-2 shows two networks, one of which does not follow this rule and one which does.

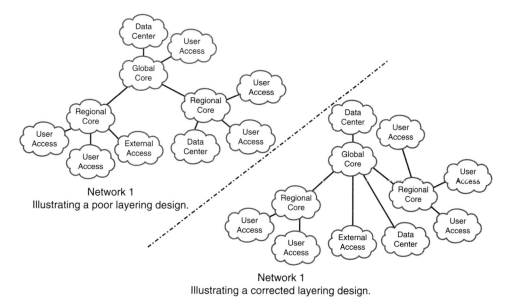

Figure 7-2   *Poor and Corrected Hierarchical Layering Designs*

Only a few connecting lines make the difference between the poorly designed hierarchical layout and the corrected one. The data center that was connected through a regional core

has been connected directly to the global core, a user access network that was connected directly to the global core has been moved so it now connects through a regional core, and the external access module has been moved from the regional core to the global core.

The key point in Figure 7-2 is that the policies and aggregation points should be consistent across all the modules of the hierarchical network plan.

Why does this matter?

One of the objectives of hierarchical network design is to allow for consistent configuration throughout the network. In the case where the global core not only connects to regional cores, but also to user access modules, the devices in the global core along the edge to this single user access module must be configured in a different way from all the remaining devices. This is not only a network management problem, it's also a network repair problem—at two in the morning, it's difficult to remember why the configuration on any specific device might be different and what the impact might be if you change the configuration. In the same way, the single user access module that connects directly to the global core must be configured in different ways than the remaining user access modules. Policy and aggregation that would normally be configured in a regional core must be handled directly within the user edge module itself.

Moving the data center and external access services so that they connect directly into the global core rather than into a regional core helps to centralize these services, allowing all users better access with shorter path lengths. It makes sense to connect them to the global core because most service modules have fewer aggregation requirements than user access modules and stronger requirements to connect to other services within the network.

Frequently, simple changes of this type can have a huge impact on the operational overhead and performance of a network.

Build Solid Redundancy at the Intermodule Level

How much redundancy is there between Modules A and L in the network shown in Figure 7-3?

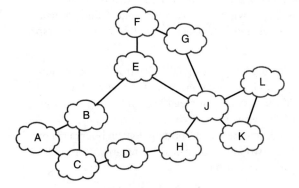

Figure 7-3 *Determining Redundancy in a Partial Mesh Topology*

It's easy to count the number of links—but it's difficult to know whether each path through this network can actually be considered a redundant path. Each path through the network must be examined individually, down to the policy level, to determine if every module along the path is configured and able to carry traffic between Modules A and L; determining the number of redundant paths becomes a matter of chasing through each available path and examining every policy to determine how it might impact traffic flow. Modifying a single policy in Module E may have the unintended side effect of removing the only redundant path between Modules A and L—and this little problem might not even be discovered until an early morning network outage.

Contrast this with a layered hub and spoke hierarchical layout with well-defined module functions. In that type of network, determining how much redundancy there is between any pair of points in the network is a simple matter of counting links combined with well-known policy sets. This greatly simplifies designing for resilience.

Another way in which a hierarchical design makes designing for resilience easier is by breaking the resilience problem into two pieces—the resilience within a module and the resilience between modules. These become two separate problems that are kept apart through clear lines of functional separation.

This leads to another general rule for hierarchical network design—build solid redundancy at the module interconnection points.

Hide Information at Module Edges

It's quite common to see a purely switched network design broken into three layers—the core, the distribution, and the access—and the design called "hierarchical." This concept of breaking a network into different pieces and simply calling those pieces different things, based on their function alone, removes one of the crucial pieces of hierarchical design theory: *information hiding.*

> If it doesn't hide information, it's not a layer.

Information hiding is crucial because it is only by hiding information about the state of one part of a network from devices in another part of the network that the designer can separate different failure domains. A single switched domain is a single failure domain, and hence it must be considered one single failure domain (or module) from the perspective of a hierarchical design.

A corollary to this is that the more information you can hide, the stronger the separation between failure domains is going to be, as changes in one area of the network will not "bleed over," or impact other areas of the network. Aggregating or blocking topology information between two sections of the network (as in the case of breaking a spanning tree into pieces or link state topology aggregation at a flooding domain boundary) provides one degree of separation between two failure domains. Aggregating reachability information provides a second degree of separation.

The stronger the separation of failure domains through information hiding, the more stability the information hiding will bring to the network.

Typical Hierarchical Design Patterns

There are two traditional hierarchical design patterns: two layer networks and three layer networks. These have been well covered in network design literature (for instance, see *Optimal Routing Design)*, so we will provide only a high level overview of these two design patterns here. Figure 7-4 illustrates two- and three-layer designs.

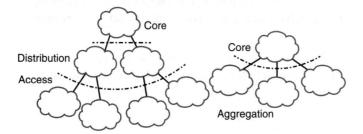

Figure 7-4 *Two- and Three-Layer Hierarchical Design Patterns*

In the traditional three-layer hierarchical design:

- The core is assigned the function of forwarding traffic between different modules within the distribution layer. Little to no control or data plane policy should be configured or implemented in the core of a traditional three-layer hierarchical design.

- The distribution layer is assigned the functions of forwarding policy and traffic aggregation. Most control plane policy, including the aggregation of reachability and topology information, should be configured in the distribution layer of the traditional three layer hierarchical design. Blocking access to specific services, or forwarding plane filtering and policy, should be left out of the distribution layer, however, simply to keep the focus on each module narrow and easy to understand.

- The access layer is assigned the functions of user attachment, user traffic aggregation, and data plane policy implementation. The access layer is where you would mark traffic for specific handling through quality of service, block specific sources from reaching specific destinations, and implement other policies of this type.

In the traditional two-layer hierarchical design:

- The core is assigned the function of forwarding traffic between different modules within the aggregation layer. The core edge, facing toward the aggregation layer, is also where any policy or aggregation toward the edge of the network is implemented.

- The aggregation layer is assigned the functions of user attachment, user traffic aggregation, and data plane policy implementation. The aggregation layer is where you would mark traffic for special handling through quality of service, block access to specific services, and otherwise implement packet and flow level filters. The edge of the aggregation layer, facing the core, is also where any policy or aggregation at the control plane is implemented moving from the edge of the network toward the core.

It's easy to describe the two-layer network design as simply collapsing the distribution layer into the edge between the core and aggregation layers, or the three-layer design as an expanded two-layer design. Often the difference between the two is sheer size—three-layer designs are often used when the aggregation layer is so large that it would overwhelm the core or require excessive links to the core. Or if it's used in a campus with multiple buildings containing large numbers of users. Geography often plays a part in choosing a three-layer design, such as a company that has regional cores connecting various sites within a given geographical area, and a global core connecting the various regional cores.

Hierarchical network design doesn't need to follow one of these design patterns, however. It's possible to build a hierarchical network using layers of layers, as illustrated in Figure 7-5.

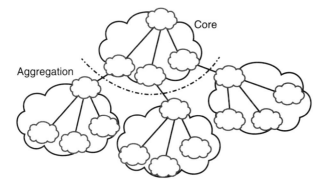

Figure 7-5   *Layers Within Layers*

Is the network shown in Figure 7-5 a four-layer design, a three-layer design with two layers within each aggregation module, a three-layer design with the distribution layer collapsed into the core, or a two-layer design with layers within each module? It really doesn't matter, so long as you're following the basic rules for hierarchical network design.

Virtualization

Virtualization is a key component of almost all modern network design. From the smallest single campus network to the largest globe-spanning service provider or enterprise, virtualization plays a key role in adapting networks to business needs.

What Is Virtualization?

Virtualization is deceptively easy to define: *the creation of virtual topologies (or information subdomains) on top of a physical topology.* But is it really this simple? Let's look at some various network situations and determine whether they are virtualization.

- A VLAN used to segregate voice traffic from other user traffic across a number of physical Ethernet segments in a network

- An MPLS-based L3VPN offered as a service by a service provider

- An MPLS-based L2VPN providing interconnect services between two data centers across an enterprise network core

- A service provider splitting customer and internal routes using an interior gateway protocol (such as IS-IS) paired with BGP

- An IPsec tunnel connecting a remote retail location to a data center across the public Internet

- A pair of physical Ethernet links bonded into a single higher bandwidth link between two switches

The first three are situations just about any network engineer would recognize as virtualization. They all involve full-blown technologies with their own control planes, tunneling mechanisms to carry traffic edge to edge, and clear-cut demarcation points. These are the types of services and configurations we normally think of when we think of virtualization.

What about the fourth situation—a service provider splitting routing information between two different routing protocols in the same network? There is no tunneling of traffic from one point in the network to another, but is tunneling really necessary in order to call a solution "virtualization"? Consider *why* a service provider would divide routing information into two different domains. Breaking up networks in this way creates multiple mutually exclusive sets of information within the networks. The idea is that internal and external routing information should not be mixed. A failure in one domain is split off from a failure in another domain (just like failures in one module of a hierarchical design are prevented from leaking into a second module in the same hierarchical design), and policy is created that prevents reachability to internal devices from external sources.

All these reasons and results sound like modularization in a hierarchical network. Thus, it only makes sense to treat the splitting of a single control plane to produce mutually exclusive sets of information as a form of virtualization. To the outside world, the entire network appears to be a single hop, edge-to-edge. The entire internal topology is hidden within the operation of BGP—hence there is a virtual topology, even if there is no tunneling.

Is MPLS Tunneling?

Is MPLS a tunneling technology? There has been a debate raging on this very topic for years within the network community, and there doesn't seem to be a clear-cut answer to the question. MPLS acts like a tunneling technology in the addition of headers between the Layer 3 transport and Layer 2 MAC headers. On the other hand, some forms of data can be placed directly into an MPLS frame and carried across an MPLS-enabled network as if MPLS were the data link layer.

The answer must be both yes and no. Tunneling is a matter of usage, rather than a matter of packet formatting. If someone built a device that switched purely on GRE headers, rather than on the outer IP packet normally carried within a GRE packet, we'd be in the same position with GRE as we are with MPLS.

When it's used as an inner header between IP and some data link layer, and when the local control plane doesn't understand the final destination—only the intermediate hops along the way—MPLS is clearly being used to tunnel. When it's used as an outer header, and the header is directly used to switch the packet (and even rewritten at each hop like all other layer two MAC headers), it's clearly not.

In most MPLS deployments, then, MPLS is both a tunneling protocol (the inner header) and not (the outer header). In both cases, MPLS is used to build virtual topologies on top of physical topologies (just like IP and a host of other protocols), so it's still a virtualization technique whether or not it's used to tunnel packets.

The fifth situation, a single IPsec tunnel from a retail store location into a data center, seems like it might even be too simple to be considered a case of virtualization. On the other hand, all the elements of virtualization are present, aren't they? We have the hiding of information from the control plane—the end site control plane doesn't need to be aware of the topology of the public Internet to reach the data center, and the routers along the path through the public Internet don't know about the internal topology of the data center to which they're forwarding packets. We have what is apparently a point-to-point link across multiple physical hops, so we also have a virtual topology, even if that topology is limited to a single link.

The answer, then, is yes, this is virtualization. Anytime you encounter a tunnel, you are encountering virtualization—although tunneling isn't a necessary part of virtualization.

With the sixth situation—bonding multiple physical links into a single Layer 2 link connecting two switches—again we have a virtual link that runs across multiple physical links, so this is virtualization as well.

Essentially, virtualization appears anytime we have the following:

- A logical topology that appears to be different from the physical topology

- More than one control plane (one for each topology), even if one of the two control planes is manually configured (such as static routes)

- Information hiding between the virtual topologies

Virtualization as Vertical Hierarchy

One way of looking at virtualization is as *vertical hierarchy* as Figure 7-6 illustrates.

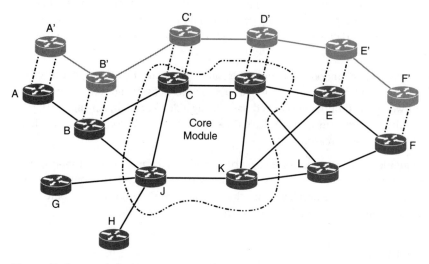

Figure 7-6   *Virtualization as Vertical Hierarchy*

In this network, Routers A through F are not only a part of the physical topology, they are also part of a virtual topology, shown offset and in a lighter shade of gray. The primary topology is divided into three modules:

- Routers A, B, G, and H

- Routers C, D, J, and K (the network core)

- Routers E, F, and L

What's important to note is that the virtual topology cuts across the hierarchical modules in the physical topology, overlaying across all of them, to form a separate information domain within the network. This virtual topology, then, can be seen as yet another module within the hierarchical system—but because it cuts across the modules in the physical topology, it can be seen as "rising out of" the physical topology—a vertical module rather than a topological module, built on top of the network, cutting through the network.

How does seeing virtualization in this way help us? Being able to understand virtualization in this way allows us to understand virtual topologies in terms of the same requirements, solutions, and problems as hierarchical modules. Virtualization is just another mechanism network designers can use to hide information.

Why We Virtualize

What business problem can we solve through virtualization? If you listen to the chatter in modern network design circles, the answer is "almost anything." But like any overused tool (hammer, anyone?), virtualization has some uses for which it's very apt and others for which it's not really such a good idea. Let's examine two specific use cases.

Communities of Interest

Within any large organization there will invariably be multiple communities of interest—groups of users who would like to have a small part of the network they can call their own. This type of application is normally geared around the ability to control access to specific applications or data so only a small subset of the entire organization can reach these resources.

For instance, it's quite common for a human resources department to ask for a relatively secure "network within the network." They need a way to transfer and store information without worrying about unauthorized users being able to reach it. An engineering, design, or animation department might have the same requirements for a "network within the network" for the same reasons.

These communities of interest can often best be served by creating a virtual topology that only people within this group can access. Building a virtual topology for a community of interest can, of course, cause problems with the capability to share common resources—see the section "Consequences of Network Virtualization" later in the chapter.

Network Desegmentation

Network designers often segment networks by creating modules for various reasons (as explained in the previous sections of this chapter). Sometimes, however, a network can be unintentionally segmented. For instance, if the only (or most cost effective) way to connect a remote site to a headquarters or regional site is to connect them both to the public Internet, the corporate network is now unintentionally segmented. Building virtual networks that pass over (over the top of) the network in the middle is the only way to desegment the network in this situation.

Common examples here include the following:

- Connecting two data centers through a Layer 3 VPN service (provided by a service provider)

- Connecting remote offices through the public Internet

- Connecting specific subsets of the network between two partner networks connected through a single service provider

Separation of Failure Domains

As we've seen in the first part of this chapter, designers modularize networks to break large failure domains into smaller pieces. Because virtualization is just another form of hiding information, it can also be used to break large failure domains into smaller pieces.

A perfect example of this is building a virtual topology for a community of interest that has a long record of "trying new things." For instance, the animation department in a large entertainment company might have a habit of deploying new applications that sometimes adversely impact other applications running on the same network. By first

separating a department that often deploys innovative new technology into its own community of interest, or making it a "network within the network," the network designer can reduce or eliminate the impact of new applications deployed by this one department.

Another version of this is the separation of customer and internal routes across two separate routing protocols (or rather two different control planes) by a service provider. This separation protects the service provider's network from being impacted by modifications in any particular customer's network.

Consequences of Network Virtualization

Just as modularizing a network has negative side effects, so does virtualization—and the first rule to return to is the one about hiding information and its effect on stretch in networks. Just as aggregation of control plane information to reduce state can increase the stretch in a network (or rather cause the routing of traffic through a network to be suboptimal), virtualization's hiding of control plane information has the same potential effect. To understand this phenomenon, take a look at the network in Figure 7-7.

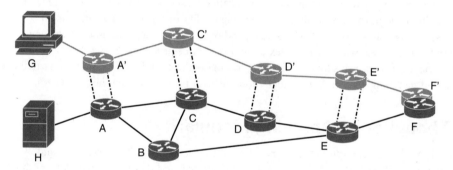

Figure 7-7   *Example of Stretch Through Virtualized Topologies*

In this case, host G is trying to reach a service on a server located in the rack represented by H. If both the host and the server were on the same virtual topology, the path between them would be one hop. Because they are on different topologies, however, traffic between the two devices must travel to the point where the two topologies meet, at Router F/F', to be routed between the two topologies (to leak between the VLANs).

If there are not services that need to be reached by all the hosts on the network, or each virtual topology acts as a complete island of its own, this problem may not arise in this specific form. But other forms exist, particularly when traffic must pass through filtering and other security devices while traveling through the network, or in the case of link or device failures along the path.

A second consequence of virtualization is *fate sharing*. Fate sharing exists anytime there are two or more logical topologies that share the same physical infrastructure—so fate sharing and virtualization go hand in hand, no matter what the physical layer and logical overlays look like. For instance, fate sharing occurs when several VLANs run across the same physical Ethernet wire, just as much as it occurs when several L3VPN circuits run

across the same provider edge router or when multiple frame relay circuits are routed across a single switch. There is also fate sharing purely at the physical level, such as two optical strands running through the same conduit. The concepts and solutions are the same in both cases.

To return to the example in Figure 7-7, when the link between Routers E and F fails, the link between Routers E' and F' also fails. This may seem like a logical conclusion on its face, but fate sharing problems aren't always so obvious, or easy to see.

The final consequence of virtualization isn't so much a technology or implementation problem as it is an attitude or set of habits on the part of network engineers, designers, and architects. RFC1925, rule 6, and the corollary rule 6a, state: "It is easier to move a problem around (for example, by moving the problem to a different part of the overall network architecture) than it is to solve it. ...It is always possible to add another level of indirection."

In the case of network design and architecture, it's often (apparently) easier to add another virtual topology than it is to resolve a difficult and immediately present problem. For instance, suppose you're deploying a new application with quality of service requirements that will be difficult to manage alongside existing quality of service configurations. It might seem easier to deploy a new topology, and push the new application onto the new topology, than to deal with the complex quality of service problems. Network architects need to be careful with this kind of thinking, though—the complexity of multiple virtual topologies can easily end up being much more difficult to manage than the alternative.

Final Thoughts on Applying Modularity

Network modularization provides clear and obvious points at which to configure and manage policy, clear trade-offs between state and stretch, and predictable reactions within the network to specific changes in the network topology. The general rules for using hierarchical design are as follows:

- Break the network into modules, using information hiding to divide module from module. Layer edges exist only where information is hidden.

- Assign each module as few functions as possible to promote clarity and repeatability in configurations, and reduce the unintended consequences of complex policy interactions.

- Build networks using hub-and-spoke configurations of modules.

- All modules at a given layer within a network should have similar functionality to promote ease of troubleshooting and reduce configuration complexity.

- Build solid redundancy at module interconnection points.

Overall, remember to be flexible with the modularization. Rather than focusing on a single design pattern as *the* solution to all design problems, focus on finding the best fit for the problem at hand.

Weathering Storms

Why isn't your CEO asking for six 9s of uptime? Because no one in the networking industry press is talking about how six 9s of availability are so much better than five 9s.

Resilience is a big issue in network architecture—so big it's almost the only thing many businesses are willing to put a lot of money into achieving. How do you build a resilient network? The traditional answer, widely used in almost every other field of architecture, is to overengineer the solution. If the floor needs to be able to handle one person walking across it, design the floor to support four or five people walking across it. If the highest wind a roof might encounter in a storm is 100 miles per hour, then design the roof to handle winds of 200 miles per hour.

Network architecture is no different in this regard—if we want to prevent a single link's failure from cutting off access to the network, we put in a second parallel link. Or maybe a third, just for good measure.

But if adding parallel links and devices is all there is to building a resilient network, we wouldn't need a chapter on the topic. So what else is there?

We begin this chapter with a hard look at redundancy because it is the primary tool used to build resilience into a network. To really understand the limits of redundancy, though, we need to examine one of the not-so-common measures of network resilience—Mean Time to Repair (MTTR). After redundancy, this chapter will delve into reducing the MTTR by optimizing the operation of the control plane, including fast convergence techniques.

Of course, resilience goes beyond the reaction of the control plane and into human factors; to build a truly resilient network, we need to chase those human factors down as well. Although resilience is also impacted by management practices and security, these two areas aren't covered here because they have their own chapters (Chapter 10, "Measure Twice," and Chapter 9, "Securing the Premises").

Redundancy as Resilience

Adding a parallel path between any two points in a network will obviously increase resilience by removing a single point of failure; however, to get at a real understanding of resilience, we need to be able to measure just how much adding this second link increases resilience by reducing potential downtime.

Network Availability Basics

To get this answer, we must begin with an understanding of two key measures of network availability: Mean Time Between Failures (MTBF) and Mean Time to Repair (MTTR). Figure 8-1 illustrates these two concepts.

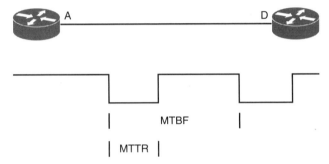

Figure 8-1   *MTBF and MTTR*

MTBF is based on the amount of time that passes between failures in a system; just divide the number of failures in any slice of time into the total amount of time, and you have the MTBF for that system (during that time slice!). The longer the time slice (without changes in the system) you use, the more accurate the MTBF will be.

MTTR is the amount of time it takes to bring the system back up after it has failed. To find the MTTR, divide the total length of all outages by the total number of outages.

Availability is the total time the system should have been operational (without counting outages) divided by the amount of time the system was not operational. To get to availability from MTBF and MTTR, you can take the MTBF as a single operational period and divide it by the MTTR, like this:

$$Availability = \frac{MTBF}{MTTR}$$

Note Most of the time, you'll see availability calculated by adding the uptime to the downtime, and then dividing the result by the downtime. This arrives at the same number, however, because the total uptime added to the total downtime should (in the case of networks) be the total amount of time the network should have been operational. You might also see this expressed using the idea of Mean Time to Failure (MTTF), which is just the MTBF minus the MTTR—so adding the MTTF and the MTTR should result in the same number as the MTBF.

Note Although it's common to exclude scheduled downtime from the total network outage time, there are a number of networks on which no scheduled downtime is possible, or for which there are no planned outages. It is a local policy whether to include scheduled downtime as part of the MTBF and MTTR calculations or not (to use total downtime or just unscheduled downtime).

Adding Redundancy

How does redundancy aim to increase availability? Figure 8-2 illustrates.

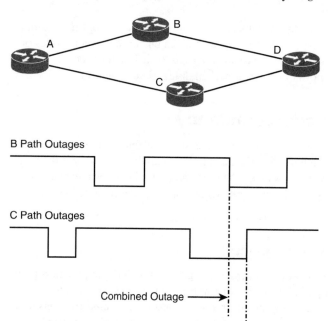

Figure 8-2 *Redundancy and Availability*

When you add redundancy, you are essentially betting outages of the original path and the alternate path will not occur at the same time. How can we calculate the odds of both links failing at the same time? The math is deceptively simple:

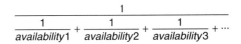

To put this in perspective, assume the paths through Routers B and C are each down for one second in every year. The total amount of time you can expect both paths to be down at the same time during the year is about 500 milliseconds. What would be the impact of adding a third path with similar characteristics? The total downtime you could expect in a year—the amount of time all three paths are likely to be down at the same time—would be around 250 milliseconds.

> **Note** This assumes the additional paths do not fate share with an existing path—that when the path through Router B fails, the path through Router C will not also fail because they share some common underlying infrastructure, such as two links passing through the same conduit, and a backhoe fade occurring across the entire conduit.

> **Note** This shouldn't assume a backup path will be immediately available. Stateful devices in the path, for instance, can require sessions along the path to be reset or restarted.

This "halving effect" for every additional link is a general rule you can adopt throughout your network designs, unless you're adding links with much higher than average rates of failure (such as satellite or long haul wireless) and are used to backfill for specific operational situations (large-scale power outages or natural disasters, for instance).

MTTR, Resilience, and Redundancy

Up to this point, we have a nice clean picture of increasing availability. Simply figure out what the availability is for each link type, then add links in parallel until you get the number of 9s you need to make your boss happy. This will work until your plan encounters the real world of complex systems, including limits on control plane convergence and feedback loops.

Limits on Control Plane Convergence

Time for a short review—the network's control plane is tasked with finding the best path (not necessarily the shortest path, but the best path) from any given source to any given destination in the network. To do this, the control plane must react to modifications in the network topology quickly, but in a way that doesn't cause more problems than it solves. We can break the reaction of the control plane to topology changes into four specific steps:

1. Detecting the topology change

2. Notifying the rest of the network about the change

3. Calculating a new best path

4. Switching to the new best path

We'll dive into each of these steps in more detail in the section "Fast Convergence Techniques" later in the chapter, but for now it's important to see that the middle two steps in this process—notifying and calculating—are both affected by the amount of information that must be transmitted and calculated. Algorithms can be modified and adjusted to deal with larger amounts of information, but no matter how much tweaking you do, dealing with more information will always mean taking longer to converge.

Reaching back into the discussion on redundancy, it's easy enough to see how adding more links into the network adds information to the control plane. Hence, every link added will, ultimately, slow down the convergence of the control plane in some measurable amount. The entire time eliminating overlapping outages by adding redundancy, we're also increasing the odds of having an overlapping outage by making the MTTR longer, as Figure 8-3 shows.

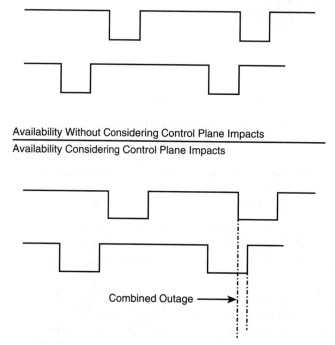

Availability Without Considering Control Plane Impacts

Availability Considering Control Plane Impacts

Combined Outage ⟶

Figure 8-3 *Impact of MTTR Through Additional Work in the Control Plane on Availability*

The actual amount of time each link is unavailable (because of physical outages, for instance), is shown in the top diagram. In the bottom diagram, the unavailable periods are longer. The outages are longer because of the time it takes for the control plane to converge so the link is used in the actual flow of traffic. When you add in this consideration, there is an overlapping outage.

Feedback Loops

The second important factor to consider when adding redundant links is the problem of positive feedback loops. Figure 8-4 illustrates a positive feedback loop in the control plane of a network.

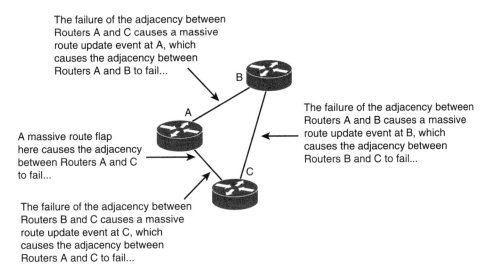

The failure of the adjacency between Routers A and C causes a massive route update event at A, which causes the adjacency between Routers A and B to fail...

The failure of the adjacency between Routers A and B causes a massive route update event at B, which causes the adjacency between Routers B and C to fail...

A massive route flap here causes the adjacency between Routers A and C to fail...

The failure of the adjacency between Routers B and C causes a massive route update event at C, which causes the adjacency between Routers A and C to fail...

Figure 8-4   *Positive Feedback Loop Resulting in a Network Failure*

In Figure 8-4, some event has caused the routing adjacency between Routers A and C to fail. This causes a massive routing recalculation at A and a huge routing update from Router A to Router B. The update is so large it brings down the adjacency between A and B. This causes B to go through the same process and send a huge update to Router C. Router C then does its own recalculations and sends a huge update to Router A, causing that adjacency to fail and sending these three routers into a positive feedback loop.

Positive feedback loops of this sort don't generally last long enough to bring a network down completely (as in no longer forwarding traffic), but they can last long enough to disrupt traffic flow, or to cause the network to converge more slowly than it should.

Note   There are two cases where a positive feedback loop can be both long lived and devastating to the network's control plane. The first is when redistribution of reachability information between multiple control planes is involved. Redistribution removes the information needed for a routing protocol to find loop-free paths, which can cause a permanent positive feedback loop. The second is when there are more paths available in any given routing process than are actually installed in the routing table. Distance vector routing protocols can interact with the routing table and split horizon rules in a way that prevents the routing protocol from effectively breaking a positive feedback loop.

For there to be a positive feedback loop, there must, of course, be a loop in the topology. Each parallel link or path added to the topology to provide additional resilience (availability) represents a potential feedback loop. Modifying routing protocol metrics though policy also heightens the possibility of positive feedback loops.

> **Note** To increase the chances of a good positive feedback loop, make certain there's a flapping link someplace that keeps changes flowing into the control plane. Constant changes in the control plane feed positive feedback loops, making control plane failure more certain.

The Interaction Between MTTR and Redundancy

The chart in Figure 8-5 puts the interaction between MTTR and redundancy into perspective.

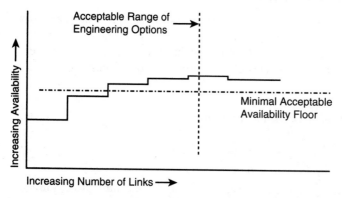

Figure 8-5 *Trade-offs in Redundancy and High Availability*

Moving from the left to the right along this chart represents an increasing number of links or paths in parallel. Moving from the bottom to the top represents increasing availability. You'll notice that each additional path or link doesn't increase availability as much as the last one. At the high end of additional links, the graph begins moving downward because of the impact of the additional links on control plane convergence time.

The vertical line represents the upper end of the range of acceptable engineering solutions to the availability/redundancy trade-off. Within this range, the amount of configuration and maintenance required are acceptable; outside this range, maintaining the network becomes more expensive than providing the additional availability.

The horizontal line across the graph represents the minimal acceptable availability floor. Any availability level below this line won't satisfy the business requirements at hand.

To correctly plan the number of redundant paths or links in a network design, the architect must find the best fit between the various points on this graph. Too many parallel paths, and the network becomes too complex and expensive to operate, especially given the diminishing nature of the return on each additional redundant link or path installed in

the network. Too little redundancy, and the network will not meet the minimal business requirements.

The process implied in this graph might appear to be complex—the architect must figure out what the minimal availability is, then calculate the level of availability for each proposed level of redundancy, consider the trade-off in additional complexity by adding redundancy (in network operations and in control plane convergence times), and then decide what level of redundancy is right. The right answer, in terms of trading off redundancy verses availability, is there should be two or three paths between any two points in the network. If you want to add redundancy between two specific devices, two or three links will be the (generally) optimal level of redundancy to provide for most network failures. The fourth link is not only likely to cost more money than it's worth, it's also likely to actually make the network converge more slowly.

Fast Convergence Techniques

A second route network engineers can take to increase availability is to make the network react more quickly to changes in the topology. These options are generally called *fast convergence techniques*, although they fall into many different categories. Fast convergence techniques address the four elements of convergence listed previously:

- Detecting the topology change
- Notifying the rest of the network about the change
- Calculating a new best path
- Switching to the new best path

Each one has specific techniques that can be applied to make the control plane converge more quickly.

Detecting the Topology Change

The first and foremost problem facing the control plane is quickly detecting topology changes. Although detection can be made almost infinitely fast, infinitely fast detection also produces infinitely fast false failure reports and requires infinite amounts of processing power. Fast detection, then, is a trade-off, rather than an absolute good (like most things in the real world).

There are a number of techniques that can be used to detect link failures, but they all come down to two basic types:

- **Event driven notifications:** Includes the loss of carrier when a physical wire is cut, or when one element of the network detects a failure and notifies other networking devices.
- **Polling driven notifications:** Generally "hello protocols," which periodically test a path for reachability. Examples of polling mechanisms are routing protocol hello packets, Bidirectional Forwarding Detection (BFD), and TCP keepalives.

Because of the requirement to reduce false positives, virtually all polling driven failure detection mechanisms wait until three polls (or three packets, in more common terms) are lost before declaring a path down. Because of this, event driven notification mechanisms will always outpace polling systems for fast and accurate path failure detection. Network engineers should always focus on finding event driven solutions and fall back to polling mechanisms only when an event driven mechanism cannot be found.

Propagating Information About the Change

When a change in the topology has been detected by the control plane, information about that topology change must be transmitted throughout the rest of the network. Figure 8-6 illustrates the difference between the propagation of information through a distance or path vector protocol and a link state protocol, highlighting the different techniques required to improve convergence in these two different environments.

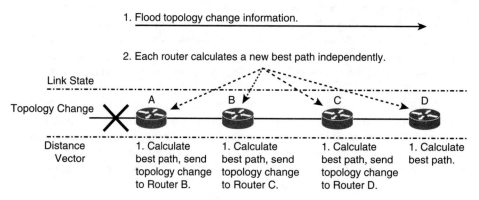

Figure 8-6 *Distance Vector and Link State Convergence*

Link state protocols must flood information about the topology to every device in the network, and distance (and path) vector protocols must process the topology change information at every hop through the network. The operation of the two different kinds of protocols suggests they require two different sets of techniques to provide optimal convergence times.

Note It might seem natural to conclude, from this description of the operation of these different types of protocols, that link state protocols will always converge more quickly than distance or path vector protocols. This isn't really the case—both types of protocols can converge very quickly given a network design optimized for their operation.

For link state protocols, it's important to flood information about topology changes as quickly as possible while preventing false information about link failures from causing major disruptions throughout the network. Fast propagation techniques for link state protocols, then, revolve around providing fast propagation for a small number of changes

in the network topology, while slowing down the rate at which information is flooded as the number of changes in the topology rises. In OSPF and IS-IS, this is accomplished with link state flooding timer tuning combined with exponential backoff systems. These techniques provide the necessary speed in flooding new topology information, without information overload or the risk of a positive feedback loop in the control plane.

> **Note**   The timers in link state protocols are there to prevent a control plane meltdown due to rapidly changing state. Generally speaking, you want to configure these times so the reaction to the first change is almost immediate—assuming the first change is normally a singular event in the state of the network. If multiple events normally happen close together in time, you're better off to set these timers to react more slowly, so more information can be gathered before the first reaction; the more information SPF has when running, and the more closely all the router's databases across the network match before SPF is run, the less likely routing loops will form for any length of time. Generally speaking, to set these timers, you need to examine the amount of time it takes for information to flow through the network, the amount of time it takes to calculate SPF, and the number of events that occur together (on average). From these, you can determine how long to wait before flooding a change in topology, and then how long to wait after receiving a new piece of topology information before running SPF.

For distance vector protocols, it's important to reduce the number of routers that must be notified of any given topology change. EIGRP's primary means of producing better convergence times, in terms of information distribution, is to reduce the number of devices that must be told about the topology change. This is accomplished through the aggregation and filtering of routing (or reachability) information—such as creating a summary route or designating a router as a Stub.

Calculating the New Best Path

The third step in fast convergence is to calculate a new best path through the network for destinations affected by the topology change. The first option for improving the calculation of new best paths is to improve routing algorithms and implementations—but this is outside the scope of the work of a network architect, so we'll skip this step here.

The second option, for a link state protocol specifically, is to improve the timing of the calculation of the best path after information about a topology change has been received. This is where exponential backoff—configuring and adjusting the amount of time OSPF or IS-IS wait after receiving new topology information before calculating the best path—comes into play. Exponential backoff plays a big role in making certain the information is processed as quickly as possible, while not causing information or processor overload.

But beyond these techniques, what could be faster than simply calculating a new path before the old path fails? We'll leave this topic for the "Fast Reroute" section of this chapter.

Switching to the New Best Path

Finally, after the topology change has been detected, information about the topology change has been propagated throughout the network, and the new best path has been calculated, the new best path must be installed and used. This might seem like a trivial issue, but in modern routers and switches it may, in fact, be a rather complex process. Most actual packet switching occurs in hardware on line cards, rather than software on the main processing card. Changes to the path traffic should take through the network because of a topology change must move from a routing process to the routing table, from the routing table to the central forwarding table, and from the central forwarding table through interprocess communication to the actual distributed forwarding tables on individual line cards. Most vendors now offer features that will install a new—or precomputed backup—path into the forwarding table so switching from one path to another can be done in a matter of milliseconds.

The Impact of Fast Convergence

What impact does fast convergence have on the trade-off between MTTR and redundancy? Figure 8-7 provides an updated graph to illustrate.

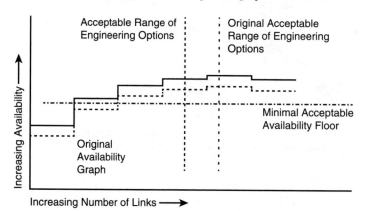

Figure 8-7   *Impact of Adding Fast Convergence Techniques to the Availability Versus Redundancy Graph*

Adding fast convergence techniques modifies the graph in two ways. First, the entire availability curve is pushed up, because deploying fast convergence techniques will allow the control plane to converge more quickly with the same number of parallel links. Previously, we said adding a fourth parallel path will often result in slower convergence; the addition of fast convergence alters this evaluation significantly. In practical applications, a network with two paths and well-designed fast convergence may converge more quickly than a network with three parallel paths and no fast convergence. The second impact is that the range of acceptable engineering options is narrowed a bit, simply because of the complexity of deploying and managing fast convergence techniques in the first place.

The bottom line doesn't change   the optimal spot on the chart is always going to be between two and three parallel paths through the network between any pair of destinations. Fast convergence techniques can raise network availability without a lot of additional management overhead, however, if properly designed and deployed.

Fast Reroute

One component of fast convergence is finding an alternate path on which to send traffic in the case of a network topology change. Why not precompute this path, rather than waiting for the actual change to occur? This is what Fast Reroute mechanisms aim to do.

Fast Reroute (FRR), particularly IP Fast Reroute (IP/FRR), tends to be difficult math wrapped in even more difficult math. From a complexity perspective, FRR technologies seem to be something only the most accomplished network engineers would want to tackle, and hence they seem to be limited to only the largest networks. FRR is important to building well-architected networks with minimal amounts of parallelism, and to building networks that can converge in packets, rather than seconds. Let's demystify FRR, beginning with Figure 8-8.

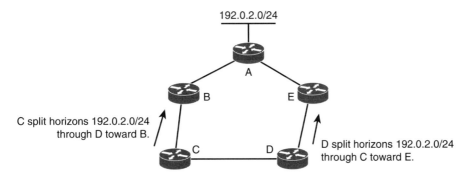

Figure 8-8   *The Fast Reroute Problem*

The simplest way to explain the problem FRR solves is by returning to a feature of all distance-vector routing protocols, split horizon. The split horizon rule is very simple:

> A router will not advertise a route to a destination through an interface it is using to reach that destination.

Why should this rule be adopted in distance-vector protocols? In Figure 8-8, if Router B forwards traffic destined to 192.0.2.0/24 to Router C (trying to follow the path through Router D), the packets will simply be looped back to Router B itself. The easiest way to prevent this loop from forming is for Router C not to tell Router B that 192.0.2.0/24 is reachable through this path. What happens if the link between Routers A and B fails?

> Router B believes there is no alternate path to 192.0.2.0/24.

When the link between Routers A and B fails, then, Router B must notify the rest of the routers in the network about the change in topology, and then wait for updates that might provide an alternate path to the destination it's interested in. Although we've used

a distance-vector protocol to illustrate the problem, it's not limited to distance-vector protocols. If a link-state protocol, such as IS-IS, were deployed on this network, Router B would know about the alternate path, but it still couldn't use the alternate path—Router C would still loop traffic destined to 192.0.2.0/24 back to Router B.

The simplest solution to this problem is for Router B to tunnel any traffic destined to 192.0.2.0/24 to Router D, which has an alternate path that doesn't pass through Router B itself. Essentially, all FRR mechanisms are designed to find this second path. Most then tunnel traffic to some point in the network that will cause packets to continue to be forwarded toward the right destination, rather than loop.

With this in the background, let's examine a few FRR mechanisms that have either been proposed or implemented. This overview isn't intended to provide a complete listing of every proposed mechanism, but rather to show how a few representative mechanisms resolve this problem.

P/Q Space

Using the concept shown in Figure 8-8, we can divide any topology into two "spaces," the *P space* and the *Q space*. Figure 8-9 illustrates.

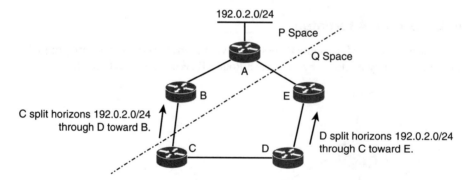

Figure 8-9   *P Space and Q Space*

In FRR parlance, the P space is the area within the network where Router B can forward traffic and expect it to reach the destination without looping. If Router B attempts to forward traffic toward 192.0.2.0/24 by way of Router C, however, the packets will be looped back to Router B itself. In these terms, the point of FRR is to find a router in the Q space that Router B can forward traffic through without the traffic being forwarded back to Router B itself.

> **Note**   Another way to say this is the P space is the space that the destination router can reach without crossing the failed or protected link—in this case, the question could be phrased, "Which routers and links can Router A reach without passing through a potentially failed link, such as (D,E)?"

Because every router in a flooding domain in a link state protocol has a complete view of the entire topology, it's possible to calculate the closest point in the network to which a router can tunnel traffic without the traffic looping. In Figure 8-8, for instance, Router B could simply calculate the best path to 192.0.2.0/24 from Router D's perspective. On finding Router D's path does not pass through Router B itself, Router B can add this as a backup path in its local forwarding table. If the Router A to Router B link fails, Router B can build a temporary tunnel (using MPLS) to Router D and forward traffic to 192.0.2.0/24 through that tunnel. When the network converges, the tunnel can be torn down.

Loop-Free Alternates

Loop-Free Alternates (LFA), known as *Feasible Successors* in EIGRP, don't resolve the FRR problem with tunneling. Rather, an LFA is simply an alternate loop-free route as calculated at any router in the network. In Figure 8-8, if Router C's best path is through Router D rather than through Router B, then Router B can safely switch to Router C as its next hop when the Router A to Router B link fails. You'll notice this can be true for only one direction in the ring—Routers B and D cannot both be using Router C as an LFA (or Feasible Successor).

Remote Loop-Free Alternates

In this network illustrated in Figure 8-10, we're trying to make certain that traffic originating someplace beyond Router A can reach Router E even if the A to E link fails.

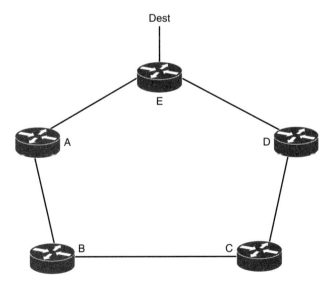

Figure 8-10 *Remote LFA Operation*

We can begin be examining Router A's neighbors—in this case, only Router B—to determine whether there is an LFA available toward E. If all the link costs here are 1, we'll find there isn't an LFA from Router A toward Router E; Router B is using A as its best path, so any traffic forwarded by Router A toward Router E via Router B will simply be forwarded back to Router A itself.

How can we solve this problem? We need to begin by recognizing that we'll have to tunnel the traffic—but how can we figure out where to tunnel the traffic to? From the diagram, we can see the correct point to tunnel the traffic to is Router C, but the router can't precisely look at a diagram of a network and figure it out. What other alternative is left? What's needed is to calculate, at Router A, the closest node in the network to which traffic toward Router E can be forwarded without it looping back to Router A itself.

We could simply remove the (A,E) link from the database and run SPF, but this won't help us find anything more than the LFA—and we already know there isn't an LFA here. What if we removed the A->E link and calculated the LFA of Router A's neighbor, though? Because A has precisely the same information as its neighbor, in this case only Router B, Router A can calculate the best path from B's perspective. If A were to calculate the best path to Router E from B's perspective after removing the A->E link from the database, then A Router could discover what alternate paths Router B has (remember that once the (A,E) link is removed, Router B can no longer calculate the best path through Router A).

Using this technique, Router A can quickly discover that Router B does, in fact, have an LFA—Router C. Moving to Router C, Router A performs the same calculation and finds the cost from (D,E) is the same or lower than the cost A->E, meaning the traffic cannot loop back through Router A if it is forwarded directly to Router C. Knowing this, A can now build a tunnel to Router C and place traffic with a next hop of Router E onto that tunnel if the (A,E) link fails. This is called the remote LFA because although Router C is not A's LFA, it is Router A's neighbor's LFA—hence it is an LFA that is remote from Router A itself.

What sort of tunnel should Router A use? The type of tunnel doesn't really matter—it could be a GRE tunnel, an MPLS tunnel, an IP-in-IP tunnel, or just about any other encapsulation. All that matters is that Router D accepts the packets tunneled from Router A, removes the tunnel header, and then forwards the packets as normal. In practice, MPLS is the type of tunnel implemented by vendors, and hence used by network operators, for remote LFA.

Not-Via Fast Reroute

To understand Not-Via, consider the network illustrated in Figure 8-11.

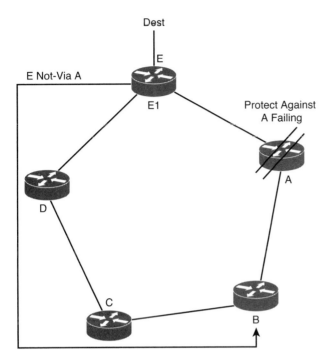

Figure 8-11 *Not-Via Operation*

In this case, we're trying to protect against Router A. To provide this protection, Router E is configured with an extra IP address on the E1 interface, which is then only advertised toward D (not A). This is called the not-via address, because it is advertised as Router E not-via Router A.

When Router B receives this special update, it will examine its local routes and find out what specific destinations are reachable through Router E. For each of these routes, it can now install a backup path with a next hop of this specific IP address. Of course, Router B must tunnel traffic to this not-via address, because it can't be certain the traffic sent toward the destination beyond Router E won't be forwarded back to Router B itself after it reaches Router C (for instance).

Not-via is, on the whole, a really clever solution to the problem of finding a tunnel end-point in the Q space onto which to drop traffic into an alternate path. As with all these solutions, however, there are trade-offs.

First, you have to know what you're protecting, and how to protect it. The actual calculation of where to drop the traffic is in the designer's head, rather than the algorithm itself. If every node in the network were advertising not-via addresses, there are ways to calculate the best place to drop traffic into the Q space without forming a data plane loop, but not-via was rejected by the IETF before the design reached that level of maturity.

The second trade-off is that each interface on every device in the network must advertise a separate not-via address for every protected neighboring node. The amount of additional state was thought to overshadow the overall usefulness of the scheme. Of course, there

are ways to optimize not-via to minimize this effect, but again, the idea was essentially rejected before any serious optimization work was done.

Finally, not-via dumps the traffic at a point that's suboptimal in the network. In this small network it doesn't really matter, but if the ring were a couple of hops longer, if the failure point was B, the traffic can be pulled past the exit point to the tunnel tail end, then released to backtrack along the same path toward the destination.

Maximally Redundant Trees

The general idea behind IP fast reroute is to precalculate a set of alternate paths that can reach a specific destination without using the shortest path. MRTs take this one step further by building two entire topologies that touch every node in the network (note—not every edge, just every node). If the shortest path fails, traffic can be moved onto one of these two overlay topologies to be forwarded along a "less than best path" toward the destination.

Let's look at the two connected topologies in Figure 8-12 and sort out how this works.

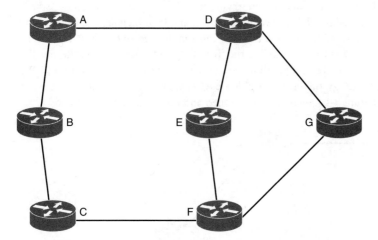

Figure 8-12   *Sample Network for MRT*

Let's begin at Router B and choose one link to remove from our local database; say the link between Routers B and C. After we've removed this link, Router B can calculate a path back to the neighbor reachable through the removed link (essentially finding a path back to itself, but breaking the path by removing a single link to prevent a cycle or loop in the topology). We can say this path is directed at Router B from Router C's vantage point, so the path runs counterclockwise around the ring, in the direction [C,F,E,D,A,B]. Figure 8-13 illustrates.

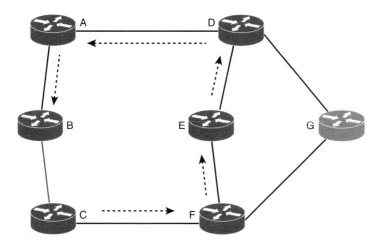

Figure 8-13   *The First Tree Built Through MRT*

From this point, we can examine any rings attached to this first ring; in this case, we have the ring containing Router G. Because we are trying to build a topology directed toward Router B, we would choose the link between Routers G and D to include. We can call this the dashed topology. To build the second tree, we can simply reverse the direction when calculating from Router B; start by removing the [B,A] link, and calculate from Router B to Router C. Finally, include the [G,F] path to bring the second ring into the topology. We can call this second topology the dotted topology. After we reach this point, we have the topology shown in Figure 8-14, including the dashed and dotted overlay topologies.

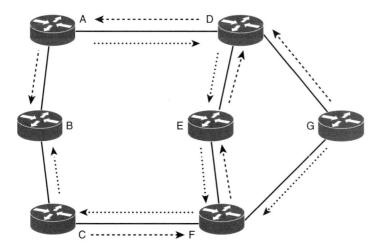

Figure 8-14   *Final Blue and Red Trees Built by MRT*

Note   MRT doesn't build these two trees in precisely the same way; instead, a Depth First Search (DFS) is performed across the topology, and each node (router) is assigned a number. Each router computes a low point and a high point, and then builds a tree based on the low and high points in the tree. Finally "ears," which are the outlying rings attached to the main topology, are added. The result, however, is the same as what's described here.

What is interesting about this calculation is that it doesn't interact with the SPF algorithm used by either OSPF or IS-IS. Because of the differences in the way SPF and MRT compute the shortest path tree, they will produce trees that only overlap sometimes (on the back of a napkin, I'd expect either of the two MRT topologies to overlap with the normal shortest path computed by Dijkstra about 50% of the time).

This means that by building a shortest path tree in the normal way, and then overlaying it with a pair of maximally redundant trees built using this process, you create three different topologies. These topologies will, of course, share some edges (links) and nodes (routers), but at least one of the three topologies will be able to reach any destination in the network in the case of a single link or router failure. If a link fails, then, the local router can place any traffic it would normally send across the failed link on an MRT topology that hasn't been impacted by the failure.

The one point to remember here is that after a packet has entered either of the two overlay topologies, it cannot leave that topology until it reaches its final destination. If it does leave the overlay topology before all the routers in the network have been notified of the failure, SPF has been run, and a new shortest path tree computed, there is a chance of a loop.

Final Thoughts on Fast Reroute

Although FRR might seem complex, it's actually a simple set of concepts embedded in complex mechanisms with the goal of making certain the control plane does the right thing in the case of network failures. Should you design around FRR techniques, or deploy them in your network designs? The answer is mostly going to depend on the requirements of your applications and your business.

FRR can, however, get you past the five 9s barrier with less topological complexity, and FRR is the only way to build a network that can truly converge in a matter of packets, rather than seconds. Don't be overwhelmed by the apparent complexity of these mechanisms. Learn the underlying principles, and don't be afraid to use them where they make sense.

The Human Side of Resilience

Resilience doesn't just mean a faster control plane, or faster detection of link failures—MTTR, in the larger sense, includes the human element of finding and correcting problems in the network, and even the mistakes humans make when dealing with changes in

complex configurations. Although there's no official measure in the network world for this, network architects need to think in terms of Mean Time Between Mistakes (MTBM).

What can network architects do to increase the MTBM and reduce the human element in MTTR? Although much of this is covered in more detail later in Chapter 10, "Measure Twice," here is a short list to get you started:

- **Simplify:** In general, when you're considering whether to deploy a new feature, or even how to deploy a new feature, remember the 2 a.m./15 minute rule: *If it takes more than 15 minutes to explain at 2 a.m., while under the pressure of a network outage, it's probably too complex.*

- **Document:** Solid documentation is important for understanding what the intent of the design was in the first place. It's almost impossible to understand the configuration of a particular device in the network without understanding the intent of the configuration.

- **Baseline:** Not only is it important to document what the intent of each element of a design is, it's also important to document what really exists, not only in terms of wiring and configuration, but also in terms of traffic flow and current operation.

- **Train:** The more the network operations staff understands the technologies in use, the intent of the network design, and the actual operation of the network, the better able they will be to run the network effectively. Further, just because a particular network runs IS-IS rather than OSPF doesn't mean training in OSPF, or even EIGRP and BGP, won't be helpful to the overall skill set of the engineers who are tasked with operating the network on a day-to-day basis.

Remember that a network is not just a system, but a system of systems; small changes in one system can have a huge impact in other systems. Try to decouple systems from one another through information hiding as much as possible.

Securing the Premises

*Someone walks in through your front door and takes your television, so you put a
lock on the front door. The next time, they break a window to get in, so you put in
better window locks and hurricane glass. They bump your front door lock, so you
replace it with a higher quality model that can't be bumped. They kick the door in, so
you replace the latch and jamb with stronger ones...*

Security, in the real world, is like this—threat and attack, closing holes, and reacting
to attacks. It's a never-ending cycle (or even war) between attacker and defender; the
attacker is always trying to find some new vulnerability to take advantage of, and the
defender is always trying to remove vulnerabilities before they are exploited.

It's almost a cliché to say that security should be "built in" to a design from the beginning, rather than "bolted on" at the very end, but what does the cliché actually mean?
How do you "design security in from the beginning?" How, precisely, do you build security in from the beginning? There are a number of answers to this question; this chapter
will approach the problem from three different directions.

We'll begin by exploring the Observe, Orient, Decide, Act (OODA) loop and how it
applies to this never-ending cycle of attack and defense. The OODA loop provides a solid
paradigm for understanding the attack/defense cycle in the larger sense (understanding
how to manage security threats in the strategic sense), but also how to manage security
breaches in real time. Models like the OODA loop are powerful tools in the hands of
good architects.

Next we'll discuss brittleness. This isn't a topic that's often discussed in security
circles, but it's a core part of designing security into a system. Finally, we'll address the
intersection of design tools and security. Specifically, we'll see how modularization and
resilience interact with security concepts.

There are probably a number of concepts here you've never encountered when considering network security—but the point of the art of network architecture is to think
through problems in different ways and to find solutions that address real concerns that
face your network now.

The OODA Loop

Although there are a number of models network engineers can use to understand security, perhaps none is more useful than the OODA loop for addressing the process of managing the threat/defense cycle. The OODA loop can be applied in two ways to network security:

- **In a larger, or more strategic sense:** The OODA loop can be applied to the "realm of security," in terms of where the security world is, what common threats are, and how to react to them.

- **In a more immediate, or more tactical sense:** The OODA loop was originally designed to handle threats in real time, so it's a perfect model to deal with a DDoS or other attack happening right now.

The OODA loop was first developed by a military strategist, Colonel John Boyd, in the context of air warfare. When it comes to air-to-air combat, how can one pilot gain the advantage needed to win on a consistent basis? Breaking the process into pieces, so it can be understood and managed, would allow pilots to address each part of the process as an independent "thing." Understanding each step independently allows each part of the reaction process to be understood and optimized independently. The key question, when examining the OODA loop for any particular situation, is: *How much of my reaction can I stage and prepare before the attack actually happens?*

Figure 9-1 shows the OODA loop.

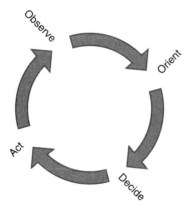

Figure 9-1   *OODA Loop*

Attackers want to either "get inside the loop," or "cut through the loop," to achieve their goals.

- **Observe:** If I can keep you from seeing what I'm doing (so you don't notice at all), I have the ability to launch a successful attack. Here we see the use of open tunnels to reach into a network, or IPv6 attacks in networks where only IPv4 is being monitored, attacks against inside interfaces, and the like.

- **Orient:** If I can make you think I'm trying to overwhelm your server with traffic, but I'm actually trying to install a Trojan by overflowing the input interface buffers, then you will react to the wrong problem, possibly even opening the door to the real attack. All sorts of feints fall into the category of orient, including most social engineering attacks.

- **Decide:** If I can attack you when I know your decision process will be slow, I can take advantage of my speed of attack to act before you can put the proper defenses in place. For instance, a long holiday weekend at 2 o'clock in the morning might be ideal, because the people who know what to do will be out on a remote beach enjoying their time off.

- **Act:** If I can prevent you from acting, or I can anticipate your action and use it against you, then I can launch a devastating attack against your network. For instance, if I can make an edge router unreachable from inside your network, I can use that moment to install a back door that allows me access later (whenever I want). Social engineering often uses peer pressure or social norms to prevent someone from acting when they should.

Defense, in terms of the OODA loop, is to make the loop work right—to observe the attack, orient to the attack (understand what type of attack it is), decide how to act, and then to implement modifications in network policy to stop the attack from damaging the network or the business. The defense wants to contain the attacker within the OODA loop; the loop itself provides the means of controlling and addressing the attack with the minimal amount of damage possible. The "tighter" the loop, the more effective the defense against any particular attack will be.

Let's consider each of these four steps within the realm of security, considering both the larger and narrower sense in turn.

Observe

What should you observe? To answer this question, ask another question: *What information is likely to be useful when diagnosing an attack on my network?*

But doesn't this answer depend on the type of attack? Of course—and that's why answering the question, "What should I observe," never has a really good answer. "Observe everything," isn't really practical in real life, so we leave it on the side and consider some other possibilities.

The first thing you should measure (or observe) is a general network baseline. For this first step, you want to ask yourself, "In what ways can I characterize network performance, and how can I produce a baseline of them?" Some examples might be:

- **The speed at which the network converges:**
  - Measuring the delay and jitter of a stream as it passes across an intentionally failed path during a maintenance window.

- Determining the average amount of time it takes for an active route to move into the passive state in an EIGRP network, which can be determined by examining the EIGRP event log across a number of events on a widely dispersed set of routers within the network.

- Determining how long an average link state Shortest Path First (SPF) calculation takes. You can normally find this information through a *show* command on the router.

- Determining how long it takes for BGP to converge on a new path when an old path fails. You can discover this by adding a new prefix and removing it, then watching how long it takes for specific routers to receive and act on the modifications to the BGP table.

- **The rate at which changes occur in the network:**

  - How often do links of each type change state, and why?

  - How often does external routing information being fed into the network change? The speed at which BGP routes change from your ISP, partner, or other peer can be an important piece of information to consider when you're facing an attack against a peering edge.

- **The utilization of links throughout the network:**

  - Although you might not want to keep track of the utilization of every link in a truly large network, being able to classify links based on what role they play, where they are in the network, and what types of traffic pass over them, and relate this classification to a "normal load," is very important.

  - A more complex—but probably just as important—measure is the utilization pattern across common periods of time. Hourly, daily, weekly, and monthly utilization rates can be very useful in determining whether there's really a problem, or if what you're seeing is actually normal network operation.

  - Who are the top talkers in each topological area of the network, and how often do they change?

- **The quality of traffic flow through the network:** Applications rely on consistent jitter and delay to work correctly; you can't know what "wrong" looks like unless you know what "correct" looks like.

Beyond a network baseline, you should also have the following on hand:

- Layer 3 network diagrams

- Layer 2 network diagrams

- Configurations for each device

One of the most difficult things to document—and to keep current—is the policies implemented on the network. This documentation should include not only what the policy is, but where it's implemented and what the intent of the policy is.

Note   The mechanisms used to observe these and other network measurements will be discussed in Chapter 10, "Measure Twice."

Although this is a long list, most network engineers can recite it by heart—because it's all about the network itself. There is another area that most network engineers miss in the realm of observing, however: the *external* security environment.

Here you can ask questions such as these:

- What attacks are other network operators seeing right now?

- What are the political and economic trends that might impact network security?

- What is the morale level within the company, and what impact will that have on the security of your network?

- What processes are in place to gain physical access to buildings, and how do these policies interact with access to network resources? There are a lot of networks that require a password to connect to wireless access, but you can plug in to any random Ethernet jack in any building and gain access to the entire network.

- Are there political events within the company planned or in progress that will impact network security, such as a massive layoff, the relocation of a major facility, or a merger with some other company?

- Is there a sickness "going around," and how will you respond to security incidents if half the network staff is out sick?

- If, for some reason, network operations folks can't leave the facility for several days (in the case of a lockdown or natural disaster), is there sufficient food and sanitary supplies to support them?

- What kind of security training is supplied to the people who work on and around the network (including users of applications that have access to even moderately sensitive data)? If the training is minimal, what is the impact of social engineering attacks, and are there specific ways you can design your system to minimize these threats?

In short, you should not limit yourself to observations about the network itself when considering the overall security of your systems. External factors can often play a bigger role in your ability to secure your network than internal ones—social engineering is probably a bigger factor in network security breaches than outright Distributed Denial of Service (DDoS) or other attacks.

In the narrower sense, you want to be able to observe a specific attack within the context of the internal baseline information and external environment information you have on hand when the attack actually occurs. Because you can't predict everything you might want to measure, the key here is to be open minded and flexible. Like a carpenter who has a lot of different tools, 80% of which are never used in the course of day-to-day work, a network engineer should have a wide array of measurement tools at hand.

Quite often, the larger and narrower views of observation will involve the regular sampling of measurements combined with the ability to perform more specific, narrow measurements in a more complete way reserved for specific circumstances. An example of this might be the regular sampling of traffic patterns using NetFlow combined with the ability to span a port or insert a packet analyzer on-the-fly to measure traffic flows on an actual packet-by-packet basis.

Sources for Security Information

There are a number of sources for information on the current and projected state of security throughout the world, covering topics from computer viruses to attacks against the Internet routing system to terrorist attacks to natural disasters. As a network architect, it's useful to keep up with at least one or two of these reports on a regular basis, just to have a good idea of current and projected problems. Some useful sources include the following:

- The Symantic Internet Security Threat Report, published yearly at http://www.symantec.com/security_response/publications/threatreport.jsp.

- The Microsoft Security Intelligence Report, published at http://www.microsoft.com/security/sir/default.aspx.

- Cisco Security publishes yearly and interim reports on a wide variety of topics at http://www.cisco.com/en/US/prod/vpndevc/annual_security_report.html.

- Arbor publishes an annual infrastructure security report, which mostly covers Internet-level threats to networks as a system, at http://www.arbornetworks.com/resources/infrastructure-security-report.

- Verisign's iDefense organization publishes reports on threats to the global Internet architecture at http://www.verisigninc.com/en_US/products-and-services/network-intelligence-availability/idefense/why-idefense-intelligence/index.xhtml.

- Verizon publishes a yearly report covering public and private data breaches and/or leaks at http://www.verizonenterprise.com/Resources/Reports.

There are a number of other large companies and organizations that build and publish reports yearly (or more often) that can be helpful to understanding the security environment, and hence to the observation stage of the OODA loop.

Orient

Orienting yourself to an attack is probably the most difficult part of the OODA loop, both in the larger and narrower senses. We all know the feeling of "sipping from the fire hose," in terms of the amount of information our world throws at us moment to moment.

It does no good to gather a lot of data that you can't ultimately analyze and use.

How do engineers deal with a flood of email and other information? By relying on filtering and machine learning techniques to bring the information that really counts to the top of our inboxes.

How should engineers deal with the flood of information being produced by a network monitoring system? It's easy to say "throw machine learning and automation at the problem"; however, it's much harder to actually implement these ideas. A few suggestions follow:

- Lump data together based on the type of information being gathered, rather than based on from where it was gathered. It's really tempting to put all the information gathered in a particular data center in one pile, and all the data gathered at the network edge into another, but solid analytics will work better if they are run across a larger pool of like data. Put all the traffic statistics from the data center in with the traffic statistics from the network edge—correlations between the two sets of traffic data might break out of the noise level more quickly, and machine learning will be more effective at finding anomalies that really stand out.

- Feed the "larger" strategic OODA loop into the monitoring and parsing process. If particular types of attacks are showing up in other company's networks, it's best to assume those same attacks are happening in your network—so you should look for their signatures specifically. This isn't to say that you won't find something completely new in your network, only that you should inject current trends and known problems into the data analysis phase to try to increase accuracy, both in terms of finding common problems and in terms of finding things that don't fit any of the known patterns.

- Layer data from the more abstract to the less. Don't try to perform analysis on a seven tuple packet-level capture across several months of network traffic. Choose smaller data sets, and then when you find an interesting pattern, dive deeper.

- When you find an anomaly, don't let go until you've explained it. If necessary, keep a "dead cases file" of interesting events on your network that you can't explain. You might find a relationship between multiple events you don't understand that lead to an attack you weren't expecting. Remember, attackers want to prevent you from observing what they are doing, so relating multiple apparently unrelated events might provide the key to understanding and shutting down a specific attack.

- Practice with the data on a regular basis. There's no substitute for working with the tools you intend to deploy in the face of a real attack on a regular basis.

In large part, orienting yourself to the information flow during a specific attack (at the tactical level) is going to depend on how well you've oriented yourself before the attack (at the strategic level). There is no direct substitute for real experience in the trenches, of course, but an hour studying how a particular attack works could well save many hours in reaction time when that attack is in progress.

Decide

What do you do with the data you've collected and analyzed? *You decide!* But if you thought orienting yourself to huge data flows was the hardest part of the OODA loop, you're wrong—deciding actually is.

The bottom line problem is this: security is not checkers. Security is, instead, more like chess. Although both are played on the same board, there are massive differences between the two games.

Checkers is a fairly easy game to learn and play; every piece has pretty much the same set of moves available, and games run pretty fast. There are, sometimes, unintended consequences, such as moving several pieces into a position where your opponent can take multiple pieces and crown a new king all in one turn; these are generally fairly obvious to the experienced observer.

Chess, on the other hand, is a very complex game (although game theory people will tell you chess is not a game, because there is no real random chance involved). There are six different types of pieces on the board, each of which moves and takes other pieces in a distinct way. Some pieces can jump over other pieces, and others can't. Lines of attack often cannot be direct, and feints are common. The key point to remember in a game of chess—particularly against a very good opponent—is that unintended consequences abound. It's very easy to become focused on executing a particular plan, to the point where your opponent's moves end up drawing you into a trap of your own devising. In fact, most chess games are lost because the loser is playing one side of the board, rather than both sides of the board.

Playing defense in the security game is a lot like this: if you don't play both sides of the board, you're going to lose. You not only have to decide what you're going to do, you have to decide what you think your opponent, the attacker, might do as well.

How can we make the job of defending easier?

First, use automation where possible to tighten the loop. Automating your response to a number of common, and well understood, attack situations will allow you to focus on the things that are different.

Second, cycle back to observe and orient often. If your attacker draws you down one path to the point where you develop tunnel vision, then you're likely to miss the second attack that comes from another angle. It's only by moving back to observe and orient on a regular basis that you can prevent tunnel vision from setting in.

Finally, build up a set of preset responses and policies around your network security. Policies are like muscle memory developed over years of practice in shooting or racing; they're short cuts that allow you to tighten the OODA loop to a minimal size. If you've built the right policies, you'll be able to react quickly to a wide range of situations.

There's another side to policies, however, that might not be so obvious. Returning to our previous metaphor, chess is full of situations where you face unintended consequences. When you're in the middle of countering an attack, it's very hard (if not impossible) to

analyze all the possible unintended consequences and steer clear of them. Policies that are developed outside the attack time frame, especially when they take into account the larger, more strategic aspects of the OODA loop, are a guardrail against unintended consequences.

Act

Finally, you need to act. If you've done the other parts of the OODA loop well, acting should be the simplest piece of the puzzle. The main problem we all face when acting is holding our pattern, or trusting the work we've done when getting to the point of acting.

Remember that losing your nerve can cost you.

Two points to consider in the realm of acting:

- Automation can help you tighten the loop, just like in the *observe, orient,* and *decide* phases of the OODA loop.

- You should return through the loop as quickly as possible after taking action. Don't rest on the action; go back to step one fast and re-execute the first three phases of the loop. The attacker might be counting on you deciding that the night is late, and the attack finished, to loosen up your network's defenses.

Brittleness

The game of security, the back and forth between attack and defense, with spiraling ideas, openings, and tools, is a lot like chess. Building security systems, however, is more like working steel. If you're trying to make something simple, say a blade for that perfect chef's knife, you first rough shape the steel, then you harden it. The hardening process is both chemical and reactionary; you choose the right materials to start with, then you heat the metal to a particular point, and finally quench it.

But if you stopped there in the process, you'd have a rather useless knife. It wouldn't hold an edge very well, and it would break the first time you dropped it on a concrete floor. Optimally hardened steel is fairly useless in any sort of tool. So the blade maker softens the steel a bit, through another heating and annealing process, to produce a workable tool.

We've spent some time discussing the use of automation as a tool to tighten the OODA loop in the previous sections—but there is a downside to automation.

Automation is brittle.

Just like an overhardened piece of steel needs to be drawn to make a useful tool, an overautomated security system needs regular human input. There need to be points in the defense system where the system itself doesn't react, but rather it raises a flag that a human must respond to. And maybe it's good, sometimes, to go in and check on the observation, orientation, and decide pieces you've built into your security system to make certain things haven't changed.

To think about this problem in a different way, consider that any security system you build is simply a static representation of your thinking about what sorts of attacks the network is going to face, and how to counter those attacks, at any moment in time. Although we might think of a security system as dynamic, in that it can have many different responses to any given attack, the reality is that the range of options the system has available is limited to the number of options you thought of when putting it together.

And if you match a static system against a dynamic human or a team of humans who can explore the limits of the system, trigger responses, and adjust their attack based on the landscape they find through these explorations, the dynamic side will eventually win—every time. This is the problem of brittleness in a nutshell—a dynamic and learning attacker addressing a static responder. No matter how broadly the security system is, there will be holes, edges, and places where the attacker can gain a foothold inside the system.

The simple solution to brittleness is to have at least some human involvement in different parts of the system.

Building Defense In

The point of the OODA loop is to short circuit the reaction process; in other words, to think through possible attack avenues and stage the equipment, monitoring points, and other information needed in the case of an attack before the attack occurs. This is great if you're working specifically in the space of network security (or even management, as we'll learn in the next chapter), but what about the network design itself? Where does security interact with the network design?

There are two specific points to consider when thinking through the intersection of network design and network security: modularization and resilience. These two are the "natural defenses" of a well-designed network, particularly if they are thought out with security in mind from the very beginning.

The Power of Unintended Consequences

The Cisco Global Escalation Team is often called into some very difficult—and unusual—network problems. In one particular case, a large bank called into the Technical Assistance Center (TAC) because they were having massive failures in EIGRP routing throughout their network. The engineer who owned the case quickly realized this was something that was simply too big to handle in a couple of phone calls, so the case was escalated.

The problem was manifesting itself as constant and widespread neighbor failures between EIGRP peers. Watching a small number of routers over a period of days closely, the failures were caught "in the act," so we could examine the state of the links and peers when a neighbor relationship failed. Close examination showed the problem was not a link failure issue; unicast and multicast pings received quick replies, even when the EIGRP neighbors were failing across the same link. There was no heavy congestion that could explain the problem, either.

Digging deeper, we discovered the input queues on the routers were filling up, resulting in a lot of the packets destined for the router itself being dropped. Clearly this was the source of the problem, as EIGRP counted on traffic being processed through the IP input queues to maintain neighbor relationships. But what was filling up these input queues?

Watching the input queues on several routers carefully, we captured a number of packets for examination. The packets all seemed to be sourced from a small number of machines, and we didn't recognize the formats of the captured traffic. The customer couldn't figure out what this set of source IP addresses represented—their documentation was sloppy in this area.

After several hours of tracing through the routing table to find each of the source addresses, we finally found the set of originating servers. Each of them was a RADIUS server; the customer had configured per command authentication on all of their routers to improve network security several weeks before, and the documentation hadn't yet caught up with the changes.

What we were seeing in the input queue each time we captured the packets waiting there were the replies from the RADIUS server giving us permission to capture the contents of the input queues. This was, in itself, a memorable lesson in the power of unintended consequences in the effort to provide bulletproof security for a network—but there was yet another lesson waiting for us when we finally discovered the root cause of the problem.

After turning off the per command authentication process, we finally captured some of the packets that were clogging up the input queues, which in turn was causing massive EIGRP failures throughout the customer's network. These packets exhibited several odd qualities; they were from a wide range of addresses, and the destination address was always along a classful IP address boundary. We isolated a small number of hosts that were among the wide array of available source addresses and traced the traffic between the host and its default gateway.

The host was sending a series of packets destined to each subnet broadcast in the entire IP address space. On further investigation, we found the piece of software that was causing all of this havoc was a backup package. The company had mistakenly installed a server version of the software on every computer in their network; a part of the server's functionality was to sweep the entire IP address range looking for hosts with clients installed that needed to be backed up.

Two attempts to ensure the correct handling of data and the security of the network together resulted in days' worth of network instability and many hours spent chasing down and resolving the problems.

Modularization

Modularization, as a design tool, is primarily aimed at the following:

- Breaking up failure domains, which improves network resilience
- Breaking up complexity, which allows for better reuse of design in multiple places, as well as designs that are more tuned to local and service requirements
- Breaking up functionality, so any given device is performing a smaller number of functions, which limits cost and management complexity

We've already discussed hierarchical design in Chapter 7, "Applying Modularity," and we'll discuss virtualization as a method of modularization in Chapter 12, "Building the Second Floor." But what does modularization have to do with security? Security interacts with each of these modularity drivers in different ways.

Modularity, Failure Domains, and Security

From the perspective of control plane design, breaking a network up into multiple failure domains creates a set of "firewalls." Failures that occur on one side of a failure domain boundary should impact the control plane on the other side of that same boundary in as minimal a way as possible.

This type of separation between failure domains is also a solid design principle in security. Even if an attacker successfully takes down one set of servers or services, it should take some effort to spread the problem to other areas of the network—breaks in the control plane at the failure domain boundaries should act as a barrier to at least slow down the spread of the attack to the entire network.

Modularity, Complexity, and Security

One of the hardest points to consider in securing a system—a point made previously when discussing the similarities between the game of chess and network security—is unintended consequences. At some point, a system can become so large, and so complex, that you don't really understand what all the various consequences of a specific action might be. When you're in a middle of dealing with a large-scale attack that threatens the very usability of a network, the last question you want to ask is, "If I change the policy configured on this router, can I really know what the impact will be on all the applications and users?"

How can you answer this question before it's asked? By separating complexity from complexity. The same points that factor into modularization as generally good design practice will also factor into good security design. The simpler the configuration of any given device, the more likely you are to understand any possible side effects of modifying that configuration.

Creating multiple simpler modules in your network helps you to react to security issues more quickly—because it allows you to understand the configuration and policy already in place faster, and to see and react to the consequences of a policy change more easily.

Modularity, Functionality, and Security

All the intersections between complexity and security apply to assigning modules specific functions, as well—by narrowing down the functional breadth of a given network module, you simplify configuration and make it easier to understand and work around the potential side effects of implementing a specific policy in reaction to an attack on the network. Beyond this, however, breaking up functionality provides one other beneficial side effect from a security perspective.

Assigning modules within the network-specific functions provides a set of well-understood points at which to implement security policy on the fly. If a network is well divided along functional boundaries, applying defenses designed for one module to other similar modules should be a simple matter of small adaptations. When you're fighting an attack in real time, you want to be able to quickly pinpoint a small number of devices on which to deploy policy across the network; functional separation enables this capability.

Resilience

Resilience is often first considered a business support and continuity issue—a network that isn't available all the time, or can't consistently support the applications the business needs to run, isn't worth building. But there's a security angle to network resilience, as well. Although it might not be obvious from a pure security perspective, the first line of defense against any sort of denial of service attack is the resilience built in to the network from the ground up.

What this means is that you should build resilience not only around the possibility of network failures, but also to react to attacks. Being able to move an important application off a path congested by an attack to a possibly less optimal, but also untouched, path quickly is a key security response mechanism in the network design.

Some Practical Considerations

There are a number of places network engineers look by default for security holes; there are others that aren't so obvious. In this section, we'll try to cover some of the less obvious places to look for security holes so that you don't find them the hard way.

Close a Door, Open a Door

One of the most important things to remember when building out a security system is that security—like all network design—is always a trade-off. For instance:

- To prevent rogue routers from injecting false routing information, HMAC/SHA signatures are deployed across all the routing processes in a network.

- To ensure compliance with change control mandates throughout a network, RADIUS authentication is enabled on all routers, and command logging per user is enabled as well.

- To counter prefix hijacking, a service provider implements a global RPKI system and ties it to BGP policy so any route that isn't authenticated is automatically rejected out of the BGP table.

- To counter spam, a company connects its firewall to a whitelist/blacklist service, and sets its email servers to reject any email from domains that are not listed in the whitelist.

Each of these may (or may not, depending on your point of view) be perfectly valid options in the war against security breaches in a network. But they all come with some form of costs. Before reading the following list, try to find the door that's being opened to new attacks in the process of closing the door against other attacks.

What new forms of attack have been added through these actions?

- The amount of work required to process an HMAC/SHA (or otherwise cryptographically signed) packet is much higher than the work required to process an unsigned version of the very same packet. By turning encrypted signatures on, you're opening each router in the network to a denial of service attack through overflowing the processor by streaming a high rate of cryptographically signed packets into a router's interface.

- If the RADIUS server itself is not reachable, what capability do network engineers have to modify the configurations on each individual router? If there is no "back door," you've given the attacker a single point to attack that will cut off the network engineering team's ability to manage the network—probably not a good thing.

- If the global RPKI system becomes unreachable, what happens to the routing system itself? Will all routes be accepted, or all rejected? What can the attacker accomplish by bringing down the RPKI itself?

- If all the mail servers in the network are configured to reject any mail that's not on a whitelist provided by an external provider, what will happen when access to that provider fails? Will all email be rejected? The attacker, rather than focusing on hundreds of separate email accounts, now only has to focus on the connection to a single service to disrupt email throughout the entire enterprise.

Each time a door is closed, a door is opened. It's not that these secondary doors can't be closed as well—but they do need to be considered. The cost of the first door needs to be weighed against the danger of opening the second door, the cost of closing that door, and any doors that might be opened by closing that second door.

A useful way to think about this is to consider the entire security perimeter of the network an *attack surface*. What is the shape of that surface? Will closing a hole here open a hole there? Security is a system, not a set of individual components.

There's always a trade-off. The job of the network architect, the security professional, the network engineer, is to find that trade-off and consider it. There's never a time when there isn't a trade-off, so if you've not found it, you're not done thinking through the implications of implementing some specific form of security.

Beware of Virtualization

When the IETF set about deliberating a new version of the Internet Protocol, one problem they ran into was the question, "How do we deploy this new protocol?" The answer the engineers involved in the process came to was, "We tunnel it over IPv4." Tunneling, of course, is a fine answer; tunneling and tunneled protocols are widely deployed in the real world to meet all sorts of different needs. From backhaul to deploying new protocols and services to security, tunneling is almost ubiquitous.

But as with all things in the real world, there are trade-offs. IPv6 transition mechanisms are a case in point. For instance, RFC6324 documents an attack using disjointed control plane information on either side of an automatic 6to4 tunnel to loop packets along an IPv6 tunnel indefinitely, eating bandwidth and potentially acting as a denial of service attack against the path along which the tunnel travels.

The only way to really be safe about tunnels is to treat each tunnel as if it were a physical link for security purposes.

Now we know this is actually impossible; there are too many tunnels between too many devices using too many protocols to track every tunnel and monitor it for security breaches. There are just too many tunnel types, and too many places they're used—SSL, IPsec, GRE, LISP, IPv6 transition, and a hundred other besides, running from routers to hosts, hosts to hosts, servers to hosts, and in many other combinations.

Tunneling mechanisms, by providing virtual topologies attackers can take advantage of, create a major hole in the attack surface of your network. There is little you can do other than deploy effective monitoring to find as much of the tunnel traffic as you can and monitor and manage it as effectively as possible.

Social Engineering

The same property that allows humans in the security process to counter brittleness also creates holes in the security process through social engineering, a form of attack that leverages perceived trust to convince the people in your company to open security holes or provide information that can be used to open the right doors for the attacker to operate successfully within your network. Here are some examples of social engineering:

- Calling an employee from an (apparently) internal line and asking for the employee's current password to fix a problem the employee hasn't noticed. If the attacker can convince the person that the attacker is a valid member of the company's staff, there is a good chance the employee will work with the attacker to be helpful, or to correct the unseen problem.

- Walking into a store wearing the right name badge or the right clothes (uniform) and asking to borrow a particular piece of equipment for some special project, or to transfer equipment from one store to another. Most people are going to trust the appearance of sincerity, rather than questioning and appearing to be unreasonable or unhelpful.

- Posing as someone who should rightly be able to ask for specific information, or to access specific areas, such as a police officer, fireman, auditor, or a member of a partnering company's staff.

Don't ever underestimate the power of social engineering.

Even the best trained people can be caught in the web of trusting those they shouldn't trust, particularly when the attacker poses as someone who is in desperate need, or someone who can really help them in some way. On the other hand, that doesn't mean you shouldn't put the right policies in place, and provide the right training, to cull out as many social engineering attacks as possible. For instance:

- Have clear, written policies about who an employee can give any sort of information to, from phone numbers to passwords.

- Get people in the habit of asking someone else, even if it's just a co-worker, before helping anyone with anything that seems remotely unusual. In detecting scams, two heads are almost always better than one.

- Encourage people to work horizontally within the company, rather than strictly vertically. The more people know the IT staff, the more likely they are to recognize an intruder or attacker as someone who doesn't belong in the right group to be asking questions.

Summary

Yes, you should build security in, rather than bolting it on after. But how can a network architect actually build security in?

First, use the OODA loop as a tool to help you analyze where and how you can provide the tools to tighten up your response times in the case of an attack. Second, remember that a lot of the good design principles you're using to make the network scalable and resilient are also effective security tools. Think about modularization and resilience not only in terms of good design, but also in terms of secure design. Finally, watch your attack surface, and remember that when you close one hole, you're most likely opening another. Never implement something new in security until you've chased down and studied the trade-off. *There's always a trade-off.*

Although this chapter hasn't provided you with every tool you'll ever need to be an effective security engineer, it has, hopefully, given you enough tools to interact with real security engineers effectively, and to think through where and how to build security in to the network design from the start.

Measure Twice

If there were a poll taken for the least favorite topic among network engineers, network management would surely win without much trouble. And yet...without solid management, network engineers are running blind, like a builder without a level or a tape measure. It's not good enough to have a blueprint; you need to know how your current building stacks up against that blueprint, and what and where to change to bring things into line.

This chapter aims to minimize the pain of network management while maximizing the gain. In a perfect world, the measurements and analysis network architects need to manage a network would just "fall out" of the process of building the network. But networks are never perfect worlds, whether virtual or real. To begin, we'll examine the "why" of network management; why trouble with measuring things? After this, we'll consider some models to try and come to grips with the network management world a little better. In the third section of this chapter, we'll look at some practical considerations in deployment management, and then finally we'll take a tour of the documentation you should have on hand.

Why Manage?

There are five primary reasons to measure and manage the state of your network:

- Justifying the cost of the network
- Planning
- Decreasing the Mean Time to Repair (MTTR)
- Increasing the Mean Time Between Mistakes (MTBM)
- Security

Security is covered in depth in Chapter 9, "Securing the Premises," so we won't spend any time on it here.

Justifying the Cost of the Network

The first, and primary, reason should be to *justify the cost of the network* to those who are paying for it. This might seem like an unintuitive—or even counterintuitive—statement, but consider the consequences of failing to justify the cost of the network (and the technologies associated with it). To put it in the most essential of terms, nothing survives (or nothing should survive) in the business world unless it adds value. Networks are not an exception to this rule.

The ability to point to "general goodness statements," such as "the network allows us to stay in business," or "the network allows email to work," or even "the network supports this specific business critical application," isn't, in the end, sufficient justification for spending money on it. This might sound odd, but consider this: there is always someone willing to provide those very same services (even "business critical applications"), as a service of some sort. Outsourcing, in other words, is always an option.

> If the network architect cannot justify the cost of maintaining the network as an internal function, then the network architect should expect his job to be outsourced.

An alternative way to look at this is in terms of return on investment (ROI)—how much money does the network cost versus how much does the network bring into the company? How do you measure such a thing? Because cloud computing is really just another form of outsourcing, some of the questions you need to ask when comparing outsourced solutions versus running and managing services within your organizations will be dealt with in Chapter 16, "On Psychologists, Unicorns, and Clouds."

There are several things to pay close attention to in this area.

First, make certain to account for the monetary value of time. Even small differentials in time can make a huge difference in productivity; when considering a large number of employees, small differences in productivity can account for large amounts of money. This is an issue both in outsourcing and in network operational upgrades. As an example, shaving a second off the handling time of each call in a call center might seem like a small bit of savings, not really worth making an investment in. But saving one second per call across 30,000 calls a day is, essentially, saving the cost of a full-time employee.

Second, take into account the value of addressing unique business opportunities. If your company runs a chain of retail stores that cater to the outdoors (camping, hunting, fishing, and shooting) markets, consider the value of being the preferred supplier in severe weather events. What is the potential and historic upside to being open just after a hurricane or tornado, both in terms of goodwill within the community, and in terms of real sales when people are rebuilding or responding to such events? The cost of network upgrades designed to support operations during and after severe weather events, such as additional redundancy and hardened equipment, may easily be offset by such considerations.

Third, take stock of the advantages of better security. There are only a few applications in the world that cannot be outsourced in terms of actual processing; with the advent of cloud computing, raw processing power on which you can run your own applications can

be just a few clicks away. But the security assumptions of outsourced platforms are often a hidden, or unaddressed, cost. What is the additional cost to encrypt data and manage encrypted data? The cost of local storage and compute power must be weighed against the cost of the outsourced service plus the additional security requirements.

Most of the ROI trade-offs around network management are going to be around improved network efficiency and increased availability, but make certain you pay attention to the less-common areas where big gains in savings or new revenue can be found.

Planning

"The past may not repeat itself, but it sure does rhyme"—Mark Twain

As counterintuitive as it might seem, the key to understanding how and where your network will need to grow to meet current and future business challenges lies in the past. Although you can't predict everything that might happen in a network through measurement and analysis, the growing emphasis on "big data" is resulting in the creation and improvement in a number of tools that can help. There are several places where the network architect should be looking for trends in network utilization to better understand what future improvements might be needed, or where the network is overbuilt (allowing investment to be shifted).

Measuring real life Mean Time Between Failures (MTBF) should be one focus of the analysis by network engineers. Rather than depending on the "stated numbers" for the failure rate of a particular piece of equipment or link type, the historical data about link and equipment failures should be analyzed to gain a better understanding of how often failures can be expected. This type of analysis can help to reduce network costs by providing insight into how much redundancy is needed at each point in the network.

Note   Examples of mining past performance to better understand the MTBF can be found in many unexpected areas, including theme parks and transportation companies. Large theme park operators can project the lifetime of the light bulbs they use in the various venues and replace them just before they fail, preventing unsafe conditions. In the transportation industry, long haul transportation (trucking) companies use data analysis to determine what type of accident each driver is likely to have, and how often these accidents will occur. By taking proactive steps to train their drivers, and routing trucks through specific paths at specific times, they can decrease the number of accidents per mile, thus reducing their cost of operations, increasing the longevity of their drivers, and increasing their operation efficiency.

Time and region based traffic shifts are another area to which network engineers should pay careful attention. Understanding traffic patterns can help determine the best time to make changes in the network, and also project when areas of the network might need to be upgraded (or downgraded). Beyond this, as the ability to measure traffic levels in real time is ramped up, the ability to use a higher percentage of the available network bandwidth increases. The ultimate goal of any traffic engineering effort in a network

should be to buy only the bandwidth that is really needed to transport the traffic actually offered, plus some small amount of redundant path capability. The better your traffic history is, the more closely you'll be able to match capacity against demand.

Shifts in traffic caused by the deployment of a new application, protocol, or service can prove very helpful over time. While analysis of packet sizes, usage levels, and other projections can be useful, all of these suffer from a major flaw common to all technology—applications and protocols aren't ever used the way their designers think they will be used. Rather, the use of a new application or protocol is limited only by the imagination and needs of those who will be using it. Mining data around changes in network patterns caused by the deployment of a new application or protocol can provide a real-life check point (or information source) when considering what network changes will be needed.

Decreasing the Mean Time to Repair

Fault management may be the most obvious use of network management software and processes, but that doesn't mean it's well understood—or even well defined. In fact, most network management software and processes are still far behind the curve when it comes to detecting, understanding, and alerting network operators to problems in the network. In particular, be careful to go beyond measuring total failures. Brownouts, increases in jitter and delay, link overloading, traffic leaking from one virtual network into another, and even slow control plane convergence are areas that are often overlooked.

In general, network management should not only be useful for finding problems quickly, but also for resolving problems quickly.

Increasing the Mean Time Between Mistakes

There are two areas where network management can help increase the MTBM: change management and configuration automation. Change management generally works on the principle that two heads are better than one—the more people who look at a change before it's put in place, the less likely it is there will be mistakes in the configuration or intent of the change itself. Configuration management attempts to battle policy dispersion (see Chapter 14, "Considering Complexity," for more information on policy dispersion), as well as providing an "abstraction layer" between humans and raw configurations. Networks are often made up of devices from many different vendors, running different versions of software, each with its own command-line interface (CLI) and nuances; a configuration management system can provide a common way to manage all these disparate devices through a single interface and with a single syntax.

Change Management Gone Wrong

Although change management can be very beneficial to the operations of a network, it's often easy to get wrapped up in the process of managing change because it reduces personal or institutional risk—even when it doesn't produce good results. Consider this example of network management gone wrong based on a real-life experience:

After checking in through the front desk, I walked in to the area where the network engineering staff was located. Lugging a laptop and projector—this was the first day of a multiday workshop on EIGRP—I passed through the cubicles looking for the conference room that had been booked the week before. At the end of one row, I noticed a lot of people gathered around the opening of one of the cubicles, all apparently intent on something going on inside. The small crowd, in fact, consisted of just about every network engineer the company had.

Approaching the cubicle, I asked, "What's going on?"

One of the engineers turned around. "Oh we're working on a problem..."

"Oh...What is it?" I set the laptop and projector on the floor, assuming the training class would be delayed until this problem was resolved. "Maybe I can help."

"There's a routing loop that's preventing access to one of the terminal servers, so a lot of people can't get to the mainframe."

"Well, let's fix it, so we can get on with this class."

The engineer continued looking over the shoulder of the person in front of him, into the surrounded cubicle. I could just see two people squeezed into the space in front of the desk, and two monitors with various real-time graphs displayed. "We know what the problem is. A static route was configured during this morning's change window. It was misconfigured, so we have a routing loop."

"Why don't you take the static route out?"

The engineer turned to look at me again. "We can't until the emergency change control board meets."

Management Models

Management models, like network models, provide a framework within which to think about the purpose and deployment of network management. The first model we'll discuss is Fault, Configuration, Accounting, Performance, and Security (FCAPS), which is widely used and well understood. The second model we'll discuss is one we've looked at before, in the context of security, the Observe, Orient, Decide, and Act (OODA) loop.

Fault, Configuration, Accounting, Performance, and Security

FCAPS was first defined in ISO 10400 in the mid 1980s as a classification system for managing an entire IT infrastructure. It has, since then, been modified through various documents; the most recent version can be found in ITU-T M.3400, which deals with telecommunications network management. The Enhanced Telecommunications

Operations Map (ETOM) has incorporated the ideas behind FCAPS into the Fulfillment, Assurance, and Billing (FAB) model, with each function of FCAPS being mapped to one of the functions of the FAB model.

The focus in this model is on the various functions management provides, rather than on the methods, tools, or processes used to provide that functionality—so although this is a good structure to build a list of "what should I ask," questions, it isn't as useful for laying out what and how to measure. FCAPS approaches network management from the business, rather than operational, perspective, which means it can often provide a good model for interfacing with corporate management.

FCAPS is a fairly straightforward model; what each section measures and manages is implied by the names themselves.

- Fault management deals with the detection of faults and notification of fault conditions to network operators for repair. If corrective action to restore a network to full operation is taken automatically, the FCAPS model still mandates the logging of fault data for future analysis. This area of FCAPS overlaps with the previous section "Decreasing the Mean Time to Repair."

- Configuration management gathers the analysis and modification of device configurations across a broad spectrum of devices into one management console, or one system. Although the ideal solution would be a single device or application managing the configuration of every device in a network, the reality is often multiple configuration management stations with overlapping spans of control. This area of FCAPS overlaps with the previous section "Increasing Mean Time Between Mistakes."

- Accounting is primarily focused on determining how much to bill specific users for specific services provided through the network. Hence accounting, in a network management system, deals with things like total bandwidth used, peak versus non-peak usage, types of traffic offered to the network, and other measures of network utilization. This section of the FCAPS model is a superset of the previous section "Justifying the Cost of the Network."

- Performance management is focused on determining the current efficiency of the network and projecting the needs of the network in the future. This section of the FCAPS model overlaps with the previous section "Planning."

- Security, in the FCAPS model, is focused on system security, particularly at the level of authorizing individual users to access and use specific services available through the network. Network security tends to be more focused on infrastructure security than the security contained in the FCAPS model. This section of the FCAPS model is closely related to Authorization, Authentication, and Accounting (AAA) services, commonly implemented through RADIUS and other protocols and services.

Observe, Orient, Decide, and Act (OODA)

The OODA loop is described in Chapter 9 in some detail; rather than examining the history and the theory at a general level, we'll consider how it can be applied to management

here. Rather than focusing on what needs to be measured or managed, the OODA loop focuses on the management process itself—how does a network administrator determine what needs to be acted on, how to act on it, and what action needs to be taken? The OODA loop is complementary to the FCAPS model previously described—for example:

- In the realm of fault management, the network engineer must first *observe* the current state of the network (build a network baseline) and the fault (fault notification). After the fault has been observed, *orientation* is required by troubleshooting the problem and determining the root cause. When the fault has been diagnosed, the correct form of action must be determined *(decide),* and action must be taken to resolve the problem *(act).*

- In the realm of configuration management, the network engineer *observes* the configuration, policy, and policy dispersion within the network. *Orientation* requires the engineer to consider the commonality and differentials between the various policies and the configurations required to effect those policies. To *decide,* the network engineer must consider which of these policies can and should be gathered up into a centralized system, and how to divide the policies and configurations across a wide array of equipment into a single unified (and possibly abstract) interface or system. Finally, *action* must be taken to implement these decisions by building and/ or deploying the appropriate configuration or network management software.

- In the realm of network accounting, the network engineer must first *observe* a set of network capabilities or services, and then *orient* to those services by determining what it costs to provide those services. *Observation,* in this realm, will also be required to determine where and how to measure the usage of the services offered, and orientation will be required to understand the limitations of the measurement, and how that will offset the value of the service as a service. *Decide* will require the network engineer, in cooperation with the business, to determine how and what to measure, and how to bill. *Act* will require the actual building and billing of the service in question.

- In the realm of performance management, the network engineer must *observe* the normal state of the network, the current state of the network, and the historical differential between the two (or changes over time). *Orientation* takes place as the network engineer determines whether current differentials are likely to continue into the future by examining why these differentials are occurring and whether the conditions causing the differentials will continue. *Orientation* will also involve examining the business environment for incipient changes and other issues that may impact the performance of the network or applications running on the network—such as a new application being deployed. The network engineer must *decide* what to do about the difference between the current performance, the ideal performance, and projected future changes to performance, and finally *act* by implementing the necessary changes to maintain network performance at some predetermined level.

The OODA loop can be used across a wider cross-section of the different processes within each area of the FCAPs model; these are just examples.

An interesting application of the OODA loop in network management is change management. A fairly standard change management process includes the following steps:

Step 1.   Define the requirement.

Step 2.   Request the change.

Step 3.   Review the change.

        a. Examine the costs and benefits.

        b. Examine the technical feasibility.

        c. Analyze the impact of the change on existing systems.

Step 4.   Plan the change.

Step 5.   Execute the change.

Step 6.   Review the change.

        a. Verify change operation.

        b. Verity change impacts.

Steps 1 and 2 in this process are *observe*; step 3 is *orient*; step 4 is *decide*; step 5 is *act*; and step 6 returns to *observe*. Rephrasing the process in terms of an OODA loop may help clarify the steps involved in change management, including answering the question, "Why are we doing this?"

Deploying Management

Deploying management takes far more than finding the right things to measure, the right place to measure them, the right way to measure them, and the right processes to control the different management areas. This section details some of the practical points network architects need to consider when deploying network management.

Loosen the Connection Between Collection and Management

One of the major problems surrounding network management is the natural affinity, or tie in, between the reason for collecting data and the data store itself. Using the FCAPS model, for instance, the interface speed might be collected multiple times—once for fault management, once for configuration management, once for accounting, and once for performance management—and processed and stored separately.

This is a *bad thing*.

Network architects should, instead, treat the measurements taken off the network as one large "pool" of data. Although specific questions might generate the original or ongoing

data set, measurement data should be stored in a way that is only loosely connected with the original purpose for which the data is collected. There should be a conscious effort to provide interfaces into the network management data so it can be used for purposes other than the original intent. In other words, data collected off the network should be placed in a store with a common set of interfaces that anyone (with the right credentials and reasons) can access.

Finally, the connection can be loosened by using monitoring information in new and unexpected ways. The entire field of data analytics can cross over from the big data and data science areas in the retail, production, or other operations area, and be used to mine for useful trends and analysis. You might know, for instance, that traffic in your network follows a working hours/off hours pattern, but are there deeper or less obvious patterns that might help you better use the bandwidth available? How can you relate network usage to energy usage in large-scale data centers, and what is the trade-off between moving loads to save energy versus the cost in terms of performance and the actual movement of the packets?

Information gathered from all around the network should be available for uses far beyond the original intent; there should be processes and mechanisms in place to find the hard data that will help you predict failures, manage cost, and adjust to growth more quickly.

Sampling Considerations

The question often arises about whether to sample data, or to gather all the information—whether at the flow level (when using Netflow, for instance), or at the control plane level (should I capture the time required to run SPF on every router, or just a few?), or in many other places. In the end, you're always going to end up sampling data; there's simply too much of it to collect wholesale. The real question network architects should be asking is, "Which samples do I want to take, and why?"

The answer to this question is the inevitable "it depends," but there are some helpful guidelines:

- How useful will the data be if it is only sampled, rather than collected wholesale? The behavior of an application that sends only a few dozen packets in each hour probably isn't going to be discernible from a sampled measurement. On the other hand, the average time each SPF run takes in an IS-IS network can probably be correctly ascertained through sampled data.

- Are you looking for trends or for hard data? Doctors often tell their patients, "Weight is a trend, not a number." At least that's what they say when they're trying to be kind to their patients—but the point still holds. Sampling is often useful for spotting trends, whereas for hard numbers, you'll need more precise wholesale monitoring.

- How self-similar is the data you're monitoring? If there is a larger network traffic pattern, such as a sudden uptick in traffic at the beginning of the workday, and a quick drop off at the end of the workday, and you already know about this daily change

through gross sampling mechanisms (such as interface counters), you might want to focus your measurement efforts at the packet level on more fine-grained changes. In this case, you might want to modify the sampling rate so it's in line with the known traffic patterns, collecting samples more frequently when the traffic levels are high, and less frequently when the traffic levels are lower.

Where and What

It's useful to not only have a model of management techniques and processes, but also of the network as a measurable object. Although network engineers often think of the network within the context of the OSI (or seven layer) model, this isn't necessarily the best model for determining what to measure, nor how to measure it (see Chapter 4, "Models," for more information on a number of different models used to describe networks). Figure 10-1 illustrates a model that's useful for thinking through network measurement techniques.

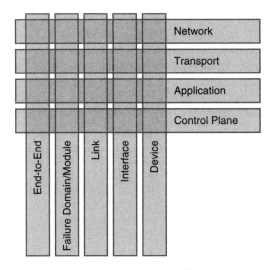

Figure 10-1 *Model of Network Measurement*

The objective of this model is to provide a framework for asking questions, rather than providing answers. At each of the intersections, there are a series of questions that can be asked, and a set of measurement techniques that will provide the answers. Along the bottom are different physical locations within the network, and along the right are different protocol layers. The key point is to determine which of these intersections need to be measured and how each measurement should be taken. Let's examine some of these intersections to see how this works.

End-to-End/Network

For any given path taken by traffic through the network, the end-to-end performance of the network protocol (IPv4 or IPv6 in most cases) can be measured in a number of ways.

For instance, the end-to-end delay, jitter, bandwidth, round-trip time, reachability, and packet loss can all be measured for each IP path through the network. Ways in which you might measure this information include the following:

■ Generating traffic along a given path and measuring the various parameters for the generated flow. This has the advantage of providing measurement traffic on demand, but it has the disadvantages of measuring traffic that's not real and adding additional load to the network. A number of management software and network testing packages can produce traffic flows with specific characteristics for measuring the performance of an end-to-end path through a network; IP/SLA is one example.

■ Passively measuring traffic generated by applications already running on the network. The advantages are that you're measuring real traffic and you're not adding additional load to the network. The disadvantage is that real application traffic might not always be available. NetFlow is probably the best known example of a measurement protocol in this area, although a number of other options might be viable in very narrow situations, such as logged access lists.

Interface/Transport

Every hop a transport layer packet, such as a Transmission Control Protocol (TCP) segment, passes through, must pass through a pair of interfaces. Each of these interfaces interacts with the packet through queuing, drops, serialization delay, and other factors. Each of these factors should (though they can't always), in turn, be measured in some way—normally through device-level **show** commands, information retrieved through SNMP or NETCONF, or some other mechanism.

Failure Domain/Control Plane

The most crucial area in which control plane performance needs to be examined is not end-to-end, at the network level, but within each failure domain. Understanding the amount of time it takes for a routing protocol to converge around a failed link within each specific failure domain can expose which failure domains are likely too large, or poorly designed, and which can be expanded in scope and size with minimal risk.

Most of the measurements taken here are going to (necessarily) be from Simple Network Management Protocol (SNMP), the Network Configuration Protocol (NETCONF), **show** commands, and other "white box" measurements. There are techniques to determine when an OSPF router has converged from within the protocol itself (see RFC 4061, RFC 4062, and RFC 4063), but these techniques are not widely deployed by testing equipment vendors. So long as information in these areas is available directly from the devices, there is little reason to add the complexity of "off box measurements," unless there's some specific situation that requires it.

Network engineers should primarily examine the amount of time required to calculate new routing information after a link or device changes state (remembering there are four steps to this process—see Chapter 8, "Weathering Storms," for more information).

Measurements should be taken both from the perspective of the network layer (IPv4 and IPv6) and from the perspective of the control plane protocols (time required to run an SPF, for instance, in an IS-IS deployment).

Bare Necessities

Every network engineer who's worked in a customer supporting role at a consulting company or a vendor has had this conversation.

"So, where in the network are you seeing the problem?"

The customer walks over to the side of the conference room and pulls the projector screen so it snaps to the ceiling, revealing a wall chart containing hundreds of pages. "Let me find the right page..." The customer flips through the pages and reaches a chart containing port and cable numbers, a chart that looks like every other chart in the stack. "Right here; see, there are two Ethernet cables connecting these two routers..."

"I thought we were looking at an OSPF problem?"

"Yes, of course. I'm just showing you how the routers are connected."

"Well, what about the IP addresses, and the area borders, and the..."

The customer starts flipping through pages, finally reaching a chart crammed with IP addresses. "Let's see, the first link is 192.0.2.0/25 and the second is 192.0.2.128/25. I'll have to look at the configurations to figure out which router is configured as the ABR..."

This leads, of course, to one of network engineering's nightmares: figuring out what the network looks like before you can actually get any work done.

What sort of documentation should every network have? A few pointers might be helpful:

- A Layer 3 network diagram indicating the points at which aggregation and other policies are configured. For bonus points, the reasoning behind deploying specific policies at specific locations could be documented, as well. These policies should include the costs of links, and what the intent was behind costing specific links in specific ways.

- A Layer 2 network diagram showing how each device is connected to each device around it. This should be a set of diagrams, rather than a single diagram, with Layer 3 references marked out, so any part of the Layer 3 diagram can be quickly correlated to a small and understandable physical wiring diagram.

- A diagram of any overlay topologies, preferably keyed so they can be quickly cross-referenced to physical and Layer 3 diagrams.

- An addressing plan marking out not only where specific addresses are deployed, but also how new addresses are chosen for specific places in the network, and why the specific process used is, in fact, used.

- A sortable database of the address space, preferably with some way to determine what routes should be visible at each device in the network (for quick comparison and examination).

■ A minable database of past problems, useful for finding correlations between current network conditions and what has happened before.

Summary

Although this chapter doesn't provide any advice on specific tools, it should give you some idea about the right questions to ask when building, evaluating, and justifying network management as a system (rather than network management systems). Network management is about far more than just measuring what's measurable, or looking for outages on a network map in an out-of-the-box network management software package. Network management takes creativity and ingenuity, but in the end measuring the network will yield insight into what needs to happen next to fulfill business needs, where problems are that need to be addressed, and other valuable information about the network.

The Floor Plan

Topologies aren't very exciting. In fact, in the realm of network design, the choice of which topology to use almost always "just happens"—it's almost never a point of intentional thought and consideration. So why should this book include an entire chapter on network topologies? Isn't stringing cables together just, well, stringing cables together?

No, stringing cables together isn't all there is to network topology, because determining which topology to use is far more than just stringing cables together. The topology is like a floor plan, in a sense; if you don't get it right, people (and packets) are going to be bumping into each other constantly, and dirt's going to be tracked into the wrong places. Traffic flow is no less a consideration when designing a network; the degree of hierarchy, the type of traffic, resilience, and other factors are crucial to supporting the business requirements and applications the network is bound to support.

Rings

Ring topologies are among the simplest to design and understand. They are also the least expensive option, especially when long haul links are involved, so they tend to predominate in wide area networks. Rings became so popular in long haul telephone networks, in fact, that there are several technologies designed around ring topologies, such as the original SONET specifications and Redundant Packet Rings (RPR).

Scaling Characteristics

Ring topologies have been scaled to large sizes; the additional cost to add a node is minimal. Generally, one new router (or switch), moving one circuit, and adding another new circuit is all that's needed. With careful planning, the addition of a new node into the ring can be accomplished without any real impact to overall network operations. Figure 11-1 depicts adding a node to a ring.

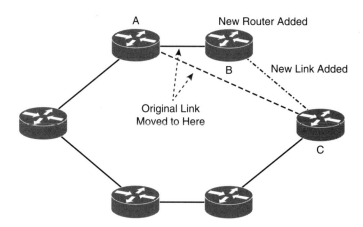

Figure 11-1 *Adding a New Node in a Ring Network*

If the original link between Routers A and C is administratively disabled before work begins (preferably during an outage window), the link can be swung to its new termination point at Router A, Router B installed, and the new link between Routers B and C installed without disturbing existing traffic. The new links and equipment can be tested without impacting operational traffic, as well. After the new equipment is tested, another outage window of short duration can be used to bring it into the production network.

Adding new nodes in a ring network, although simple enough, does increase the total number of hops through the network itself. Where before the change illustrated in Figure 11-1 Routers A and C were directly connected, they are now one hop apart. The total distance around the ring has also increased from 5 hops to 6.

Adding new nodes into a ring topology does not impact control plane scaling in any noticeable way. Each router along the ring will have precisely two neighbors, no matter how large the ring becomes. Although the total length of the path through the ring increases as nodes are added, most modern implementations of routing protocols are fast enough that the additional path length is of little concern. Shortest Path First (SPF), which is used in OSPF and IS-IS to calculate the best path to each destination in the network, will handle long path lengths with little trouble. EIGRP, as an advanced distance vector protocol, doesn't suffer from scaling issues in ring networks, either. Convergence does suffer with both of these two types of control planes, however—see the following section for a more detailed look at problems with convergence on ring topologies.

As ring size increases, it becomes difficult to manage quality of service and optimal traffic flows. Two heavy users of bandwidth connected to Routers A and B in the network illustrated in Figure 11-2 might cause the intervening link to remain constantly congested, causing problems for real-time traffic (such as VoIP) passing between Routers A and C. Forcing traffic around the "back side" of the ring, the longer path, to avoid this congestion can be very difficult, generally requiring tunneling (such as Multiprotocol Label Switching, or MPLS), and added complexity in the control plane.

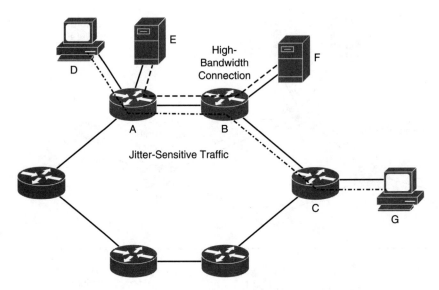

Figure 11-2 *Quality of Service Issues in Ring Topologies*

Furthermore, each additional hop in the ring represents an additional queue through which traffic must pass to reach its destination, and each queue represents an additional set of serialization delays, queuing delays, and possible queue holding time. Each additional hop in a ring network, then, will almost certainly cause not only longer delays for traffic passing through the network, but also more pronounced jitter.

Some ring technologies are designed to remove these effects by separating the ring's Layer 2 forwarding path from its Layer 3 forwarding path. Traffic from Router A destined to a host attached to Router C would be switched at Layer 2 by Router B, rather than routed at Layer 3. Configuring a ring in this way using SONET or RPR can reduce, but not wholly eliminate, the quality of service problems introduced by increasing the size of a ring topology.

Resilience Characteristics

Rings can withstand a single failure anyplace in the ring; any two failures will cause the ring to split. However, a single failure in the network can play havoc with carefully planned traffic flows, as Figure 11-3 illustrates.

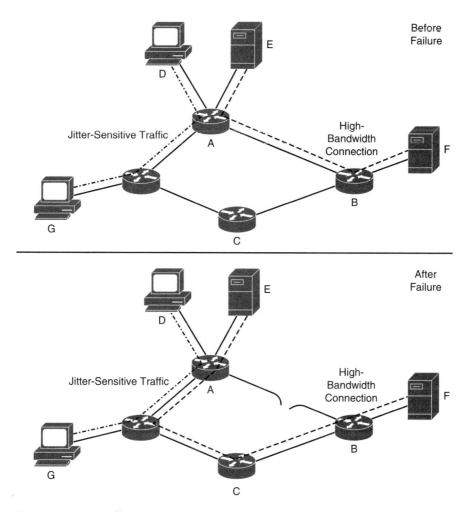

Figure 11-3   *Traffic Engineering in a Ring Network*

If the link between Routers A and B fails, the high-bandwidth flow is thrown across the
same path as the jitter-sensitive flow. This could cause major problems with the application running between Hosts D and G. To resolve these problems, ring topologies are often
deployed in overlaid pairs, as illustrated in Figure 11-4, and designed to support about
twice the normal traffic load.

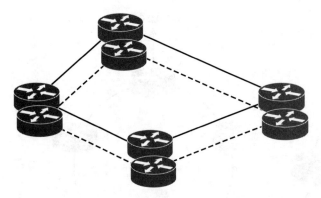

Figure 11-4   *Dual Ring Deployment*

The dual ring deployment shown in Figure 11-4 is an instance of either a *moderately* or *fully disjoint plane*, both of which are discussed in more detail in following sections.

Convergence Characteristics

Convergence in ring topologies lays the foundation for truly understanding the convergence of every other network topology ever designed or deployed. After you understand the principles of routed convergence in a ring topology, it's simple to apply these same principles to quickly understand the convergence of any other topology you might encounter.

In other words, pay attention!

The crucial point to remember when considering how any control plane protocol—routed or switched—will operate on a particular topology is to think in terms of the "prime directive": *thou shalt not loop packets!* This aversion to looping packets explains the convergence properties of ring topologies. Consider the rings in Figure 11-5.

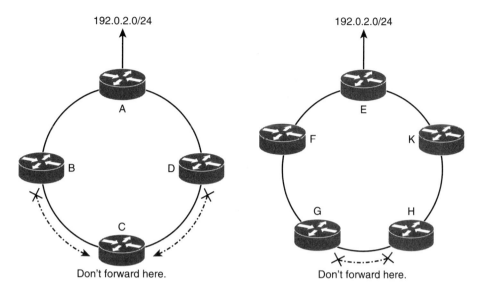

Figure 11-5 *Loop Avoidance in Ring Topologies*

In the two rings shown in Figure 11-5, the links over which a routing protocol will not forward packets toward the destination indicated are marked.

We like to think of routing as a way to use every possible link in a network topology, but routing creates a spanning tree computed per destination. For any given destination, specific links are blocked out of the path to prevent a packet forwarded toward that destination from looping in the network. The primary difference between routing and spanning tree is this blocking occurs once per destination, rather than once per topology. Because every destination has different blocked links, all the links in a network are, on average, used.

In the case of the four hop ring toward 192.0.2.0/24

■ The link between Routers B and C appears to be unidirectional toward Router B.

■ The link between Routers C and D appears to be unidirectional toward Router D.

Why are these links blocked in this way by the routing protocol? To follow the prime directive—*thou shalt not loop!*

■ If a packet destined to 192.0.2.0/24 is forwarded from Router D to Router C, the packet will loop back to Router D.

■ If a packet destined to 192.0.2.0/24 is forwarded from Router B to Router C, the packet will loop back to Router D.

In the case of the five-hop ring toward 192.0.2.0/24, the link between Routers G and H appears to be completely blocked. But why should this be? Suppose a packet destined to some host in 192.0.2.0/24 is forwarded from Router G to H. This packet will be forwarded correctly to Router F, then to Router E, and finally to the destination itself.

But what if Router G is forwarding traffic to H for 192.0.2.0/24, and Router H is also forwarding traffic to G for 192.0.2.0/24? We have a permanent routing loop.

Split Horizon and the P/Q Space

There are a number of other ways to describe the way routing protocols block links in a topology to prevent data plane loops from forming. The first, and most familiar, of these is *split horizon.*

Distance vector protocols split horizon a route advertisement by refusing to advertise a destination through an interface being used locally to forward traffic toward that destination. In the networks in Figure 11-5, Router C will split horizon the advertisement of 192.0.2.0/24 toward both Routers B and D. While Router C can forward along both of these links to reach 192.0.2.0/24, Routers B and D have no knowledge of this destination being reachable through Router C, effectively causing these two links in the topology to be unidirectional toward the destination.

Likewise, Router G will split horizon the advertisement of 192.0.2.0/24 toward Router F, and Router H will refuse to advertise this same destination toward Router K. Again, the net effect is that the Router G to F link appears to be unidirectional toward 192.0.2.0/24, and the Router G to H link isn't available to Router F at all to that network.

Another way to express this is to split the network into *P space and Q space* (see Chapter 8, "Weathering Storms," for more information about P and Q space in the context of fast convergence). To put it in the simplest terms possible, you can think of the network as a split waterfall. One side of the waterfall is the P space, the other is the Q space. The key point to remember, however, is that any packets forwarded into the P space from the Q space will be looped back to the P space.

In the four-hop ring in Figure 11-5, Routers A, B, and C would be in the P space for 192.0.2.0/24, and Routers A, D, and C would be in the Q space. In the five-hop ring in Figure 11-5, Routers E, F, and G would be in the P space, and Routers E, K, and H would be in the Q space.

This is all great theory, but what does this have to do with convergence? Let's begin with some specific observations and then generalize those into some compact convergence rules we can apply to all topologies.

> If the link between Routers A and D fails in Figure 11-5, Router D has no way to forward traffic toward 192.0.2.0/24 until the routing protocol converges.

If a distance vector protocol is deployed on this four-hop ring, the failure of the Router A to D link will cause traffic entering the ring at Router D to be dropped until the routing protocol converges. If a link state protocol is deployed on this four-hop ring, the failure of the Router A to D link will cause traffic entering the ring at Router D to be looped between it and Router C until the routing protocol converges—a microloop.

> If the link between Routers E and K fails in Figure 11-5, Router H has no way to forward traffic toward 192.0.2.0/24 until the routing protocol converges.

If a distance vector protocol is deployed on this five-hop ring, the failure of the Router F to G link will cause traffic entering the ring at Router G to be dropped until the routing protocol converges. If a link state protocol is deployed instead, this same failure will result in a routing loop between Routers G and H until the routing protocol converges—a microloop.

Generalizing Ring Convergence

Why is all this so important to understand? Because virtually every topology you can envision that has any sort of redundancy is, ultimately, made up of rings (full mesh designs are considered by many to be an exception, and Clos fabrics are exceptions). To put it another way, virtually every network topology in the world can be broken into some set of interconnected rings, and each of these rings is going to converge according to a very basic set of rules.

- Every ring has, for each destination, a set of links not used to forward traffic.

- The failure of any link or node on a ring will cause traffic to either be dropped (distance vector) or looped (link state) until the routing protocol converges.

In the "Fast Convergence" section in Chapter 8, we learned that the speed at which a routing protocol converges is directly related to the number of routers that need to be notified of a topology change. Applying this to ring topologies gives us a third rule:

- The larger the ring, the more slowly the routing protocol will converge (and thus stop throwing packets on the floor or resolve the resulting microloop).

These three rules apply to virtually every topology you encounter. Find the rings, and you've found the most basic element of network convergence.

Rings and Fast Reroute

These general rules on convergence in ring topologies wouldn't be complete without some thoughts on how they impact fast reroute technologies. In the network illustrated in Figure 11-5, it is possible for Router D to continue forwarding traffic toward 192.0.2.0/24 if the Router A to D link fails—but only if it can get the traffic to Router B, rather than Router C.

This simple insight is the foundation of every fast reroute scheme other than MPLS TE/FRR (which builds an end-to-end tunnel through the network across the "back side" of every ring in the topology between the source and destination). To quickly route around local failures, what we need is a system that allows Router D to discover that Router B is the closest "safe point" to which traffic destined to 192.0.2.0/24 can be forwarded without looping, and then a tunneling mechanism that allows Router D to actually forward traffic to Router B, skipping over Router C's forwarding table.

For instance, if Remote LFAs are deployed in the four-hop ring in Figure 11-5, Router D would use constrained SPF to discover that any traffic forwarded to Router B toward 192.0.2.0/24 will not be forwarded back to Router D itself. After this discovery is made, a tunnel is constructed from Router D to Router B using MPLS (LDP), skipping Router C's control plane. This tunnel becomes the backup path for Router D toward 192.0.2.0/24 (see draft-ietf-rtgwg-remote-lfa for more information on remote LFAs).

Final Thoughts on Ring Topologies

What's the bottom line on ring topologies?

- Rings are cheap to deploy and simple to scale.

- The larger the ring, the more difficult it is to predict and control quality of service issues resulting from link or device failures.

- Redundancy in any ring generally requires every link in the ring to be able to carry double the normally offered load to provision for link and device failures in the ring. This can be somewhat mitigated by spreading traffic over a wider set of links in the case of link and device failures, or by carefully measuring traffic flows and planning their failover paths.

- Smaller rings converge more quickly; triangles are the smallest ring possible, and therefore the "golden triangle" is the most desirable topology element for fast convergence.

- Capacity planning is difficult in a ring topology because traffic flows are additive through the ring.

Full Mesh

Now we jump from the topology cheapest to deploy and simplest to scale to the topology that is the most expensive to deploy and the most difficult to scale—the full mesh, shown in Figure 11-6. However, full mesh topologies are simpler to understand, in terms of convergence and scaling, than ring topologies.

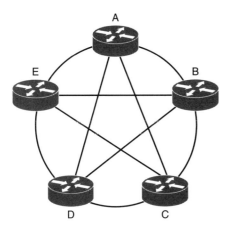

Figure 11-6   *Full Mesh Topology*

As Figure 11-6 shows, every node in a full mesh topology has a connection to every other node in the same full mesh topology. From Router A to D, there are 10 paths traffic can take:

- (A,D)

- (A,E,D)

- (A,B,D)

- (A,C,D)

- (A,B,C,D)

- (A,B,E,D)

- (A,C,B,D)

- (A,C,E,D)

- (A,E,B,D)

- (A,E,C,D)

Traffic engineering techniques can be used to direct specific traffic onto any of these paths, allowing the network designer to design traffic flows for optimal performance. The number of paths through the network, and the number of links required to build a complete mesh between a set of nodes, is given in a simple (and well-known) formula:

$$N(n-1)/2$$

For the five-node network in Figure 11-6, this is

$$5(5-1)/2 == 10$$

This property of full mesh networks, however, also points to the weaknesses of this topology: scale and expense. These two weaknesses are closely related. Each new node

added to the network means adding as many links as there are nodes already in the network. Adding a new node to the network in Figure 11-6 would mean adding five new links to bring the new node fully into the mesh.

Each new link added means not only a cable, but also a new port used, and new ports mean new line cards, and so on. Each new link also represents a new set of neighbors for the control plane to manage, increasing memory utilization and processing requirements. The MTTR/MTBF curve quickly moves toward higher MTTR in full mesh topologies (see the discussion about control plane convergence speeds versus state in the control plane in Chapter 8). For these reasons, full mesh topologies are generally limited to small sizes, on the order of 10 to 20 nodes, in most real-world applications.

There are protocol-level techniques that can reduce the control plane overhead in full mesh topologies, if they are properly managed and deployed. OSPF and IS-IS both have the capability to build a mesh group, which treats the full mesh topology similar to a broadcast network; a small number of routers at the edge of the mesh are designated to flood topology information onto the mesh, while the remainder of the attached routers passively listen.

The one place where network engineers often encounter full mesh topologies is in virtual overlays, particularly in deployments where traffic engineering is a fundamental part of the reason for deploying the virtual overlay. Although the port and link costs are reduced (or eliminated) when building a full mesh of tunnels, the cost of managing and troubleshooting a full mesh remains.

Clos Networks

Charles Clos developed the Clos multistage switching fabric in 1953 as a means to overcome the cost and lack of availability of high-speed crossbar switches in telephone networks. The general idea behind a Clos fabric is that a network capable of carrying high traffic rates can be built from components that individually support only lower packet switching speeds. Clos designs are fairly common in data center environments, where the costs of nodes can easily outstrip the cost of links and ports. A small Clos design is illustrated in Figure 11-7.

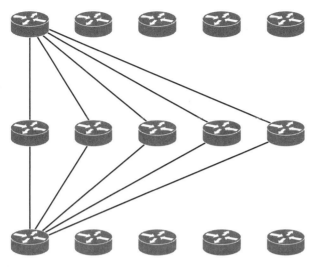

Two Devices' Connections

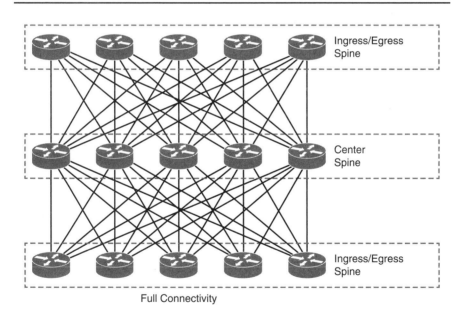

Full Connectivity

Figure 11-7   *Clos Fabric*

The top half of Figure 11-7 illustrates the connections from two devices in the ingress/egress spines to the center spine to make the connection scheme easier to understand. The bottom half illustrates the full connection scheme for completeness. This might appear to be a full mesh, but there is one specific difference: nodes on the ingress and egress spines are not connected as they would be in a full mesh network.

The effect of not including these cross-device links is to force traffic from any device attached to an ingress/egress spine to travel through the center spine to reach its

destination. In data center centric terms, all traffic from any device must travel north/south, even when trying to reach a destination that is either east or west of the originator, as shown in Figure 11-8.

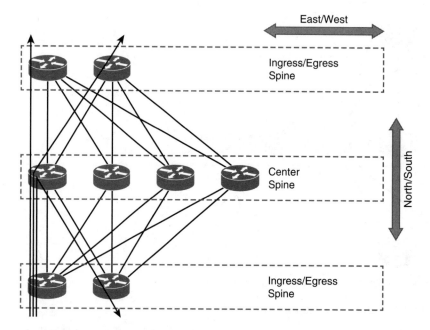

Figure 11-8   *Traffic Flow in a Clos Fabric*

Forcing traffic through the center spine might seem strange, or perhaps even a disadvantage from the perspective of managing bandwidth and quality of service. But the design has its advantages.

> **Note**   Spine and leaf designs, which are a variant of Clos designs, are covered in detail in Chapter 18, "Data Center Design."

Clos and the Control Plane

This north/south only traffic pattern, up to the core and back out, might seem familiar because it is—the Clos fabric is a set of overlapping spanning trees, each rooted in a device in the center spine. If spanning tree is properly deployed on a Clos fabric, no link is ever blocked. In fact, it's entirely possible to build a Clos fabric with no dynamic control plane at all. Simple reverse path forwarding checks configured at each interface can prevent any loops in this network topology.

Almost all Clos designs are deployed with active control planes; really large ones are almost always deployed with a routed control plane to manage the size of the broadcast domain across the Clos fabric, which can reach to the hundreds of thousands of devices.

The main challenge in these large deployments is state overlap. Figure 11-9 shows how a link state protocol operates on these highly meshed topologies.

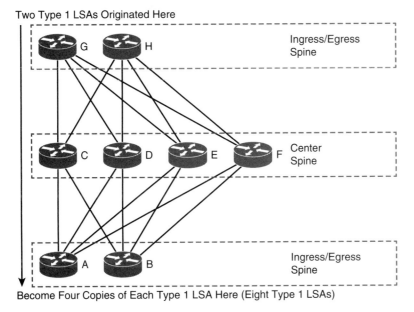

Figure 11-9 shows how a link state protocol operates on these highly meshed topologies. Two Type 1 LSAs Originated Here. Become Four Copies of Each Type 1 LSA Here (Eight Type 1 LSAs)

Figure 11-9 *LSA Flooding Replication in Clos Fabrics*

Assume OSPF is deployed on the network shown in Figure 11-9. Routers G and H will each originate a single Type 1 (Router) LSA describing local links and reachable subnets. A copy of each of these LSAs is received by devices in the center spine (Routers C, D, E, and F). These routers reflood these two LSAs to their neighbors, so that Routers A and B each receive 4 copies of Router G's Type 1 LSA, and 4 copies of Router H's Type 1 LSA. Across a large Clos fabric, this packet replication can cause a lot of packet generation, queuing, and processing—even if the replicated LSAs are discarded by the OSPF process on each device.

To make matters worse, link state protocols are designed to time their advertisements out periodically. In a network of a thousand routers and default OSPF timers, a new LSA would need to be generated and flooded every 3.5 seconds.

How can network designers avoid these problems? Eliminating the reflooding of LSAs setting the OSPF Do Not Age (DNA) bit on all advertisements would be a good start at reducing the load on the control plane. Further reductions can be found in flooding reduction mechanisms done for MANET and other highly mobile and low-bandwidth environments.

Clos and Capacity Planning

A major advantage of Clos over more traditional designs is the relative ease of capacity planning in a Clos fabric. Given that all the links in the Clos fabric have the same

bandwidth, the amount of bandwidth available for any device attached to a router on the ingress/egress spine is the total bandwidth available into the fabric divided by the number of nodes attached to each edge router. For instance, if each link in the network illustrated in Figure 11-7 is a 1GB link, the total bandwidth available from each edge device is 4GB in total. If there are four devices attached to an ingress/egress router in this network, each device would have 1GB available bandwidth throughout the entire fabric.

So long as the total amount of bandwidth available from the node within the ingress/egress spine is consistent across the entire network, and the total bandwidth offered by any node never exceeds the available bandwidth, the network will (theoretically) never block traffic between two nodes within the Clos fabric itself. This characteristic of the Clos fabric makes this topology extremely attractive in data center networks.

Partial Mesh

Partial mesh is a flexible term, generally used to describe a topology that is neither a single ring nor a full mesh. Most partial mesh topologies are collections of interconnected rings built to match the geography of the network and/or specific business needs. An example of a partial mesh topology is shown in Figure 11-10.

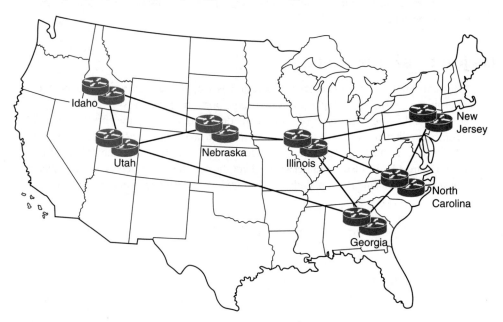

Figure 11-10 *Partial Mesh Topology*

In Figure 11-10, you can see this network can be seen as a single ring starting in Georgia, through North Carolina, New York, Illinois, Nebraska, Idaho, Utah, and then back to Georgia. Within this ring are a number of cut-through loops that were put in place to provide bandwidth for specific traffic flows. Another way to look at this topology is as a set of interconnected rings. Starting in Georgia, a ring runs through North Carolina,

to Illinois, and then back to Georgia. Starting in New York, another ring runs through Illinois, through North Carolina, and finally back to New York.

Each ring within this topology will converge as any other single ring topology with the added complexity of the interaction between the overlapping links. The network will converge more slowly if the link between Utah and Georgia fails than if the link between Georgia and North Carolina fails.

Partial mesh topologies are a good balance between traffic engineering and cost; because links can be installed just where they are needed to provide bandwidth to specific applications or sections of the network, the cost of the network can be finely tuned to the needs of the business with no outside restrictions.

Partial mesh topologies can, on the other hand, promote uncontrolled organic growth. Because there is no specific topology the network designer is following, it's tempting to simply add links wherever they are needed, as they are needed. The resulting network can be very difficult to understand, troubleshoot, and manage. Partial mesh topologies are also more difficult to easily divide into modular pieces. As new connections are made between various sites to account for growing bandwidth needs, it's often possible to string all the nodes within the distribution or access layer together, cutting the network core out of the path for most applications and ruining carefully planned addressing and aggregation schemes.

Disjoint Parallel Planes

A disjoint topology is multiple ring or partial mesh topologies that are not connected either in the control or data plane through some portion of the network topology. In most networks where this type of topology is deployed, it is only the core which is fully disjoint; the distribution, access, and/or aggregation layers of the network are designed using more conventional topologies, such as rings, partial mesh, hub-and-spoke, or full mesh. Figure 11-11 illustrates a network where the core has been deployed with fully disjoint topologies, while the remainder of the network is designed using small rings.

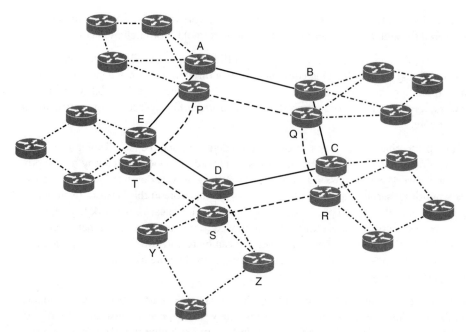

Figure 11-11 *Disjoint Parallel Ring Topology*

Routers A, B, C, D, and E are one core; Routers P, Q, R, S, and T are the second. These two cores are not connected in any way—there is no way to forward traffic from Router D to Router S, for instance, without passing through either Router Y or Z. Routers Y and Z, however, are configured so routing information is not shared between the two cores, to prevent traffic from passing through them between the cores.

In most implementations, the two cores are configured to run two different BGP processes, and routes are redistributed into and out of these separate BGP processes at the core edge. Each core may run a different IGP (generally one core will run OSPF, while the other will run IS-IS), and may even be based on a different product line or products from different vendors. Each disjoint plane, being a ring topology, will converge in the same way that a normal ring topology converges.

This type of topology is sometimes deployed in networks that require absolute availability—networks where five 9s of availability still isn't enough (such as financial services companies, which rely on their networks to make money within slices of a second).

Advantages of Disjoint Topologies

Implementing dual cores provides the opportunity to guard against monoculture software and hardware failures by deploying hardware and software from different vendors (or from different lines of equipment from a single vendor), different routing protocols, and different processes in each core. In a single plane core deployed with a single type of equipment, a single routing protocol, and a common software implementation is susceptible

to a new defect introduced across every router in the core through a software update, or discovered through a unique unanticipated (and untested) set of circumstances.

In this case, Routers A, B, C, D, and E may run IS-IS from one vendor, while Routers P, Q, R, S, and T may run OSPF using equipment from a different vendor. A defect introduced when upgrading the software on one core cannot impact the overall reliability of the network; a failure in one core simply causes the distribution layer to reroute traffic to the second core.

Beyond protecting against any sort of common defect among the two disjoint topologies, this type of design also allows services to be deployed in an incremental way on the production network without risking an outage or network service degradation. For instance, a new multicast service can be deployed across the first core in this network (Routers A through E) and placed into production. If the new service causes a network failure, or a service degradation, critical traffic can be moved to the unmodified alternate core quickly along the entire network edge. Service can be restored without backing the new service out of production, allowing network engineers the time needed to troubleshoot and repair the new service.

Each core network in a pair of disjoint topologies can also be designed using the simplest possible topology, because the network's resiliency isn't dependent on a single topology reacting correctly to every possible failure. Instead of deploying full redundancy at each core site location, for instance, the network designer can slim down the design, so each core represents the simplest design that will provide the connectivity required. Again, resilience is provided by the second core, rather than by complex backup paths and links within each core.

Added Complexity

The major (and obvious) downside to disjoint parallel topologies of this type is the added complexity—particularly when you add two routing protocols and two vendors (or two different lines of equipment running different software from two vendors). This type of doubling can verge on requiring two different support teams, one for each network. Virtualization over disjoint parallel planes can also be difficult, because each routing protocol and each implementation interacts differently with each virtualization technology.

Each failure in a single core will tend to drive greater resiliency within each disjoint topology, as well—it takes a good deal of discipline to control costs when you're supporting two cores, rather than one. Each bit of redundancy removes value from the overall design.

The Bottom Line

Disjoint topologies are a solid choice for those situations when the network simply cannot fail—ever—and where costs aren't as much of an issue. These are complex, difficult to manage topologies reserved for the largest of the large, where data processing is such an integral part of the business that a network failure costs more than the cost of deploying and managing this type of network.

Divergent Data Planes

Divergent data planes are an intermediate topology between a single ring and totally disjoint topologies. Whereas a single control plane operates over the entire topology, the data plane is intentionally split into two parts, with resiliency within each data plane preferred over alternate paths in the second data plane. Figure 11-12 provides an example of a dual data plane topology.

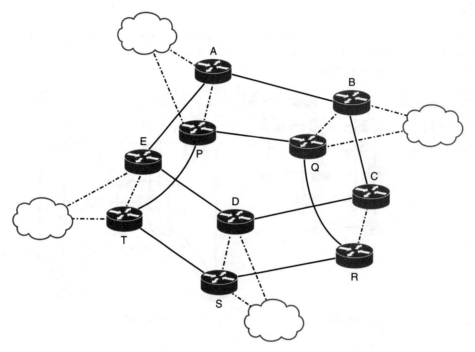

Figure 11-12   *Diverse Data Plane Topology*

This is very similar to the disjoint parallel topologies in Figure 11-11, with the addition of *shunt links* between the two planes. These shunt links are configured with a very high cost in the routing protocol so traffic crosses them only if there is no other path to a given destination.

This design allows each topology to be treated as a separate unit from a data path perspective. One plane can be taken down for maintenance without impacting traffic flow through the network (other than all traffic converging onto the single remaining path), and new applications or services can be deployed in one plane while not impacting traffic being routed through the second plane.

The order of failover in a diverse data plane topology is important; traffic should fail over within a data plane first, then between data planes from the edge (rather than across the shunt links), and finally across the shunt links. This allows for the maximum separation of services being carried on the different data planes.

Control plane failures will still impact the entire network in this design, possibly taking the entire network down in the case of a total control plane failure. Each plane, however, converges as a ring topology, with the added complexity of the shunt links.

Diverse data planes would normally be deployed in the core of a large scale network using BGP. As with fully disjoint planes deployed in parallel, it takes discipline to control costs.

Cubes

Cubes, stacked cubes, and hypercubes, like Clos fabrics, have interesting mathematical properties that make them ideal network topologies in some situations. Figure 11-13 depicts each of these topologies.

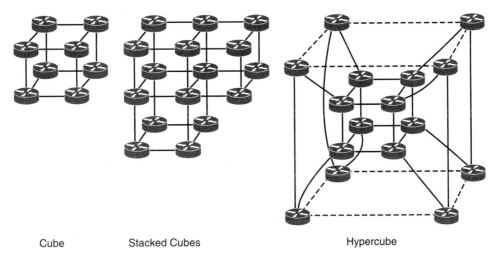

Cube   Stacked Cubes   Hypercube

Figure 11-13 *Cube Topologies*

The property that makes these designs interesting is that they represent the minimum set of links that can provide shortest (minimum stretch) paths between virtually any number of nodes. Cube designs, then, tend to be less expensive than more ad hoc partial mesh designs while providing either the same or a higher degree of connectivity. On the other hand, cube designs work only if the geographical shape of the network fits within a cube layout in some way.

In a cube design, no node is ever more than two hops from any other node, and any pair of link failures will leave connectivity intact between every pair of nodes. Cubes can be deployed with two faces configured as disjoint data planes, as well. The cube is limited to 8 nodes; this limitation often makes a cube design less than ideal for large scale wide area or data center network cores.

After the limit of 8 nodes is reached in a simple cube design, there are two ways to continue to scale the network design while remaining within the general outlines of a cube topology. The first of these is a stacked cube, illustrated in the center of the three networks in Figure 11-13. A stacked cube can be built up to larger "cubes of cubes," (the next size is

4 cubes total, 2 cubes high by 2 cubes wide) while leaving every node within two hops of every other node in the network. Each layer of "stacking" adds one more hop to the maximum hop count between any two nodes. Four cubes in a stacked topology would have 27 nodes total—large enough for most wide area and data center core designs. Stacked cubes retain the property of being able to sustain any pair of link failures within each cube and maintain full connectivity between every node in the topology.

Cubes can also be grown into hypercubes, shown on the right side of Figure 11-13. This is more difficult to conceive, and almost impossible to draw in an intelligible way on a traditional flat network diagram. Hypercubes provide full connectivity between 16 nodes with a minimum of links, while keeping the maximum length of the path between any two nodes to 1 hop. A hypercube can withstand any three link failures while maintaining full connectivity between all the nodes.

Hypercubes are a good choice for the core of a data center network, where the geographic layout of the network doesn't constrain node placement, and high availability is an absolute requirement, so long as the 12 nodes offered by this topology are sufficient from a scaling perspective. They are difficult to conceptualize and, therefore, sometimes difficult to design, cable, and manage.

Each face of each of these cube designs converges as a four-hop ring. If faster convergence is required, it is possible to put a single link across some or all of the cube's faces to produce triangles, rather than four-hop rings.

Toroid Topologies

A final topology to consider is the toroid design. Although this isn't a design most network architects will run into, toroid topologies are used in many supercomputing applications and internal fabrics in high-performance routers and switches. A two-dimensional toroid design is shown in Figure 11-14.

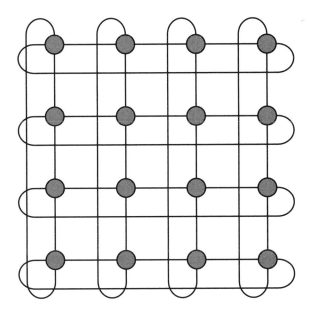

Figure 11-14   *Two-Dimensional Toroid Topology*

A two-dimensional toroid is essentially a mesh topology that has been "pulled together" along the outside edges with torus links. The significant point to note is that every node in the toroid fabric has precisely four links configured; the size of the fabric can be increased or decreased with the addition of new nodes and without increasing the number of ports required at each device. A new dimension can be added to the fabric with an increase of two ports per node, as well, making the fabric easy to scale to truly huge sizes.

Torus fabrics are typically oversubscribed at high operational loads, and hence are considered a form of blocking fabric. Two mechanisms are often used to reduce blocking in a toroid fabric. The first is to localize the workload so work with a high affinity is placed on directly adjacent nodes where possible. The second is to build virtual channels across the topology, so each node has an apparent direct connection to every other node in the fabric. This replaces physical interface with virtual ones. The physical links, in this case, can be sized to provide no blocking to the aggregate bandwidth of all the virtual links, or blocking may occur in contention among the virtual links for the capacity of the underlying physical links.

Toroid topologies are rare, but they are a solid design option for data center fabrics where work can be efficiently localized and port counts are a major scaling concern.

Summary

Network designers often "fall into" a particular topology without much thought—a little creativity can go a long way in the area of producing minimally connected networks to reduce deployment cost, or topologies optimized for resilience, or balanced topologies that match a variety of requirements. The bottom line, though, is that determining which topology to use shouldn't be a matter of doing what's always been done. The network topology must match the requirements laid on the network, allow for future scaling, and support the business in a way that makes sense.

Chapter 12

Building the Second Floor

Virtualization is building vertically with overlay topologies, rather than horizontally with a larger physical topology—this process can be described as building the "second floor" of a network. Just as a construction crew has specific tools and techniques they use to build the second floor of a building, the network architect has tools used to build the network's second floor.

To understand these tools and techniques, we need to first define tunneling—something that's harder to do than it might seem. Although there are virtualization techniques that do not rely on tunneling (such as 802.1Q in the Ethernet world), they still rely on multiple overlaying control planes, and hence often face the same sorts of control plane problems as virtualization techniques based on tunneling. After we've defined what a tunnel is, we need to consider the underlying questions any network designer or architect should ask about any virtualization technology. Finally, we'll consider MPLS-based L3VPNs as a specific example of applying these questions to a widely deployed virtualization solution.

What Is a Tunnel?

"What is a tunnel?" must rank very low on the scale of the most interesting questions in the world. Surely there are simple definitions for tunneling within the network world, right? For instance, "Anytime one packet is encapsulated inside another, the packet is being tunneled."

Yes, simple enough—but it's often easy to create a simple definition that's simply wrong. To understand why the initial definition given above is wrong, examine the normal operation of network protocols as they progress up and down a network stack, as shown in Figure 12-1.

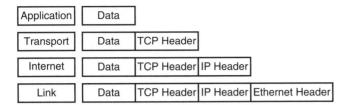

Figure 12-1 *Layered Encapsulation*

Within normal network protocol layering, IP packets are placed inside Ethernet packets, TCP packets are placed inside IP packets, and some other data format is placed inside TCP packets. If we stick with the definition "Anytime a packet is placed inside another packet, the inner packet is being tunneled," then IP tunnels TCP, and Ethernet tunnels IP. Clearly, our definition needs to be fine-tuned a bit to fit the real world.

Let's try to firm this definition up by adding a condition: "Anytime one packet is encapsulated inside another packet of the same or a higher layer, the packet is being tunneled." This is a definition we can live with, so long as we assume each protocol can live at one (and only one) layer. In the real world, this one restriction is generally true, so this definition will work out most of the time from a packet perspective.

What about from the data plane's perspective? Here we can use this definition: "A tunnel is a path through the network where the forwarding devices along the path do not know the actual destination of nor have visibility into the data." It is true that in all tunneling schemes, devices forward traffic to some intermediate device that then removes an outer header and forwards the traffic again toward its real and final destination.

And the control plane? From a control plane perspective, the crucial point to remember is that there must be more than one control plane (or perhaps more than one view of the forwarding and reachability information across every link the virtual topology crosses) for a virtual topology or a tunnel to exist. To see this last rule in action, examine Figure 12-2.

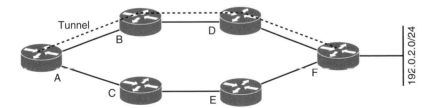

Figure 12-2 *Control Plane Interaction with Tunnels*

Router A has three paths it can take to reach 192.0.2.0/24: (A,B,D,F), (A,C,E,F), and (A,tunnel,F). Which path should it take? How can we control which traffic enters the tunnel and which does not?

The obvious answer is, of course, that you can control which traffic enters the tunnel by modifying the metrics for various destinations. The shortest path in terms of hop count to 192.0.2.0/24 from Router A would be through the tunnel, so traffic destined to hosts

on that subnet should be forwarded along the tunnel path. But wouldn't the link (E,F) also be reachable across the tunnel other than through the path (A,C,E)? If metrics are used to determine which traffic enters the tunnel and which does not, then the metrics must be carefully planned and managed to prevent routing loops or unintended suboptimal routing through the tunnel interfaces.

The less obvious answer is the one that's normally used to manage traffic flows through the tunnel—control routing so 192.0.2.0/24 is only advertised through the tunnel, and not through the underlying network. Although it is possible to filter routing information to achieve this effect, it's much simpler in larger deployments to run a second control plane. This second control plane might be as simple as two static routes, or it might be a second layer of control plane information contained in the same routing protocol (such as carrying MPLS reachability information through a link state protocol), or it might be a completely different routing protocol.

A side effect of deploying a second control plane is that the "routers in the middle" can't reach the destinations on either end of the tunnel; Routers B and D can't, in this case, reach 192.0.2.0/24 (and whatever hosts on that network are talking to beyond Router A). Normally this is the intended effect of tunneling; it reduces the forwarding information Routers B and D must carry in their tables, and helps to break the network into smaller failure domains (see Chapter 6, "Principles of Modularity").

So, then, tunneling involves three levels of definition:

- From a packet's perspective, a tunnel is created when one packet is encapsulated into another packet at an equal or higher level.

- From the data plane's perspective, tunnels allow the forwarding of traffic to destinations only some of the devices along the path know how to reach.

- From the control plane perspective, tunneling involves the deployment of a second control plane (or precise controls and policies configured on one control plane), combined with breaking the network into multiple vertical failure domains.

Is MPLS Tunneling?

How does MPLS fit into this picture? On the one side are engineers who state MPLS is tunneling, and on the other side are engineers who insist MPLS is not tunneling. Entire shows and articles have been produced addressing this question, with the result normally being a draw. Resolving this long-standing dispute is a useful exercise in understanding the concept of tunneling.

What are the attributes of MPLS that point toward its status as a tunneled solution?

- It's used to carry IP and other traffic through a network.

- MPLS is normally deployed either with a separate control plane or with control plane information that's not mixed with IP forwarding information.

- MPLS connections between the edges of the network are explicitly called tunnels, with head and tail ends at either edge of the network.

- MPLS is designed to reduce the IP forwarding information managed by the nodes in the center of the network by tunneling through them.

All of these, combined, certainly make a strong case for MPLS to be considered tunneling. On the other hand, routers and switches in the core of an MPLS network must support MPLS forwarding for MPLS to be deployed edge-to-edge in the network. If MPLS is a tunneling technology, then why must core devices be MPLS aware?

The resolution to this problem entails returning to what tunneling really means. Let's take IP as an example: is IP a tunneling protocol, or isn't it? IP normally provides end-to-end addressing and traffic delivery for higher layer protocols, and it relies on the control plane of every device an IP packet passes through to know how to reach the packet's destination. It's clearly not a tunneling protocol, correct?

On the other hand, IP packets can be encapsulated inside other IP packets, to be carried across some part of the network that might not know about the destination in the inner packet header. MPLS, in fact, can also be encapsulated into a GRE packet, which is then encapsulated into an IP packet. These are all tunneled use cases, however—so IP must be a tunneling protocol, right?

This confusion about what's a tunneling protocol and what's not comes about because we've approached the tunneling problem from the wrong end of the stick.

In reality, there are no tunneling protocols.

Tunneling is something that is done by stacking protocols; the protocols being stacked are not, in and of themselves, tunneling or "not tunneling" protocols, as Figure 12-3 illustrates.

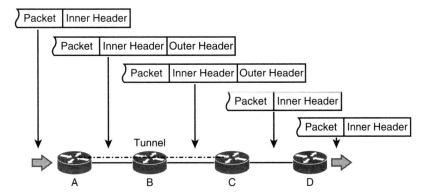

Figure 12-3 *Tunneling or Not?*

Router A in Figure 12-3 receives a packet, consults its local forwarding information, and decides the packet needs to be transmitted over a tunnel interface toward Router D, rather than over the physical interface connected to Router B. To forward this packet over the

tunnel, Router A encapsulates the packet into an outer header of some type and forwards the packet to Router B. Routers B and C forward the traffic according to this outer header (Router C removes the outer header because it is the penultimate hop, or the next to last hop, in the tunnel).

> **Note**   Penultimate label popping is something particular to MPLS; most tunneling protocols don't pop the outer label until the packet has reached the tunnel end point, or tail. This doesn't impact whether or not MPLS is a tunneling protocol, however; it's just a matter of operational details within MPLS itself. In Figure 12-3, the dashed line shows where the outer header takes the packet, rather than where the tunnel terminates from a configuration perspective.

The question we need to ask to understand the problem of MPLS being a tunneling protocol is this: *Does it matter what protocol the inner and outer headers are?*

The answer to this question must be no. What matters is that one packet is placed inside another header (the outer header) to form a second packet at the same or higher layer than the original packet, not what the inner protocol is, nor what the outer protocol is. In the case of IP in IP, the inner header is an IP header, and the outer header is an IP header.

In the case of MPLS, the inner header is MPLS (normally carrying IP, Ethernet, or some other data link or transport layer protocol). The outer header is like an Ethernet header, used to carry traffic hop by hop. The inner header in MPLS defines the end-to-end tunnel between Routers A and D; the outer header is used to carry the packet along from Router A to Router B, from Router B to Router C, and so on.

So the answer is this: MPLS is a protocol that can be used to tunnel traffic or as a data link protocol to carry packets hop by hop. The confusion in MPLS stems from the reality that the inner header is the tunneling header, while the outer header is the hop-by-hop header; normally these roles are reversed. However, if we think of the outer header just like an Ethernet header, and the inner header like a tunnel header, we get a clearer picture of what is going on.

Protocols shouldn't be classified as a "tunneling protocol" or not (with the exception of protocols specifically designed for the sole purpose of tunneling other protocols). Just as the inner label in an MPLS label stack can be defined as a tunnel, but the outer label is hop by hop and therefore not a tunnel, tunneling is defined by the way the packets are built, not by the protocols being used in the inner or outer headers.

Fundamental Virtualization Questions

Because virtualization is always going to involve inner and outer headers, there will be a number of questions network designers need to ask about the interaction of these two different headers, or tunneling protocols. In the same way, the use of multiple overlaying control planes is going to bring up a number of questions about the interactions between these control planes. Beyond these two areas, network engineers need to think through how the overlay network will interact with QoS, multicast, and security.

Data Plane Interaction

Let's deal with the easy questions first: The first fundamental question network designers need to ask about the interaction of the different protocols is what traffic can be tunneled—or rather, what type of traffic the tunnel can support. There's no point in specifying a tunneling mechanism that will not support the traffic that needs to be carried through the virtual topology. The second fundamental question network designers need to ask about the interaction of the different protocols is what transport is used to carry the tunneled traffic. Again, there's little point in specifying a tunneling mechanism that won't work on the underlying network.

The first of the more difficult problems is the Maximum Transmission Unit (MTU) through the tunneled infrastructure. The MTU of a link determines the maximum size of packet that can be transmitted through it; the link with the smallest MTU along a path limits the maximum size of packets that can be transmitted through the entire path. The MTU is normally fixed on a per-link basis, determined by the hardware interfaces and specifications for that specific link type. Adding a new header onto a packet means the amount of space available for user traffic is made smaller by the size of this additional header, as Figure 12-4 illustrates.

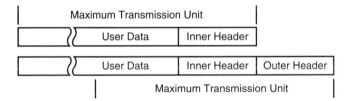

Figure 12-4   *Impact of a Tunnel Header on User Data*

The amount of data an application can send through a tunneled link in each packet can have a major impact on the performance of applications, particularly streaming media and the transfer of large amounts of data. How can the network engineer account for the impact of decreasing MTUs on application performance?

This comes back to knowing the applications running across the network, and focusing on the crucial questions you need to ask about each application in order to best understand the support it needs. It's best to test applications in the lab using links with reduced MTUs to get a good idea of what impact tunneling application traffic will have on performance in various conditions, and use this information when considering when and where to tunnel traffic over a virtualized infrastructure.

The second difficult problem network engineers face when dealing with tunneling is quality of service. There are two facets to this problem: the first is how the quality of service markings from the inner header are moved (or represented) in the outer header—if there's the possibility of representing these markings in the outer header. If traffic from a streaming real-time application is moved into a tunnel, and the quality of service markings aren't somehow transferred from the inner header to the outer, there is little chance the application will perform well over the tunnel.

Beyond this, the underlying links and protocols supporting the virtual (tunneled) topology must be able to somehow coherently mix the various quality of service parameters from the tunneled packets into a consistent overall queuing structure. Should streaming traffic from any tunnel be preferred over file transfer from any tunnel? Or should the traffic from one tunnel always be preferred over the traffic from another tunnel? The combinations are almost limitless, and the answers all depend on knowing what service parameters each application needs in order to run effectively across the tunneled infrastructure.

Control Plane Considerations

Virtualization always overlays one control plane on another: the control plane that provides reachability through the virtual topology on top of the control plane that provides reachability to the tunnel end points. This added level of complexity brings its own set of problems into network design and management. Two specific areas of concern are the interaction between these two overlaid control planes and the scaling of the two overlaid control planes.

Control Plane Interaction

Although the tunneled virtual overlay topology looks and feels very much like a network that is independent of the underlying physical and logical topology, it is most certainly not an independent topology. The control plane of the virtual topology relies entirely on the control plane of the underlying network. Interaction between these two control planes adds a level of complexity that might be hidden but can come to the surface in unexpected ways.

As an example, let's look at Figure 12-5.

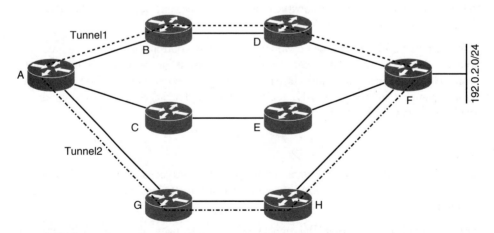

Figure 12-5   *Overlaying and Underlying Control Plane Interaction*

In Figure 12-5, there are two tunnels available between Routers A and F. The metrics across these tunnels are configured so the tunnel running through the path (A,B,D,F) is preferred over the tunnel running over the path (A,G,H,F). The paths between Routers A

and F arc configured so the (A,B,D,F) path is best, the (A,C,E,F) path is second, and the (A,G,H,F) path is the worst of the three available paths.

Assume that the link between Routers B and D fails—what are the possible results?

- The underlying control plane could converge more quickly than the overlaying control plane can detect the failure, in which case Tunnel1 will fail over to the (A,C,E,F) before the tunnel actually fails. This might cause an interruption in the application's data flow without any corresponding notification at the tunnel interface level.

- The underlying control plane could converge more slowly than the overlaying control plane can detect the failure, in which case the traffic will switch from Tunnel1 at the moment of failure to Tunnel2, then back to Tunnel1 when the underlying network has converged and service across Tunnel1 has been restored.

- The underlying control plane could detect the failure at about the same time as the overlaying control plane, in which case convergence becomes a mess of switches between different tunnels, or temporary loss of traffic flow, while the various elements converge on some available path.

In all these cases, a good deal of time and trouble could be spent trying to find problems in the performance of the application(s) running across the virtual topology. The tunnel interface may or may not fail, depending on the circumstances and the order in which the different control planes detect any given failure and react to it (such as the amount of time it takes for the overlay control plane to time out any keepalives and declare the virtual link down).

To prevent very difficult convergence problems in virtual topologies, network engineers need to consider every possible convergence scenario, and either rule it out through careful configuration or document how the two control planes interact to help when that fateful call comes at two in the morning.

It is generally best to design the network so the overlay control plane detects and reacts to network failures faster than the underlying control plane, or so the underlying control plane detects and reacts to failures faster than the overlay control plane. Allowing the two control planes to interplay freely is a recipe for long hard nights of troubleshooting difficult to understand and find problems.

Scaling

Scaling is the second most important control plane factor to consider when using tunneled overlays to build a virtualized network. Two specific factors need to be considered in this area.

First, the number of endpoints the tunnel will be connecting needs to be considered. Unless hierarchy is specifically called out in the basic design of the overlay network, the entire virtual topology ends up looking like one flat broadcast domain in the case of Layer 2 overlays, and a single subnet or full mesh of point-to-point links in the case

of Layer 3 overlays. This means the overlay control plane must scale with the size of the overlay in real terms.

Overlay networks can be scaled by adding hierarchy (just as the underlying network is scaled), but hierarchy is generally difficult to deploy in overlay networks. Deploying hierarchy in an overlay network normally means pulling traffic out of a tunnel, switching it through a router or switch, and then reinjecting it into another set of tunnels. Matching up the correct sets of tunnels, handling the modifications to quality of service parameters into and out of the tunnels, and other control plane issues are generally left to the network engineer to work out through configuration on individual devices.

Second, the configuration required to deploy and maintain large scale tunneled overlay environments must be considered. Each tunnel end point must be configured (and reconfigured for changes), and a second control plane must be configured and managed. As the size of the virtual topology increases over time, the sheer amount of configuration can often become daunting. Solutions to this problem generally revolve around using some automated configuration system, or an overlay control plane designed specifically to handle the necessary tunnel setup and teardown. Although these can ease configuration management costs, they cannot erase the cost entirely.

Multicast

Multicast is always tricky to successfully deploy and manage; overlay networks just make the problem more complex. There are two questions network engineers must ask about virtual topologies in regard to multicast.

First, how are multicast groups advertised through the control plane (or rather how is multicast routing information carried)? Is a separate control plane required, such as Protocol Independent Multicast (PIM), or can multicast routing information be carried in the overlay control plane? For overlays that rely on standard IGPs, the answer is almost always that an additional control plane will be needed, making the total number of control planes involved in deploying a virtual topology 4 (2 for unicast, and 2 for multicast). Some virtualization technologies, however, have the capability to advertise multicast routing information through the overlay control plane. An example of this is BGP, which can carry multicast and unicast routing information in separate address families.

The second question relates primarily to the performance of multicast across a virtual topology; Figure 12-6 illustrates.

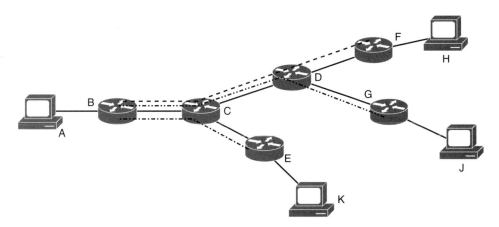

Figure 12-6 *Multicast Replication in a Virtual Topology*

If multicast were being carried across the underlying network, Router C would replicate the multicast stream into two streams, one of which is transmitted toward Router D, the other of which is transmitted toward Router E. Router D would, in turn, replicate the multicast traffic into two streams again, one of which would be transmitted to Router F, and the other of which would be transmitted to Router G.

Overlaying the three point-to-point tunnels shown in Figure 12-6 changes where multicast replication is performed. Instead of Routers C and D sharing the load of replication, the full weight of replication falls on Router B itself. As the head end of all three tunnels, Router B must replicate the single stream into three streams and transmit the traffic along all three tunnels. Note this also means that while the multicast traffic only passed along the Router B to Router C link once on the underlying topology, three copies of each packet in the stream must now pass along this same link, one in each tunnel.

Security in a Virtual Topology

Security, like all the other network design problems we've dealt with so far, is also more complex in a tunneled virtual topology—if the tunneled virtual topology is put into place to provide a secure topology on which to transmit sensitive information. There are two points that need to be considered in relation to virtual topologies and security.

Does the tunnel increase the security of the information transmitted over the virtual topology? There has long been the impression that IP is somehow inherently insecure, so moving information off of IP and onto some other transport will make the network more secure. For instance, some companies consider an L3VPN service offered by a service provider to be more secure than a straight IP tunnel across that same service provider's network.

Why? Because there is a feeling that placing traffic inside an MPLS tunnel separates the traffic streams of different users at some fundamental level; that attackers can't "get at" traffic within an MPLS tunnel in the same way they can traffic in an IP tunnel. Back in the real world, the type of encapsulation placed around a packet—unless that encapsulation

includes some form of encryption—makes no difference. The traffic might be slightly harder to intercept, but one type of header is just as easy as another to strip off so the attacker can get to the underlying data. There is, in other words, no inherent security advantage to using one form of tunneling over another.

Tunnels, however, do hide the path traffic is actually taking—a possible security risk. Figure 12-7 illustrates.

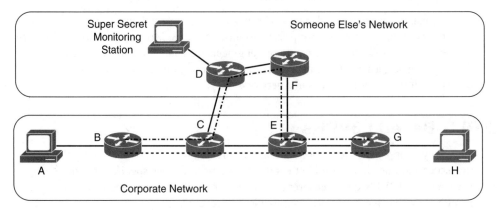

Figure 12-7   *Tunnel Path Insecurity*

Because tunnels hide the underlying network topology, it's possible for a tunnel originally set up to pass along one route to be moved to another route without either the network administrator or the users realizing the traffic has been shifted. In Figure 12-7, for instance, the lower tunnel is the original path intended for traffic between Hosts A and H. The tunnel, however, has been rerouted through Routers D and F so a monitoring station can snoop on the traffic as it passes by. Most of the time, this type of traffic misdirection is a mistake, but it is possible for an attacker to take advantage of traffic passing along an unintended path.

How can you prevent this problem from happening? Routing is a hop-by-hop affair; each router in a network makes an independent decision about where traffic should be routed. This characteristic of packet-based switching is important to fast recovery from failures, or rather rapid adjustment to changes in network topology—the primary reason this form of switching was adopted in the original Internet architecture. Moving to a more circuit-based approach in order to circumvent problems with misdirected tunnels opens the network up to an entirely different set of problems; there is no relief in that direction.

If the information in a stream is worth protecting, protect it with encryption. Don't expect the network to magically protect information you've put on the wire by keeping it within some preset bounds. Even if the traffic is "inside" your corporate network, it's still vulnerable. Sensitive data should be encrypted using a tunneling protocol specifically designed to protect it, such as IPsec.

Virtual overlay networks can not only hide the physical routers, switches, and links between any two points on a network, they can also hide any security devices, or policy

checkpoints, along the path. When small home routers first began adding firewalls into their software, many applications broke because these new firewalls wouldn't allow the application's traffic to pass. Rather than fixing the application (by installing a small local stub that would source connections from the local computer out through the firewall, or some other means), most application developers moved all their traffic to port 80. Why? Because all firewalls leave port 80 open to allow the Hypertext Transport Protocol (HTTP) through to support web browsing.

IPv6 tunnels are particularly dangerous in this regard, primarily because a large number of network administrators are not paying attention to IPv6. Most devices now come with IPv6 enabled by default, but few network engineers have intentionally configured IPv6 security policies, leaving the attacker the perfect opportunity to set up a tunnel that bypasses all the security checks in a network.

MPLS-Based L3VPNs

How do you apply the ideas covered so far in this chapter? This section works through all the issues and questions raised in the previous sections for one specific type of overlay network—an L3VPN deployed over an MPLS core. Both self-deployed L3VPNs and an L3VPN service offered by a service provider are covered.

The section begins with a short overview of the technology for readers who aren't familiar with L3VPN operation, followed by a discussion of each specific question or issue raised in considering virtual overlay solutions.

Operational Overview

Figure 12-8 provides a simplified overview of the operation of an L3VPN provisioned over an MPLS core.

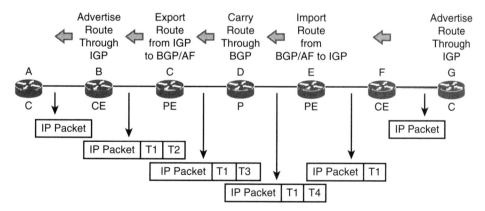

Figure 12-8   *Overview of MPLS-Based L3VPN Operation*

There are two flows of information to follow through any virtual overlay network—the flow of information being transmitted through the network, and the flow of control plane information that carries routing information through the network. Figure 12-8 shows both of these flows.. The upper labels on the routers shown are used to differentiate one router from another in the diagram; the lower labels indicate the function of the router within the network. These roles are the following:

- **C Router:** Customer router, which only participates in the edge routing protocol, typically an Interior Gateway Protocol (IGP), such as IS-IS.

- **CE Router:** Customer Edge router, which may only participate in the edge routing protocol, or may act as the point at which routing information is redistributed from the edge IGP into the PE to CE protocol. The PE to CE protocol is typically BGP, provisioned and managed either by the customer or the provider.

- **PE Router:** Provider Edge router, which places routes learned from the CE into a per-customer routing table (a Virtual Routing and Forwarding instance, or VRF). The term VRF is often used loosely to refer to a virtual topology across the network core, as well as designating this separate routing table.

- **P Router:** Provider router, which may run an IGP internal to the provider network, does not share routing information with the customer network at all, and also may run BGP. However, the customer routes learned from BGP are not installed in the local table on P routers.

Although MPLS L3VPNs can be (and often are) deployed in large-scale enterprise networks, the names for the roles played by various routers have become fixed in the world of service provider networks. In an enterprise network, the role of the provider is played by the network core and whatever groups maintain and manage the network core. The role of the customer is played by business units, geographic sites, and other business users of the network.

Begin at the right side of Figure 12-8 with a reachable destination being advertised by Router G. This route is advertised through the local (customer owned) IGP to the CE router, which is Router F in this network. The route may be redistributed into BGP, or otherwise processed by Router F, before it is advertised to the PE router, Router E.

Router E places the route learned from the customer into a routing table specific to that customer network (or specific to that VRF). The local BGP process picks this new route up and marks it so BGP can associate this particular route with a particular virtual topology; these markings are called the *Route Distinguisher* and the *Route Tag*. The route is now carried across the provider network, either through the P router or through a separate path through a route reflector, to the other edge of the provider network at Router C. Here the route is exported from the BGP table into the correct local routing table (VRF) based on the information carried within the BGP route advertisement. The PE router, Router C, now advertises the route to Router B, using the configured PE to CE protocol. Router B performs whatever processing is needed on the route (redistribution, and so on), and advertises it into the customer's local routing process.

Note   For those unfamiliar with MPLS L3VPNs, the RD provides differentiation between multiple reachable destinations using the same address space, and the RT provides information about which virtual network a particular reachable destination belongs to. The RD combined with the actual IP address assigned to the reachable destination is called the VPNv4 address for the destination. For instance, 192.0.2.0/24 might be used to address two different networks attached to the same MPLS/L3VPN. The first of these two destinations might be assigned the RD 00FD:E901, while the second is assigned the RD 00FD:E902; BGP speakers along the path will combine these two RDs with the destination address itself, creating the destinations 00FD:E901/192.0.2.0 and 00FD:E902/192.0.2.0, which will appear as two different destinations within their routing tables. The RT, on the other hand, is simply a number assigned by the MPLS/L3VPN network operator on a per virtual topology basis. This combination of numbers allows a single virtual network to have multiple logical destinations with the same IP address (which is useful for load sharing and multipath, among other things), and also to distinguish between different destinations on different virtual topologies that happen to share the same address space.

After the route is advertised into the customer network at Router B, traffic is drawn into the network toward Router G. Packets arriving at the PE (Router C) from the CE (Router B) are routed based on the VRF associated with the interface on which they arrived. This VRF contains two tags for any given destination, a tag that provides information about which VRF (or virtual topology) the packet belongs in and a tag that indicates how to reach the next hop toward the PE representing the exit point from the network to reach this destination.

The tag indicating the topology to which this packet belongs is prepended to the packet as the *inner tag* (IT in the illustration) and is carried edge-to-edge in the provider's network. This is the *tunnel* tag in the L3VPN system; it provides the virtual topology context that separates flows from one another within the system and allows the edge routers to forward the packet out the correct interface.

The tag indicating the next hop is the *outer tag*. Each router that receives the packet strips off the outer tag and replaces it with a new outer tag indicating the next hop toward the destination. To put these two tags in context, the inner tag is much like the IP header of a packet travelling across a multihop Ethernet network, and the outer tag is much like the Ethernet header that is replaced at each hop to provide hop-by-hop forwarding through the network.

Note   Another way to look at the separation of tunnels and tunneling protocols is to ask this question: What information is being used to switch the packet? As an example, packets passing through an MPLS/L3VPN network will have at least four headers: an IP header, the inner MPLS header, the outer MPLS header, and a Layer 2 header (assume it's Ethernet for ease of discussion here). When a router receives a packet, what header is it using to decide how to forward the packet? For routers in the middle of the MPLS/L3VPN loud (P routers, in MPLS/L3VPN parlance), the outer MPLS header is the only one being switched on, so the inner MPLS header is being tunneled by the outer one. The IP header, however, is being tunneled by the inner MPLS header because the IP header is not used to make a forwarding decision either. The outer Ethernet header is not used for switching at all—only to decide whether to accept the packet into the local interface—and hence is not a tunneling header. This type of distinction still leaves some questions to answer; for instance: Is the outer Ethernet header thus a tunneled header in a pure Layer 2 network? But we already know there is no single, clean definition for what tunneling is that will work in every possible situation, so we just have to take the definitions we have as useful general rules and live with the ambiguities along the way.

Fundamental Questions

What type of traffic can an MPLS tunnel support? Virtually every protocol of note has a specification for running over MPLS, including Ethernet, IP, and many others. In the case of L3VPNs, however, support is built around tunneling IP over a provider's network through a virtual topology. This focus is based on the control plane, however, rather than on the data plane.

What type of transport is used to carry the tunneled traffic? MPLS is used both for the inner tag (the tunnel tag) and the outer tag (the forwarding tag) in an MPLS L3VPN. Again, remember that protocols (other than a few designed specifically for tunneling) are not really "tunneling protocols," but rather that just about any protocol can be used to build a tunnel.

The Maximum Transmission Unit

MTU normally isn't an issue in L3VPNs for two reasons. First, the MPLS header was designed to be minimal in size, so adding two MPLS headers to each packet represents very little decrease in overall packet-carrying capability.

Second, most L3VPNs rely on links with large MTUs internally, while presenting an MTU at the user interface that's similar to most Ethernet links in their default configuration. Internally, most providers configure their links with an MTU of at least 1520 bytes, while they present a 1500 byte MTU—the standard default MTU on most Ethernet links—at the PE edge interface facing the customer network. If the customer network has configured larger frame sizes, then it is possible for the MPLS headers to impose an MTU penalty on the total packet size available along the link, however. This is something network engineers need to take into consideration when implementing or planning around an MPLS-based L3VPN.

Quality of Service

Quality of service can be quite tricky with MPLS, primarily because there are only three bits with which to represent all possible classes of service in the MPLS header (the EXP bits). There can easily be many more classes of service among the various customer networks connected to the L3VPN network, so some aggregating is normally in order to translate the various classes of service in customer networks into a manageable set within the MPLS overlay.

Most providers limit the available classes of service to three or four, labeling each with a specific color and providing bandwidth, delay, and jitter guarantees for these four classes. Each class of service can be placed on a different tunnel within the MPLS network (packets can be tagged so they can follow one tunnel within the provider's network rather than another, so that packets with a higher class of service are grouped along less congested or shorter paths—although providers don't normally provide one tunnel per class of service).

When QoS is enabled on your MPLS WAN, the first three bits from the Type of Service byte (the IP Precedence [IPP] bits) in the IP header of packets received on the inbound interface of the PE are mapped into the EXP field of the inner tag. The packet is then placed into one of the classes offered by the provider based on the value of this field. These tags are copied, hop by hop, into the inner header as the packet is forwarded through the MPLS network. Providers also have the option to change the markings as they map them into the EXP field, based on the contracted level of service. For instance, if you contract for two classes, Expedited and Best Effort, the provider could mark all traffic that wasn't IPP 5 down to 0. Or if you have contracted for specific bandwidth levels within each class, traffic that is above those levels might be marked so that they can map to a lower class or be dropped.

It is critical to keep this process in mind when designing your network QoS. Your MPLS provider will tell you which bits it maps into each class; make sure your markings are set so that the right traffic is placed into each class. If your network has already deployed a QoS scheme that doesn't fit into the provider's mappings, you will need to re-mark traffic outbound from the CE to the PE.

Control Plane Interaction

There are, in reality, three (and possibly four) control planes in an MPLS-based L3VPN. The first control plane is the IGP, or the routing protocol deployed at the customer edge sites. This protocol only interacts with the L3VPN control plane through redistribution or import/export. The interaction along this edge primarily must deal with the speed at which routes can be moved between the IGP in the customer network and BGP in the L3VPN overlay.

This movement isn't as simple as redistribution; normally there are timers here that prevent the customer's control plane from overwhelming the provider's control plane with route changes. This dampening effect can have a major impact on the end-to-end convergence of the network, so it's well worth examining when deploying an MPLS-based L3VPN.

There is also the interaction within the provider's network between the provider's IGP and BGP. The primary goal here is to prevent BGP from ever converging by provisioning very fast IGP convergence times within the provider's network, so BGP never loses edge-to-edge (peer-to-peer) reachability, no matter what type of failure occurs in the provider network.

Finally, there is BGP itself, which is carrying the customer's routes through the provider network. BGP convergence tends to be very slow, limited by the hop-by-hop processing of a path-vector routing protocol combined with various timers that rate limit the speed at which BGP can send routing information. BGP can be tuned to converge within most networks in less than a few seconds, but it's better to design the network so BGP never converges (if possible). This focuses all the fast convergence work in the network on one place: the IGP that provides BGP peer-to-peer reachability.

Using BGP to carry customer routes through the provider network has a downside in terms of optimal routing, as well. Each BGP speaker in the network will choose only one route among the various available routes for any given destination. This prevents customers from being able to load share traffic across multiple links into the L3VPN topology, and it can lead to suboptimal routing between networks connected to the L3VPN. There are solutions providers can deploy to allow more than one route to any given destination, but these will necessarily increase the BGP table size within the provider network, which can become a control plane scaling issue.

Scaling

Control plane scaling can be a major issue in MPLS-based L3VPN deployments. Because each customer can see only one part of the total routing table being carried through BGP, there is a temptation to load a full set of internal routes into this table and "let the provider worry about the details." Adding more routes into the L3VPN tables will increase the optimality of routing through the network, so there is an advantage to adding more routing information from the customer's perspective.

In large-scale deployments, it's possible for hundreds or thousands of individual customers with small- to medium-sized routing tables to overwhelm the BGP processes carrying customer routes through the provider network. Most providers place some form of limits on the amount of information a single customer can inject into the virtual control plane to prevent problems in this area.

A second scaling issue is that the MPLS tunnels carrying customer traffic (the inner label) are actually point-to-point, from a PE at one edge of the network to another PE at the opposite edge. The point-to-point nature of MPLS tunnels means that in order to build a full mesh of connectivity between all the PEs connected to a single virtual topology, every pair of PEs that participate in the topology must be connected with a tunnel— there must be a full mesh of tunnels to produce a full mesh topology on top of which customer traffic rides. This is obviously a scaling issue from a configuration and management perspective.

To resolve this, most MPLS networks are deployed with automatic label distribution of some type to build the mesh of tunnels needed to create an edge-to-edge virtual topology.

Either a special protocol is deployed (Label Distribution Protocol, or LDP), labels are distributed through an IGP (such as IS-IS), or labels are distributed through BGP. Using a label distribution protocol simplifies the configuration and provisioning of labels, but it adds a level of complexity to the overall deployment because "yet another control plane" must be deployed.

Finally, from the customer's perspective, L3VPNs provide excellent scaling characteristics; each edge site must maintain peering with only one other router, the PE, to reach every other destination available through the virtual topology.

Multicast

Because MPLS is based on point-to-point tunnels, the problem illustrated in Figure 12-6 applies; the PE is normally responsible for replicating packets into the various tunnels needed to reach all the receivers of any given multicast stream.

Security in MPLS-Based L3VPNs

Encapsulating traffic into an MPLS shim header to separate different virtual topologies (or VRFs) doesn't really add any security to the network in terms of protecting data flowing through the L3VPN. In theory, if the network is configured correctly, the customer edge routers attached to one VRF can never receive traffic that's within another VRF, but a simple misconfiguration of the Route Target, Route Distinguisher, route import, route export, or other filters can cause traffic from different customers to be mixed or misrouted.

Within the provider's network, all traffic (including MPLS tagged traffic) is open for inspection by anyone with access to the devices or the links themselves. It's very difficult for traffic to be routed through an outside network with an MPLS deployment, however, because the tags used to identify the end-to-end tunnels, and to provide for hop-by-hop forwarding, are local to the provider network itself.

MPLS-Based L3VPN Summary

In general, we can make a few observations about MPLS-based L3VPN services based on the answers to the virtualization questions asked in the first part of this chapter. L3VPNs provide good scaling and simple configuration to customer networks, at the cost of much higher complexity and management costs in the provider network. The trade-off for this simplicity to the customer is lack of control over the path traffic takes in the provider network (potential suboptimal routing), and little control over the convergence speed, including potentially complex interactions between the L3VPN control plane and the customer's control plane at the edge.

Where enterprises deploy L3VPNs to provide virtual topologies across a network core to their customers, such as business units, there is more transparency in the process that can allow the virtual topologies to be better adjusted to fit application and business

requirements. The cost of complexity is often worth the improved service levels and virtualization options for large enterprise networks considering large scale core virtualization options.

VXLAN

To further illustrate the concepts outlined here, let's work through a second example, this time using VXLAN as the subject of our study. VXLAN has been specifically designed to provide Layer 2 over Layer 3 tunneling in the data center environment and is normally deployed from hypervisor to hypervisor (although some hardware implementations, such as the new Insieme line of Cisco switches, support VXLAN tunneling in hardware).

Operational Overview

VXLAN is, operationally, much simpler than an MPLS/L3VPN, because there is less interaction between the overlay and underlying control planes. Figure 12-9 illustrates.

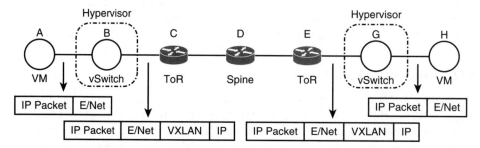

Figure 12-9   *VXLAN Traffic Flow*

Packets are transmitted by a virtual machine (VM) in a given pod to the local hypervisor, which then passes them to a local vSwitch for processing. The vSwitch examines the destination Ethernet address and determines the packet is destined to a VM located in some other pod within the data center, so it encapsulates the packet into a VXLAN header, and then places an outer IP header on the packet with the IP address of the vSwitch within the hypervisor on the pod where the destination VM is located. The packet is switched based on this outer IP header across the Top of Rack and Spine switches in the data center fabric (assuming this is a spine and leaf data center, rather than a toroid, or some other design) to the destination vSwitch, where the outer IP and VXLAN headers are removed, and the packet is delivered using the original Ethernet header.

How does a vSwitch know about what VXLAN header and destination vSwitch IP address to use when switching the packet? VXLAN's control plane is much like the spanning tree control plane. If the vSwitch receives a packet destined to an unknown address, the vSwitch will forward the packet to an IP address that floods the packet to all the other vSwitches in the data center—the broadcast and unknown IP address. This IP address is, in turn, mapped to a multicast group across the IP network, under which lies the data center fabric. On receiving a packet from a remote vSwitch, the local vSwitch will cache the source MAC address/vSwitch IP address pair for future use.

Fundamental Questions

What type of traffic can a VXLAN tunnel support? The answer to this question is simple: Ethernet traffic. Of course, IP, CLNS, and other traffic can be carried across the Ethernet connection (that's the point of the Ethernet connection in the first place!), but as far as the VXLAN tunnel is concerned, all this traffic is "just Ethernet."

What type of transport is used to carry the tunneled traffic? Again, the answer to this question is simple: IP. VXLAN is interesting because it really uses a "shim header," rather than a full tunnel header. The tunnel header in VXLAN doesn't really carry the tunnel endpoint information, but rather just the information needed to properly classify and direct the traffic at the tunnel tail (or termination point). The actual tunnel destination is carried in the IP header.

This (once again) shows the difficulty in crafting a straightforward answer to the question, "What is a tunnel?" In the case of VXLAN, traffic is switched on the outer IP header, not the VXLAN header, so technically the outer IP header should be considered the tunnel header, not the VXLAN shim. It's probably best to think of the tunnel header in a VXLAN network as the combined IP and VXLAN shim headers—because it takes both of these headers to properly manage the tunneled traffic through the overlay network.

Control Plane Interaction

Although VXLAN more cleanly separates the overlay and underlay control planes than MPLS/L3VPNs, there are still some complexities the network designer needs to think through when deploying this tunneling technology. Although the size and rate of change in the overlaying topology has no impact on the underlying control plane, the rate of change and convergence characteristics of the underlying control plane still have a major impact on the capability of the overlaying tunnels to support the applications running on the virtual topology. If the underlying IP network cannot converge quickly enough, not only can packets be dropped by VXLAN, but cache timeouts might be triggered, causing more work in the form of additional packets forwarded to the broadcast and unknown multicast group. The additional requirement of a multicast group added to the unicast IP control plane also adds complexity to the underlying control plane.

Finally, it's interesting to note the extended "reach" of the underlying control plane required for VXLAN operation. In a normal data center deployment, the designer might expect the fabric control plane to end at the ToR, and hence to plan scaling and other factors at this level. With VXLAN, however, the vSwitches below the ToR devices must have IP reachability visibility to every other vSwitch in the network. The only clear way to provide this reachability information is to extend the fabric control plane to the vSwitches themselves.

Scaling

There are a number of important scaling questions network designers can ask about VXLAN.

First, there is the question of the number of multicast groups required in the underlying IP control plane providing reachability for the data center fabric. Each VXLAN virtual network (VLAN) configured over the IP fabric needs its own multicast group for broadcast and unknown packets (unless you're going to mix broadcast and unknown traffic between virtual topologies—not a good idea). How many IP multicast groups can the IP control plane support, versus how many VLANs are needed within the data center? How much additional state, and how many additional protocols, will this multicast require? There are complexity questions here that need to be weighed carefully when deploying VXLAN.

Second, there is the question of the cache size and speed of updates at the vSwitch. How many hosts will live on any given VLAN, and how large of a cache can the vSwitch support? Cached control planes are notorious for failing in unusual and unexpected ways. How will you monitor and manage this cache to prevent catastrophic failures? How do you plan around troubleshooting the operation of a traffic driven control plane?

Finally, there is the fabric control plane extension mentioned above. How will you extend IP reachability into the vSwitch, or will you allow the vSwitch to send all VXLAN encapsulated traffic to its default gateway? Will traffic flow optimally through the network if the vSwitch is sending all VXLAN traffic to a single ToR, or will you need to provide more intelligence to the vSwitch—and how will you provide this intelligence, if it's needed?

VXLAN Summary

VXLAN is an interesting (and useful) addition to the set of tools available to a network designer working in the data center space. As with any tool, however, there are scaling and other design challenges that need to be dealt with. The separation between control planes is cleaner, and the protocol is more clearly a tunneling protocol, but there are still control plane interactions that need to be considered.

Summary

Virtualization on a large scale often involves tunneling combined with multiple control planes. There are a number of crucial questions network engineers need to ask about any given virtualization solution before they determine which solution is best (or whether virtualization is needed at all), including questions about the interaction between multiple data planes, the interaction between multiple control planes, security, and scalability.

Deploying virtual topologies can seem like a simple solution to complex problems—and sometimes they are, in fact, simple solutions to complex problems. But without proper planning, and unless the right questions are asked up front, virtualization can turn into a real mess.

Routing Choices

In the early days of networking, huge projects were undertaken to determine the best routing protocol—for some definition of "best." For instance, one project commissioned by the US Air Force attempted to measure the speed of convergence for each of the primary routing protocols (OSPF, IS-IS, and EIGRP), how much bandwidth each protocol used under normal operation, how much bandwidth was required when the protocol was converging (given a specific network topology and breakage scenarios), how many network engineers knew each of the protocols under investigation, and a number of other factors. Ultimately, the project was designed to churn all these factors together and produce a single answer.

Underlying all these calculations was always some set of assumptions—assumptions rarely ever brought out into the light of day and clearly examined, much less fully justified. These assumptions are, in reality, the interesting piece of the "which routing protocol" puzzle. Here you will find the real intersection between the business and technology choices.

The first part of this chapter will deal with the "which routing protocol is best" question, but we'll be concerned with exposing the questions network architects need to ask in order to answer that question, rather than providing a one size fits all solution.

Beyond choosing a routing protocol, there are questions around best practices in deploying routing; this is where the second part of this chapter concentrates. For instance, how should flooding domain boundaries be set up in a link state protocol? Are there trade-offs in different plans or designs?

Finally, we'll consider a different set of questions about routing protocol deployment, specifically related to the current "BGP everywhere" trend so common in large scale networks designs. Is end-to-end BGP really the best answer to resolve the routing problems modern networks face? What problems do networks designed with end-to-end BGP face?

Which Routing Protocol?

What are the traditional questions surrounding the choice of a routing protocol? Most network operators will jump to two questions:

■ How fast does it converge?

■ Is it proprietary?

These two questions quickly become the center of virtually any discussion on choosing a routing protocol. But are they the right questions? There is another set of questions every network designer should consider—questions that bring the relationship between the business and technology more into view. These questions include the following:

■ Which protocol is easier to configure?

■ Which protocol is easier to troubleshoot?

■ Which protocol degrades in a way that provides the best support for the business works during failures?

■ Which protocol works best on the topology the business usually builds?

Let's consider each of these questions in turn.

How Fast Does the Routing Protocol Converge?

Convergence speed, although often discussed, debated, and discovered, is a rather slippery concept to define. We must begin with the rather benign sounding question: What does it mean for the network to be converged? When testing for convergence, engineers often set up small, simple test beds that make for easy control and measurement. They then use various methods (such as those outlined in RFC 4061, 4062, and 4063), to determine when the routing protocol has finished calculating the best path to each possible destination within the (simple) network. Or the engineer might use a traffic generator to determine how many packets are dropped in the (simple) network during a convergence event.

While all this measurement is fine, it doesn't really answer real-world questions. As a counterexample, let's consider the global Internet. The global Internet is made up of tens of thousands (if not hundreds of thousands) of autonomous systems. These autonomous systems are interconnected by somewhere between 250,000 and 1 million eBGP speakers. The number of BGP speakers within the global Internet (which would include iBGP speakers, route reflectors, and other BGP speaking devices) easily numbers over a million, and the total number of routers—adding routers that are not BGP speakers at all—is at least double the total number of BGP speakers.

This scale, combined with the constant churn of modified policies, changing connectivity, and simple failures, produces a network that never converges. Does this mean BGP is a "bad" protocol from a convergence speed perspective? No, it simply means designers

need to be realistic about network convergence. To get a handle on the real world, you need to turn the question around.

The first question you need to ask is: *How fast do you need the network to converge?*

In the real world, there won't be one answer to this question—there will be one answer for every application, every business requirement, and every area of the network. With careful planning, you can build tiers of convergence requirements. The fastest convergence times should be contained in a small slice of the network (see Chapter 14, "Considering Complexity," for a more complete discussion of the trade-off between speed and stability).

The second question you need to ask is: *How much are you willing to pay for faster convergence?*

Given a baseline of redundant links and equipment, fast convergence reverts to software and configuration. It's often easy to see the additional software and configuration as "free," in terms of investment, which skews the trade-off between fast convergence and faster convergence. Remember the design, configuration, and equipment investment in faster convergence can be much higher than it appears in many areas.

For instance, faster converging networks may be more brittle—although minor failures may be handled more quickly, major failures may not be handled at all. Modifying the topology in a network designed around fast convergence isn't as simple as adding a new link here or there; real analysis work must be done to ensure that the overall convergence properties of the network remain stable or improve. Finally, fast convergence configurations aren't often well understood by support personnel, even at the network vendor; this could make for long and difficult troubleshooting sessions over the smallest of problems.

When all the right questions have been asked—and answered—we can return to the question at hand: *Which protocol converges more quickly?*

EIGRP can converge around single link or node failures, given the correct design, in well under a second. The crucial point to consider in EIGRP fast convergence is the depth of the query process, or rather how many routers must process a query before the network can converge. As a general rule, EIGRP normally adds about 200 milliseconds to the convergence time for each hop that must process a query, so to converge in less than one second, you need to keep the query scope down in the two hop range.

The upside to EIGRP fast convergence is there is almost no configuration required to produce a fast converging network. So long as the EIGRP process can detect the failed link quickly, and the network is designed correctly, EIGRP will do its part. The downside is the network must be designed correctly, which means a lot of thought needs to go into where and how to place links when the network is being changed for any reason.

OSPF can converge around single link or node failures, given the correct design and configuration, in well under a second, as well. There are several key points to remember when designing around OSPF convergence, including the placement of flooding domain boundaries, the speed at which Link State Advertisements (LSA) are generated, the frequency

and timing of Shortest Path First (SPF) calculations, and the path and timing of flooding through the network.

The upside to OSPF fast convergence is that it's better understood than EIGRP fast convergence, and also that it converges quickly on a wider variety of network topologies (at press time, there are techniques that would allow EIGRP to converge just as quickly on the same set of topologies, but they have not been implemented). The downside is that OSPF fast convergence is a delicate dance between configuration and design. The design gains a little more latitude at the cost of extra configuration and extra database information, both of which can make configuring and troubleshooting fast convergence more difficult.

IS-IS can converge around single link or node failures, given the correct design and configuration, in well under a second, just as OSPF and EIGRP can. The key points to remember (upsides and downsides) about fast convergence in IS-IS are similar enough to OSPF that they don't need to be repeated. The main difference to consider is that IS-IS has a little more deployment latitude on various network topologies, which can make fast convergence design either easier or more difficult.

Is the Routing Protocol Proprietary?

Another key question most businesses are concerned about when choosing a routing protocol is whether the protocol is proprietary; however, what does the concept of a proprietary protocol really mean? Generally speaking, if the design of the protocol is supported and managed by some form of standards body, and the protocol is available on more than one vendor's equipment, it is considered an open, rather than proprietary, protocol.

Defining what a *proprietary* protocol is, however, is just as slippery in practice as defining *fast convergence*.

To understand why, we must begin with a better understanding of how standards bodies work, and what they propose to standardize. The IETF is the standards body most engineers associate with the development and maintenance of routing protocols—but for all the prestige and effort of the engineers who work hard at building a sustainable and solid set of protocols on which to build networks, human realities still slip in.

Funding can often drive the adoption of a protocol, rather than technical merit—particularly where a single player with some stake in the process funds the development and implementation of one specific solution, making it look like the adoption of that solution is all but inevitable. Personality can, likewise, have a major impact on the flow of the standardization process; engineers have egos just like the rest of humanity, and often cling to their work far past when the work itself has ceased to be useful. Competitive pressures can play a role, as well. Difficult-to-read standards with a large amount of implementation leeway often result from several competitors squaring off and deciding to build a standard that will allow both of them to claim standards backing while working on extensions and modifications that prevent real interoperability.

Although none of these problems are unique to the engineering community, and standards bodies often do well at rejecting the effects of these human realities, they still

imply that saying something is "standards based" is often not enough. Interoperable protocols may often come out of a standards process, but standards processes don't always result in interoperable protocols. There is a long list of protocols and ideas that have originated in standards bodies, or that have been standardized in some way, but have not survived in the wild.

The obvious solution to this is to narrow the scope of *proprietary* so it includes not only protocols that have been standardized, but also those that have been implemented by more than one vendor. Again, however, this definition is fraught with problems. If we're discussing a routing protocol, is its implementation by a router vendor and a firewall vendor enough to consider the protocol "open"?

The best solution when dealing with proprietary protocols is to turn the question around. Let's break the shorthand out into actual business requirements.

- *Is this protocol implemented on the platforms I would likely use in my network?* Instead of asking whether the protocol is a standard or not, ask whether the protocol is implemented on each of the platforms you're likely to actually use.

- *How interoperable are the various implementations of this protocol?* Even a single protocol implemented multiple times by the same vendor can have interoperability problems, either because the standard is loose enough to allow noninteroperable options, or because one or more implementations just aren't well formed.

- *How long are these interoperable versions likely to be around?* Gravitating toward protocols standardized through open processes may mean more support for a protocol, and hence a longer protocol life. Or it may not. Don't assume OSPF, IS-IS, or EIGRP will always be around—consider the support each protocol has in real life, how widely it's used, and how likely it is to be used in the future.

- *How much are you willing to pay for the ability to use multiple platforms from multiple vendors?* Standards bodies can only promise solid standards, not interoperability. Are you willing to spend the time and money required to ensure the basic functioning of each protocol, and the design effort required to avoid features that won't work across multiple platforms and implementations? Saving at the bargaining table when buying equipment is attractive, but remember to count the costs on the other end of the bargain when deciding what protocol to use.

In the end, you should choose the protocol that best fits your needs, taking full account of the costs and benefits. Quite often, the decision will sway in the direction of using only widely implemented standards-based protocols, but architects should not go into the decision process assuming this is the right choice.

How Easy Is the Routing Protocol to Configure and Troubleshoot?

Which protocol is more difficult to configure? Which is more difficult to troubleshoot? Clearly these questions cannot be answered in a more objective way than any of the previous questions we've asked. But although there are no clear-cut answers, there are still

guiding questions you can ask in this area to help you decide which protocol fits your network the best.

- *Do you tend to have routing policy spread throughout the network, or concentrated in a few small places, such as along module edges?* Because EIGRP is a distance vector protocol, policy can be implemented almost any place in the network, whereas link state protocols (IS-IS and OSPF) only allow policy, such as route filters, to be implemented at well-defined points in the network.

- *Is your network broken into many smaller IGP domains connected through BGP? Do you use a single IGP end-to-end with BGP as an overlay, or no BGP at all?* Larger scale IGP-only or IGP end-to-end networks tend to benefit from EIGRP's ability to aggregate and implement routing policy in many places throughout the network. If the IGP is isolated into smaller "pockets," interconnected with BGP, or the network scale is small enough to allow for two aggregation and/or "policy points," end-to-end, then a link state protocol will work well.

- *Do you need traffic engineering that requires an end-to-end view of the topology within the IGP itself?* If you're planning to use the IGP's capability to perform constrained SPF for traffic engineering (such as MPLS-TE), then a link state protocol is your only real option. If traffic engineering will be performed offline, then EIGRP is an option.

- *What is the network operations staff more comfortable troubleshooting?* Many people find the database of a link state protocol difficult to read and understand. EIGRP's topology table tends to be easier to read and grasp quickly, particularly for operations staff who don't need to examine or review routing protocols details on a regular basis.

- *Which protocol produces the least complex final configuration?* There is almost no way to know the answer to this question other than to build configurations for the features you'll need to deploy at several places throughout your network, and make a subjective call about which one is the least complex.

Combining these considerations with the others outlined in this chapter should provide a fairly good indication of which routing protocol will work best in your environment.

Which Protocol Degrades in a Way That Works with the Business?

One of the most common mistakes in network architecture is to fail to think about failure. There will, inevitably, be a time when the network fails to operate as it should, whether due to the weather, or equipment, or a simple mismatch between the network design and business operations. When the network does degrade, it's important for it to degrade in a way that leaves as much of the crucial parts of the business running as possible for as long as possible.

For instance, when designing a network to support a high-speed financial trading operation, a total failure might be preferred to a partial failure. It might be better to fail to

deliver any traffic than to deliver some (or all) traffic slowly. In the case of a retail store, however, it might be better to keep the retail centers up and operational, so customers can continue buying things, even if retail analytics cannot be collected in real time.

The protocol the architect chooses must provide for the right failure domain separation in the right places in the network to separate critical business functions from the rest of the network where possible. The protocol the architect decides to use must also degrade the least under network failures on the topologies and sections of the network where the most critical business functions are performed.

Which Protocol Works Best on the Topology the Business Usually Builds?

With all the different networking topologies available in the current world of design, it can seem that making a protocol decision based on the topology of your network is bound to be a very complex problem. Matching the protocol to the topology, however, is very simple.

First, you need to decide what the most important part of your network is from a convergence speed perspective. No matter how large a network is, you'll always find there is one place in the network where you cannot work around the centrality of convergence speed. For instance, in many financial organizations, the trading floor might be crucial, while the network core, or financial branches, can operate with slightly slower convergence speed. For a retail organization, individual stores might be crucial from a convergence speed perspective, while the network core might have enough flexibility to work around a less than optimal protocol choice.

Note there might be more than one area of your network where convergence speed is considered crucial. In this case, you have to make a value judgment about balancing the needs of each piece of the network in terms of convergence speed.

After this decision is made, you need to examine the topology of that section of the network to determine what the *controlling topology* is going to be—the part of the topology that is going to have the largest effect on control plane convergence. There are only three types of topologies you need to look for: a full mesh, a hub and spoke, or some form of ring. These three topology types are virtually always going to have the most impact on control plane convergence because of the ways in which routing protocols interact with them.

For instance, if the individual locations in a retail environment are the area of the network where convergence is crucial, you would expect a large-scale hub-and-spoke deployment to be the main topology that needs to be addressed. For a financial or data center centric environment, a full mesh, or some form of complex partial mesh, might be the primary factor in choosing a protocol. If the network core is the most critical area from a control plane convergence perspective, the set of rings that make up what is likely a partial mesh might be the primary factor in choosing a protocol. When considering this step, remember that it's not the larger topology you're seeking. Rather, it's the primary topology components involved—whether rings, full mesh, or hub and spoke.

After you've determined the primary topology component you need to work around, you can examine the way in which different protocols interact with these topology components, and thus choose the best protocol from a network convergence standpoint.

- Link state protocols tend to perform better in full mesh networks than distance vector (specifically EIGRP), simply because they flood then calculate, rather than calculating hop by hop as information about topology changes is being distributed.

- Distance-vector protocols tend to support large-scale hub-and-spoke networks better than link state protocols, because distance vector protocols only carry reachability information, rather than reachability and topology information. This immediate and natural level of information hiding helps distance vector protocols perform better in environments where reachability information is all that's required to make optimal routing decisions.

- Link state protocols will create microloops when converging on ring topologies, and distance vector protocols will drop some amount of traffic when converging in the same environment. Choosing a protocol for deployment in large rings, therefore, is a matter of whether it's better to drop traffic or loop traffic for short periods of time (while the routing protocol is converging).

- IS-IS provides more flexibility in the design of flooding domain boundaries than OSPF. This is sometimes a consideration when dealing with designs where optimal routing along flooding domain boundaries is a crucial consideration in managing traffic flow.

- Link state protocols only allow the hiding of information at flooding domain boundaries, rather than anywhere in the network; EIGRP, on the other hand, allows information hiding to be configured just about any place the network designer desires. EIGRP, then, is going to be easier to deploy and provision for fast convergence in networks with a lot of depth, or a lot of edge-to-edge hops.

Of course, none of these general rules can be considered permanent attributes of any given protocol. For instance, it's possible for OSPF to provide at least some of the same flexibility that IS-IS currently provides in dealing with flooding domain boundaries, and it's possible to modify OSPF to perform better in hub-and-spoke network environments.

No matter how each protocol develops, however, the process of choosing the best protocol for a specific network, in terms of topology support, remains constant. Choose the most crucial part of the network in terms of convergence, determine the prevalent (or controlling) topology element within that area of the network, and then evaluate how each protocol would perform in that controlling topology.

Which Protocol is Right?

Given all these techniques, can you determine which protocol is "right" for any particular network? Although each of these methods provides guidance, no method can provide the right answer in every situation; no method can definitively answer the question, "Which protocol is right for this network?"

There are a few things you can safely ignore for all modern protocols, such as the following:

■ **Protocol Degradation Modes:** For many years, some protocols (such as OSPF) degraded in a graceful way, while others (EIGRP, for instance), were known to "fall off the cliff." The choice was between a protocol that would continue running, even if it wasn't running optimally, under a wide variety of network conditions, and a protocol that would run nearly optimally until network conditions were so poor that it simply failed to converge at all. Modern implementations of all the interior gateway protocols now degrade in a generally graceful way (especially given all the work that has been done on the EIGRP active process), so protocol degradation modes are no longer a real issue.

■ **On-the-Wire Performance:** The number of packets a protocol takes to converge in specific network conditions was once a huge issue; network engineers would spend hours with network analyzers trying to figure out the protocol that most efficiently used bandwidth. The increases in data traffic rates and available bandwidth across the network, from edge to core, have put this concern into a different perspective, however. While the routing protocol might have actually consumed 20% or more of the available bandwidth connecting different devices in a lower bandwidth world, they would be hard pressed to consume 1% of the bandwidth on higher speed links. Bandwidth utilization is no longer the issue it once was.

■ **Memory Utilization:** Again, in the "bad old days," memory was very expensive, and routers with a lot of memory simply weren't available. To counter this, many routing protocols used clever tricks to reduce the amount of memory they used or held by compacting their tables, or interesting (and complex) encoding schemes, or even not holding on to data as long as they really should have. Memory is now (relatively speaking) cheap, and most routers are designed with more than enough memory to handle routing tables in the millions of routes. Memory consumption—outside of memory leaks or memory usage far out of the ordinary—is simply no longer an issue that needs to be addressed when considering which routing protocol to use.

Ignore concerns about protocol failure modes, bandwidth utilization, and memory utilization when choosing a routing protocol. Instead, focus on the various points discussed in this chapter, including the following:

■ *How fast does the protocol converge?* But remember that fast enough is fast enough; adding complexity to get to convergence speeds you don't need is a recipe for failure at some point in the future.

■ *Is it proprietary?* But remember that proprietary is in the eye of the beholder; there is no clear and fixed way to value the availability of a single protocol from multiple vendors versus a protocol that is available from only one vendor.

■ *Which protocol is going to be the easiest to configure and troubleshoot in my environment?*

■ *Which protocol will fit best with the most crucial topologies in my network?*

If you can answer these questions, you will be well on your way to determining which protocol fits best in your network.

There is one more element to consider when choosing a routing protocol: *Which protocol best fits the IPv6 deployment most likely to be used in this network?* The next section discusses the relationship of IPv6 and routing protocols in more detail.

IPv6 Considerations

If IPv6 isn't a factor in your network designs, it should be—there is clearly going to come a point where IPv6 is going to replace IPv4 as the dominant network transport protocol. There are a number of differences between IPv4 and IPv6 you need to be concerned with as a network engineer, including security and addressing, but this section will only consider the issues involved in deploying an IPv6 control plane. As with the other issues covered thus far, IPv6 control plane deployment needs to be thought through in two distinct stages.

The first stage in IPv6 deployment is to consider how your business requirements interact with IPv6.

What Is the Shape of the Deployment?

How large will the initial IPv6 deployment be? How many endpoints will be connected via IPv6, and where are they located in the network? A small number of devices within an easily contained portion of the network (within a single module, for instance), can be easily connected using dual-stack IPv4 and IPv6 across a minimal number of devices. Larger numbers of devices, or devices that are spread across a wide topological area, will require some form of tunneling for connectivity. The choice of whether to run dual-stack in a small area of the network or create some form of virtual topology or tunneled overlay will drive key decisions in the control plane.

If your initial deployment is going to be a number of hosts connected within a single network module, or topological area, then configuring a routing protocol across the minimal set of devices to exchange IPv6 routing information and build IPv6 forwarding tables is probably going to be the easiest deployment path. On the other hand, if the initial IPv6 deployment is going to involve devices spread throughout the network, a virtual topology of some type (whether using MPLS or some form of 6 over 4 tunneling) must be configured and managed. If tunnels are deployed, then multiple control planes must be deployed, as well, and traffic correctly steered into and out of those tunnels.

How Does Your Deployment Grow?

Before deploying IPv6, you need to think through how this initial deployment will transfer to the network at large in terms of skills and technology.

Topological Deployment

If you are working in a network environment that has little virtualization "at large," it is probably best to begin in a small geographical area using a dual stack deployment (unless you're using the IPv6 deployment to bring virtualization into the network; however, it's never a good idea to deploy two new major classes of technology at the same time). Deploying dual stack IPv4 and IPv6 will build the skills and test the protocols needed to deploy IPv6 throughout the rest of the network—tunneling is going to hide some of the complexity involved in a real deployment, and introduce complexity you're not going to face in the real network.

Topological deployments need a growth path that is edge and topology oriented, as well. After you've deployed IPv6 in one corner of the network, how do you expand the range of the new transport into the rest of the network? Where do you place flooding domain boundaries, aggregation points, and redistribution points? Where is policy implemented, and how do you manage traffic flow, particularly with the interaction of IPv4 and IPv6 traffic running in parallel across the same wire? What about quality of service?

Virtual Topology Deployment

If you are working in a heavily virtualized environment, it is probably best to deploy IPv6 on a parallel set of virtual topologies. The virtualization skill sets are already in place, and the long-term plan will probably be to run IPv6 within its own virtual topologies anyway (or in parallel with IPv4 using dual stack deployments on each virtual topology). Understanding the interaction between the tunneling technology in use to build virtual topologies and IPv6 will provide valuable lessons and skills as the IPv6 deployment grows.

A plan developed to grow this type of deployment needs to consider whether IPv4 and IPv6 will run forever on multiple parallel topologies, or if all the virtual topologies built across the network will eventually need to run IPv4 and IPv6 in dual stack mode.

Where Are the Policy Edges?

The third set of questions network engineers need to ask before turning IPv6 on is how this new transport and its associated control plane are going to interact with the policy edges in the network—specifically security choke points, aggregation and flooding domain boundaries, and traffic engineering mechanisms.

It's tempting to look at your current network and think, "We really could have done a much better job of aggregating the routing information here—let's aggregate in different places in IPv6, to make the addressing more efficient." But before moving in this direction, consider the added complexity, especially when you're awakened in the middle of the night to troubleshoot some routing problem that involves both IPv4 and IPv6. Which routers should have aggregation configured, and which ones shouldn't? What should the aggregation look like? It might be possible to answer these sorts of questions differently in IPv4 and IPv6, but answering them differently for each transport protocol could inject unintended complexity that actually harms MTTR.

Another temptation when deploying a small IPv6 pilot is to simply not plan for aggregation at all. After all, it's just a pilot, right? It won't ever grow into anything larger, or become so much a fabric of the application space that it IPv6 can't be taken down to be replaced with a "real" deployment... There are probably real estate agents out there who will sell you future prime ocean front property in Nevada, too—it'll be worth it all when that next big earthquake hits and California floats off into the ocean.

Just say no to all these temptations; plan any and all IPv6 deployments from day one as if they were real, permanent, and the future of your network. Consider the existing policy edges, where new ones might need to be created, where old ones can be removed, and build the IPv6 deployment accordingly.

Routing Protocol Interaction with IPv6

There are three ways in which a routing protocol can interact with IPv6 as a new transport protocol:

- IPv6 can be included in the protocol packet format and processing in a way that allows a single protocol process (using a single database) to provide forwarding information for both IPv4 and IPv6.

- IPv6 can be included in the protocol format so it rides alongside IPv4, but because of changes in the way the protocol interacts with the forwarding plane, IPv6 must still be carried in a separate process or instance of the same protocol.

- The protocol can be redesigned to support IPv6 using different packet formats and processing, requiring two entirely different forms of the protocol to be run across the entire network to support both IPv4 and IPv6.

All three of these options have been used, one in each of the most commonly used IGPs.

IS-IS Interaction with IPv6

IS-IS simply added IPv6 as a new set of Type-Length-Value (TLV) types, so a single IS-IS process will support both IPv4 and IPv6 forwarding. If an IPv6 next hop is available toward a particular neighbor, then IS-IS will use that neighbor for installing IPv6 routes into the local routing table; if not, IPv6 routes that would normally use that neighbor will not be installed.

How does this work? Remember IS-IS builds neighbor adjacencies using a native IS-IS encapsulation carried directly over the Layer 2 data network; in other words, IS-IS doesn't use IP as its transport. When an IS-IS router advertises the networks to which it is locally connected, it includes any IPv4 or IPv6 addresses associated with that interface. An IS-IS router receiving this information can determine if it is on the same IP subnet by comparing the included IPv4 and IPv6 information with information about its local interfaces. If two IS-IS routers are connected over an interface that shares a common subnet (or set of subnets), then it's safe for both routers to install routes in the local routing table using an address on the shared subnet as a next hop toward destinations of the same transport type (whether IPv4 or IPv6).

This mode of operation provides simplicity in the realm of routing process management, but it does create the possibility of failing to build complete paths across incongruent topologies, as Figure 13-1 illustrates.

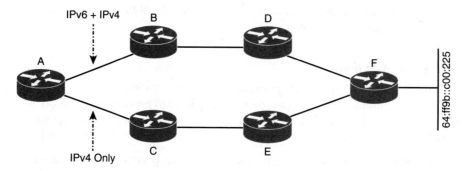

Figure 13-1   *IPv4 and IPv6 in the Same Protocol Format and Process*

In this network, Router A has two paths to the IPv6 destination (64:ff9b::c00:225); one through Router B, and one through Router C. Whether Router A can actually reach the destination depends on which of the two paths is the better path. If the path through Router B has the lower metric, Router A will install a route to 64:ff9b::c00:225 with Router B as the next hop, and IPv6 traffic will flow toward the destination correctly.

If, however, Router A calculates the best path through Router C, it will not be able to forward traffic to 64:ff9b::c00:225 at all. When IS-IS attempts to install a route toward 64:ff9b::c00:225 into the local routing table, it will find there is no IPv6 next hop through Router C (because IPv6 is not running on that link), and the route to 64:ff9b::c00:225 will not be installed in Router A's local routing table.

The only solution to this problem is to be careful and intentional in planning IPv6 deployments when using IS-IS—including making certain you understand the best path to each destination and the path traffic might take if the best path has failed. One alternative here is to deploy IPv6 in IS-IS network one flooding domain at a time.

OSPF Interaction with IPv6

The OSPF working group in the Internet Engineering Task Force (IETF) chose a completely different path—they essentially re-created the protocol from the ground up. IPv6 is not carried in the same version of OSPF as IPv4; IPv4 is carried in OSPFv2, and IPv6 is carried in OSPFv3. Although the two versions share the same algorithms for computing routes, breaking apart flooding domains, forming neighbor adjacencies, and various other operations, each of these things are performed with completely new packet types for IPv6. To deploy IPv6 in an all-OSPF environment, it essentially means running a completely new protocol, with a different database, different output, and different configuration styles and methods, on every router where IPv6 is to be forwarded.

This prevents the incongruent topology problem found in IS-IS, but at the cost of a potentially steep learning curve. Many network administrators, when deploying IPv6,

evaluate OSPFv3 against IS-IS and EIGRP as a second routing protocol—if you're going to deploy a new protocol, why not consider all the available options, rather than just one?

The OSPF working group has been adding IPv4 capabilities to OSPFv3, so a move to OSPFv3 can be used to support both IPv4 and IPv6, much like IS-IS supports both in the same process and packets.

EIGRP Interaction with IPv6

EIGRP's designers chose the second option: add IPv6 to the existing packet formats, but require a separate protocol instance (and therefore database) to provide routing information for IPv6. The primary motivation for choosing this option revolves around the way the EIGRP transport system works and the way EIGRP interacts with the routing table.

EIGRP has a separate transport process for each type of transport protocol supported—the protocol was designed from the beginning to support multiple transport protocols through this mechanism (remember when EIGRP supported Netware's IPX transport?). The protocol will form a set of neighbors for each transport mechanism enabled, using separate hello and reliable transport processes, calculate routes separately for each transport enabled, and install routes on a per transport basis. Although the configuration, output, and algorithms used are all similar, multiple EIGRP processes must be configured to support multiple transports—one for IPv4 and one for IPv6.

This avoids the IPv6 routing black hole problem described for IS-IS while also avoiding the complete dislocation of a new protocol, such as OSPv3. It's a "best of both worlds" bid, a solution that sits between the other alternatives—and for those who already run EIGRP, or are thinking about switching to EIGRP, it's a solid solution to the problem of deploying IPv6 using familiar tools while keeping the new transport separate from the existing IPv4 deployment.

There has been work proposed to allow an EIGRP mode of operation similar to the IS-IS mode of operation, for network operators who would like the simplicity of a single routing process. EIGRP, being a distance-vector protocol, would not suffer from the same routing black hole problem IS-IS encounters with this mode of operation. IPv6 routes can be advertised or not on a per hop basis, depending on the transports available on the interface over which routes are being advertised.

Deploying BGP

When your network grows too large for an IGP to support the routing requirements, it's time to deploy BGP. Right? In the minds of most network engineers, the concepts of "scale" and "BGP" are indelibly intertwined. To scale means to deploy BGP, and to deploy BGP means to scale. But if this were a test question, it would probably be one of those most often missed questions.

There are times, of course, when large scale is its own type of complexity, where the standard IGPs become too difficult to deploy and maintain without breaking them up along some set of boundaries, but to move down this path is to reinforce the notion

that BGP is an answer to complexity, rather than size. A properly designed IGP network can scale into the tens of thousands of routers (if not even larger); the key is using good design principles, breaking failure domains into small pieces, and making the right trade-offs between complexity, speed, and operations.

If all this is true, we need to rethink our reasons for deploying BGP.

Why Deploy BGP?

BGP isn't mainly an answer to scaling; it's mainly an answer to complexity—but what sorts of complexity should drive the deployment of BGP in a network? The next three sections provide a list that is more representative than exhaustive.

Complexity of Purpose

As businesses grow, so do their information needs—and what starts out as a single network with an easy to define and understand set of requirements morphs into a multiheaded hydra, each with its own appetites, problems, and requirements. There is ultimately a point in this process where it becomes easier to split requirements into smaller pieces, to "aggregate requirements," much as routing information is aggregated.

But how can these "aggregated requirements" be represented within the framework of a network? Generally they are represented as different virtual topologies. But just creating virtual topologies doesn't really solve the problem—as each business unit, set of applications, or operational need is given its own "network within the network," operational complexity rises—so while virtualization can simplify the process of understanding and meeting widely divergent sets of requirements, it takes a toll in operational complexity. BGP, as a policy-oriented control plane, can be used to control the added complexity of interacting virtual topologies and their policies.

When a business reaches the point where multiple business units present requirements that are hard to reconcile using a single set of policies throughout the entire network, then BGP can be used to tame the policy complexity into a manageable aggregation of policies. As an example, consider the network in Figure 13-2.

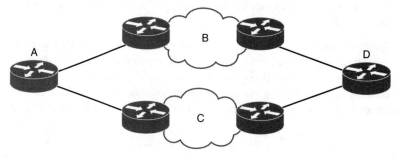

Figure 13-2   *Example of BGP Policy*

Assume two business units have locations (or networks) attached to this network at Routers A and D. For some reason (a business decision to split the two sets of traffic along multiple links, delay verses network cost, and so on), the first business unit would like its traffic to travel along [A,B,D], while the second would like its traffic to travel along [A,C,D].

To accomplish this using just an IGP, the metrics along the links must be managed on a per destination basis, or some form of tunneling and traffic engineering used to draw the traffic along the correct links from Router D. If BGP is in use, however, this logic can be encoded using local preference (if this is all one BGP AS), Multiple Exit Discriminator (if this is multiple BGP AS'), cost community, or in various other ways. What is a process of building individual metrics per destination—an almost impossible task in a link state protocol—becomes a routine application of policy.

Complexity of Place

Much as widely divergent requirements present a form of complexity, different places in the network can have their own associated complexity. In a network with a large hub-and-spoke retail environment, or a large network core to which somewhat simpler campus networks are attached, the different types of topologies might be easy to reconcile. But as networks grow, frequently the number of different types of topologies, along with their associated optimal design patterns, increase in scale and scope. Then designing within the context of a single IGP may become complex enough that it's worth adding a layer of aggregation in the overall complexity of the network.

For instance, a data center (or private cloud) may have moderately strict traffic flow requirements, so some form of tight control over the path flows take into and out of this one particular part of the network might be needed. Opposing requirements might surface in the need to reach the data and services represented by the data center/private cloud from many different locations within the network. Overlaying these types of complex requirements on top of other traffic engineering requirements (such as speed of convergence for real-time services, for instance), may present an almost insoluble set of problems to the network architect.

In this case, adding a layer of policy abstraction by deploying BGP to control specific traffic patterns can provide the policy mechanisms needed to balance the various needs in a way that's operationally obtainable.

Note that complexity of place can also include multiple business units that each run their own campus operations, and so need their campuses to form a single unified network for internal reasons. At the same time, these business units need to share the same core network and access many of the same services that make the business a "complete operation." Here complexity of place presents a different set of problems that BGP can be used to resolve.

Complexity of Policy

Beyond the two more specific realms of place and purpose are other sets of policy that might indicate the introduction of BGP into a network. For instance:

- Security, such as the requirement to be able to react to some form of denial of service attack across a global network quickly and efficiently

- The ability to separate traffic in some way, such as splitting internal and customer traffic

- Splitting a network into multiple administrative domains based on lines of business, geographic locations, security requirements, and so on

- Providing "lightweight," or very simple traffic engineering (see the preceding section for an example of this use case)

Each of these situations can create a complex maze of policy requirements that fall outside the realm of place and purpose, and BGP can provide the necessary solutions to resolve each one with the minimum of administrative overhead and operational complexity.

BGP Deployment Models

The decision to deploy BGP in a large-scale network is only the beginning of the work—throwing BGP into the mix, without fully considering the best way to deploy BGP, can have unintended consequences that far outweigh any net gains in network management and operational simplicity. Two of the primary questions network engineers need to answer are how BGP will interact with the current routing system, and how BGP will grow and change with the network over time.

These questions can be reduced to three options:

- Should BGP be overlaid on top of the existing routing system—should it augment, rather than replace?

- Should BGP be deployed as one large administrative domain, so the network appears to be a single entity to other networks to which it's connected?

- Should BGP be deployed using multiple administrative domains?

The three final sections in this chapter will consider the positive and negative aspects of each model, so you can better choose which model fits any specific BGP deployment.

iBGP Edge-to-Edge (Overlay Model)

If BGP is being used to provide a common core of policies (such as security) along all edges, or to separate external routing information (such as customer routes in the case of a service provider) from internal routing information, then an overlay may be the best deployment model. In this model, a single IGP still provides end-to-end connectivity throughout the network, while BGP provides "policy tweaks" and separation where needed to implement the necessary policies as illustrated in Figure 13-3.

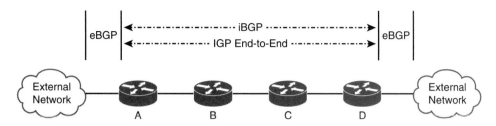

Figure 13-3   *BGP Overlaid on IGP End-to-End*

The advantages of overlaying BGP on top of an IGP are the following:

■ Provides good edge-to-edge policy within a single administrative domain

■ Provides good separation between external and internal routing information

■ Preserves end-to-end IGP routing information, allowing for well-defined traffic engineering within the context of the IGP

The disadvantage of this type of deployment is that it doesn't—without additional mechanisms such as an L3VPN—support the type of complexity described in the previous section, "Complexity of Place."

iBGP Core

To support complexity in the core while preserving the simplicity of IGP at the edges, BGP can be deployed using an iBGP core with redistribution into and out of the iBGP core at specific boundaries in the network. Figure 13-4 illustrates this type of deployment.

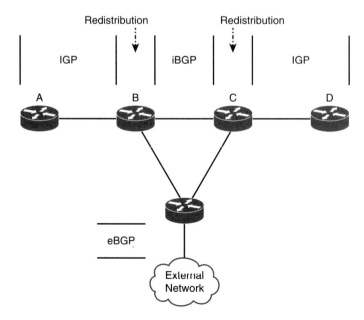

Figure 13-4   *iBGP Core Deployment*

The advantages of this model are the following:

■ Retains the simplicity of IGPs at the network edges

■ Allows the core of the network to take on the complexity of connecting different places or policies, leaving the edges, which may be administered by smaller or less-centralized engineering teams, as simple as possible

■ Provides the ability to use different IGPs in different parts of the network, allowing you to match the IGP with the topology or business requirements more closely

The disadvantages of this model are the following:

■ The loss of end-to-end IGP routing information. This could make traffic engineering more difficult.

■ The added complexity of redistribution at the iBGP core edge, which must be carefully managed and monitored to provide the performance and stability network users expect.

This deployment model is often used with self-managed L3VPN cores.

eBGP Edge-to-Edge (Core and Aggregation Model)

Finally, a network can be modeled as a set of different administrative domains, treating the network as an internetwork, as Figure 13-5 shows.

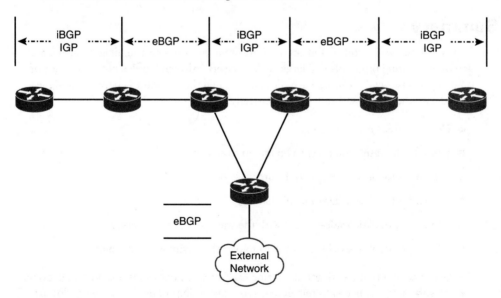

Figure 13-5 *eBGP Edge-to-Edge*

The advantages of this model are as follows:

- eBGP metrics are preserved edge-to-edge, providing a single unified way to engineer traffic through metrics and other BGP policies (such as community strings and multi-exit discriminator).

- Each section of the network is truly a separate administrative domain, allowing each set of administrators to make local decisions that will not (theoretically) have a major impact on the other parts of the network.

- The ability to use a different IGP in each part of the network, allowing the network designer to more closely align topology and business requirements with routing protocol choice.

The disadvantages of this model are as follows:

- The added complexity when interacting with external networks—should the local network appear to be a single network to the outside world, or multiple networks?

- The added complexity involved in engineering traffic through mechanisms such as L3VPNs across autonomous system boundaries.

- The added complexity of BGP on (essentially) every device in the network, along with the (possibly complex) iBGP design and deployment.

Note that some eBGP edge-to-edge networks are deployed using a single IGP end-to-end, which is primarily used to provide BGP next hop reachability information.

Summary

In this chapter, we've considered several important questions surrounding choosing and deploying routing protocols in a large scale network. Although we've not spent a lot of time in packet-level details, we have thought through the questions a network designer should ask when choosing an IGP—specifically:

- How fast does it converge?

- Does it run on the equipment you intend to run, and are there interoperability issues?

- Which protocol is easier to configure?

- Which protocol is easier to troubleshoot?

- Which protocol degrades in line with the way the business works?

- Which protocol works best on the topology the business usually builds?

We've looked at a framework for answering each of these questions, including the points the network designer needs to remember, and—just as important—what really doesn't matter when considering the answer to each one.

Finally, we've looked at some routing considerations surrounding the deployment of IPv6, and when and how to deploy BGP.

Considering Complexity

It won't scale. It's not elegant. It's too complex.

The network engineering world isn't quite science, nor is it quite art; network engineering, like most other engineering disciplines, lives on the line between art and science. Part of living in this world between science and art is living with fuzzy definitions and fuzzy ideas, dealing with instinct, making and breaking general rules, and being okay with imprecision. On the other hand, if there is any time we can think through something that's imprecise so we can get a "less fuzzy" image in our heads of what we mean, it's worth putting the time and energy into the effort.

In this chapter, we're going to try to make complexity a little less fuzzy. Because complexity interacts with scaling and elegance (engineers have an innate love of elegance that's hard for those outside the engineering world to understand), roughly outlining at least one view of network complexity can help bring those concepts into a little better focus, as well. We'll attack the problem directly; each section in the chapter considers one specific element of complexity in network design and engineering. Each section compares two competing design ideals, examining how each pair contains trade-offs against another.

By the end of this chapter, you should be able to see how they all share the same common elements of state and optimization.

Control Plane State

How much information does the routing protocol manage? Even though the concept of information load in the control plane is important, there are no good ways to put an objective number on it. There are two areas we need to look at, however, and two types of complexity you can trade off against to reduce control plane load.

Concepts of Control Plane State

The two dimensions we need to consider are these:

- The number of reachable destinations, which could be measured as the number of routes in the routing table, the switching table, or the forwarding table.

- The rate at which the information carried in the control plane changes.

The first measure can easily be expressed as the number of routes carried in the average router anyplace in the network. It's hard to be precise, of course, because devices in some parts of the network will naturally have more control plane entries than others. For instance, you would expect switches in a data center to have more switching table entries than those handling traffic across a campus or a small office.

But even though it's hard to be precise about the amount of information being carried in the control plane, it's a useful measure of complexity. More control plane information generally means more processor and memory utilization; more reachable destinations generally means more policy at the per destination level that must be configured and maintained.

A second aspect of control plane complexity—one that network engineers rarely think about—is rate of change. In very large networks, like the global Internet, the network itself is never really converged. To understand how this happens, consider a network with 10,000 links and devices, each of which changes once a day on average. If the control plane in this network takes more than 1/10,000th of a day to converge (8.64 seconds), the network will never be completely converged. In a large network that's also one large flat failure domain, it doesn't take high change rates to create changes that happen faster than the control plane can converge.

The more often the topology or set of reachable destinations changes, the more processing and memory individual devices participating in the control plane will consume. Higher rates of change also indicate a higher rate of traffic path modification within the network, which then represents more difficult problems in engineering traffic and end-to-end quality of service.

Note   One interesting study of these two aspects of network complexity is discussed in the paper "A Network Complexity Index for Networks of Networks," by Stuart Bailey and Robert L. Grossman. In this paper, the authors present a formula for computing a network complexity index by considering the number of nodes and their degree of connectivity, the number of edges, and the rate of change in connectivity and node count over time. This network complexity index can be used for a wide variety of uses, from social media networks to computer networks. Absolute measures of this sort can be used for one pole of a pair of complexity trade-offs, but it's important not to build networks around reducing one specific absolute measure of this type, because complexity must rise in some places in order to minimize complexity absolutely in one place.

Ironically, it's easier to measure this rate of change in a large flat network, like the Internet, than it is in a well-crafted network, such as a large scale enterprise, service provider, or data center. In fact, good network architecture is designed to hide the rate of change in a network by limiting the number of devices any particular change will impact (the scope of the change).

It is possible to reduce the information load in the control plane, and therefore the complexity of the network, through aggregation, or information hiding. We've discussed the techniques and ideas behind aggregation as a means of splitting up failure domains in Chapter 6, "Principles of Modularity," so we won't spend a lot of time on the same material here. In that chapter, we discussed two side effects of using aggregation to reduce control plane state:

- Reducing the optimal flow of traffic through the network

- Additional configuration complexity

We'll discuss these two side effects in more detail in the sections that follow.

Network Stretch

Now that we can at least articulate the things we'd like to measure on the control plane side of the equation, let's consider the optimal traffic flow side. How, precisely, can we express the optimality of traffic flow through a network?

By considering something called *stretch*.

> **Note**   We've touched on the concept of stretch in the context of modularity in Chapter 6 as well as in Chapter 7, "Applying Modularity." In this chapter, we'll consider stretch in the context of network complexity.

Stretch is the difference between the best possible path (for some measure of best!) through the network and the actual path the traffic takes through the network. Figure 14-1 illustrates the idea of stretch.

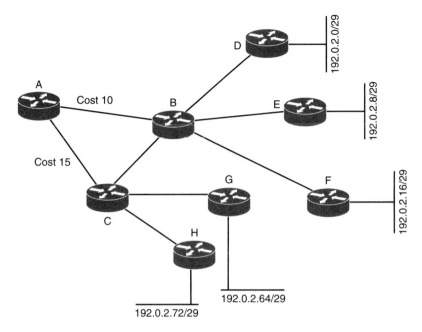

Figure 14-1   *Illustration of State Versus Stretch*

If there is no aggregation of routing information in this network, Router A will have (at least) 13 routes (counting the connecting links as reachable destinations). This number of routes—13—represents a finite amount of complexity at Router A. Each route must be stored, including metrics, tags, and other information, and the best path to each reachable destination must be calculated each time there is a change in the network topology. Of course, 13 routes might not seem very complex—but it's clearly more complex than 1 route.

To minimize the routes at Router A, the network administrator can configure Routers B and C so they both advertise the same route, 192.0.2.0/24. This reduces the number of routes in Router A's table to 3, a definite reduction in the amount of information Router A is storing and processing, but at what cost? If Routers B and C are both advertising 192.0.2.0/24, Router A will choose the path through Router B to reach every destination shown in this network, because the cost of the link (A,B) is only 10.

There is no change in the path Router A will take to reach 192.0.2.16/29, so traffic along this path will not be affected. What happens to traffic entering the network at Router A and traveling to 192.0.2.64/29? Without aggregation, this traffic would follow the path (A,C,G). With aggregation configured, however, this traffic will take the path (A,B,C,G)—an increase of one hop.

In this network, then, we can say that aggregating to 192.0.2.0/24 at Routers B and C will cause traffic flowing to 192.0.2.16/29 to travel across one extra hop to reach its destination. To put this another way, the path from Router A to the destination 192.0.2.16/29 has stretched by one hop—or the stretch has increased by 1. The stretch of the entire

network hasn't increased by 1, of course, just a subset of the paths. We can calculate the average increase in stretch from Router A by dividing the sum of the lengths of the shortest paths to every destination in the network before and after the aggregation.

Before aggregation is configured, there are 5 destinations with a hop count of 2, and 6 destinations (links between routers) with a hop count of 1, for a sum of 16. After aggregation is configured, there are two destinations with a hop count of 3, 5 destinations with a hop count of 2, and 4 destinations with a hop count of 1, for a total of 20. The average stretch caused by configuring the aggregation, in this case, is 1.25.

It's often possible to prevent stretch in some networks by configuring pairs of overlapping aggregates. For instance, in this network:

- Router B is configured to advertise 192.0.2.0/24 and 192.0.2.0/25

- Router C is configured to advertise 192.0.2.0/24 and 192.0.2.64/25

Now every path will remain optimal, and Router A will only have five routes in its local table.

Configuration State

Using overlapping aggregates to optimize routing while reducing the amount of information carried in the routing table brings us to the second trade-off in complexity—control plane state versus configuration state. In this specific case, adding overlapping aggregates to provide for optimal traffic flow through the network results in a few extra lines in configuration that must be remembered and managed when conditions in the network change. If 198.51.100.0/29 is connected to Router D, and 198.51.100.8/29 is connected to Router H, the aggregation scheme must be reconsidered, and the configurations at Routers B and C modified accordingly.

As with the other areas of control plane complexity we've discussed so far, there is no clear way to measure the complexity (or the *depth*—a term we'll use here to separate the general idea of complexity and the idea of complexity within a particular configuration), of a configuration. These two configuration snippets perform exactly the same task if applied in a similar way to routing information:

```
ip prefix-list permit 192.0.2.0/24 le 32
access-list 100 permit 192.0.2.0 0.0.0.255
```

Which is simpler to read and manage? It depends on a number of factors:

- **Which format are you are you more familiar with?** If you're more familiar with the reverse subnet mask notation, the access list is likely to be easier to work with. If you're more familiar with the prefix length notation, the prefix list is likely to be easier to work with.

- **Which format best fits with your configuration model?** It might make sense to configure all packet filters with access lists, and all route filters with prefix lists, just

to provide a notational difference that's easy to recognize when you look at a device you've not examined in a long while.

- **Which format processes more quickly on the device?** Although both forms might be roughly equivalent in terms of configuration complexity from a human standpoint, one form might execute more quickly on specific devices. This might be close to impossible to find out if you don't have access to the code involved—but it's a consideration few engineers take into account when determining how best to configure a particular policy.

Using the number of lines of configuration needed to express a specific policy is the one measure you don't want to get into the habit of using. Not only can the same set of policies be expressed in multiple ways, but configuration through alternative interfaces (such as an XML or GUI interface) and direct modification of local tables through off box processes (as in the case of a software defined network) will put a major crimp in the *number of lines versus depth* form of configuration measurement.

Control Plane Policy Dispersion

You might have noticed aggregation must be configured on both Routers B and C in the preceding examples to be effective. This is not only an issue for the management and maintenance of device configurations, it's also an issue in troubleshooting.

We can call this phenomenon *policy dispersion.*

Engineers working on the network for any reason must remember the interlocking pieces of a single policy scattered through configurations on various devices in the network. Configuration management, troubleshooting, network measurement, and modifications designed to grow the network must all take into account these interlocking policies dispersed through hundreds (or thousands) of devices, many of which might be widely separated in the network.

In general, moving policy closer to the edge, where it will necessarily be configured on more devices, will allow more optimal routing and handling of traffic. Moving policy implementation closer to the core will reduce the number of devices with which any particular policy interacts, but it will also reduce the effectiveness of the policy at steering traffic flow through the network. Figure 14-2 illustrates.

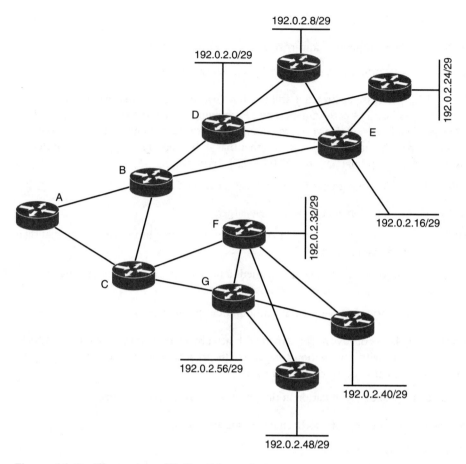

Figure 14-2   *Illustration of Policy Dispersion*

Although there are a number of places aggregation could be configured in this network, two specific configurations will illustrate the trade-off between optimal traffic flows and the dispersion of policy. The first set of aggregates follows:

- Router D is configured to advertise 192.0.2.0/28 toward Router B.
- Router E is configured to advertise 192.0.2.16/28 toward Router B.
- Router F is configured to advertise 192.0.2.32/28 toward Router C.
- Router G is configured to advertise 192.0.2.48/28 toward Router C.

In this configuration, traffic flowing from Router A toward 192.0.2.0/29 could pass along the path (A,B,E,D), rather than the shortest path, which is (A,B,D), because Router A will consider everything behind Router D to have the same cost. The worst case for any destination, from Router A, is increasing the path length by one hop.

The number of routes for which a suboptimal route could be taken using this aggregation is 4 (two behind Routers D and E, two behind Routers F and G).

The second set of aggregates follows:

- Router B is configured to advertise 192.0.2.0/27 toward Router A.

- Router C is configured to advertise 192.0.2.32/27 toward Router A.

The maximum increase in stretch is still one hop (because of the links between Routers B and C, Routers F and G, and Routers D and E, through which more specific routing information is still advertised). However, the number of paths that could be reached through a suboptimal path has now doubled to 8, rather than 4, because it's now possible for Router A to choose a suboptimal path to 192.0.2.40/29, for instance.

By moving the policy (aggregation in this case) closer to the edge:

- The core failure domain has been made larger.

- The traffic flow is more optimal than with optimal aggregation, but less optimal than with no aggregation.

- The amount of information being carried in the control plane at Router A has been decreased, but not to the minimal possible level.

- The complexity of managing the configurations has increased.

This last point is the one we're concerned with here; by increasing then number of devices in the network with aggregation configured, the total complexity level of the configuration set in the entire network has increased.

By moving the policy (aggregation in this case) closer to the core (Router A):

- The core failure domain has been made smaller.

- The traffic is less optimal.

- The amount of information carried in the control plane at Router A has been minimized.

- The complexity of managing the configuration has been minimized.

The trade-off between aggregation closer to the core and closer to the edge is the cost of added complexity in two additional router configurations versus the optimal flow of traffic through the network.

As policy is dispersed toward the edge of the network, traffic flow generally becomes more optimal. As policy is moved toward the core of the network, the number of devices on which complex configuration must be managed generally becomes smaller, reducing the overall complexity of configuring and managing the network.

Data Plane State

The control plane is not the only place where policy is implemented and managed in a network, of course—there is plenty of policy to be managed at the data plane, as well.

Various forms of packet level security, such as deep packet inspection, filtering, and black holing, are widely deployed in networks today. Quality of service is another class of policy that is often widely deployed in networks. Traffic must be marked so it is handled properly, and per hop behaviors must be configured on most (or all) of the devices through which traffic flows to meet quality of service requirements.

Let's use quality of service as an example. The first element to consider is the number of queues configured and managed to support end-to-end requirements for traffic handling; Figure 14-3 shows several queue designs placed side by side for comparison.

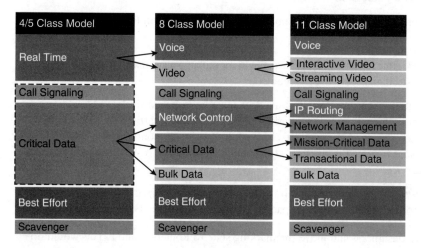

Figure 14-3   *Queue Designs Compared*

Moving from the left to the right in this illustration, the queues become more specific, and therefore more able to provide specific quality of service guarantees for each class of traffic. Moving from the left to the right in this illustration also means

- Moving from simpler configurations for marking traffic at the quality of service edge to more complex

- Moving from simpler per hop behavior configurations (scheduling, queuing, and dropping traffic) at every forwarding device in the network to more complex

- Moving up the scale in terms of processor and memory utilization both at marking and forwarding devices throughout the network

As with control plane state, finer grained control over traffic flow and handing requires additional state—state that must be configured, managed, and must be considered in troubleshooting. Also like state in the control plane, there is more involved in data plane state than how complex the configurations are. Dispersing data plane policy to a larger number of devices increases overall systemic complexity by increasing the number of interlocking pieces that must be considered and increasing the number of devices that must be configured and managed. We'll use the small network in Figure 14-4 to illustrate the principles involved.

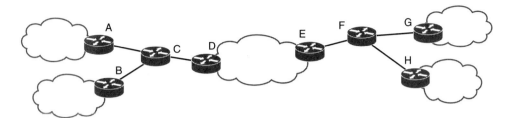

Figure 14-4   *Data Plane State*

If the network designer decides to implement packet marking on Routers A, B, G, and H, then

- There are four routers in the network with complex packet marking configurations that must be managed and maintained.

- The configurations on these four devices must be managed so they interlock properly; configuring Router G to mark Voice over IP (VoIP) traffic so it is placed in the Express Forwarding (EF) service class, while Router A is configured to mark VoIP traffic so it is placed in the best effort service class would result, at best, in uneven VoIP service.

- Routers C, D, E, and F must all be configured with the correct Per Hop Behaviors (PHB) to take advantage of the packet marking imposed at the edge of the network.

The network designer could move the marking state to Routers C and F. This would do the following:

- Decrease the number of routers on which packet marking configurations must be maintained to two

- Decrease the number of routers on which PHBs must be maintained to two

- (Most likely) reduce the consistency and quality of end-to-end traffic handling in the network

The trade-off here is between managing configurations on a wider scale versus optimizing the handling of different types of traffic flowing through the network.

> **Note**   A number of papers have been written in the area of measuring state complexity in terms of state and derived state dispersed throughout a network—a solid example is "NetComplex: A Complexity Metric for Networked System Designs," by Chun, Ratnasamy, and Kohler. By assigning a value to individual pieces of state, and then a value to the complexity of distributing and maintaining that state, an overall number describing the complexity of the entire network can be derived. As with all other "single instance" measures of network complexity, calculating a single measure of state complexity can be useful, but it won't provide you with the "whole picture," in terms of network complexity—rather it will only provide a measure for one-half of a trade-off.

Reaction Time

The final set of trade-offs to explore focuses on making the network react quickly to changes in the control plane. The example we'll use here is Fast Reroute (FRR), a set of mechanisms designed to quickly move traffic from a failed link to a backup path. Chapter 8, "Weathering Storms," explains the concepts behind FRR in detail; we won't repeat that information here. Instead, let's consider the amount of state and additional configuration planning required to implement some form of FRR system using Figure 14-5.

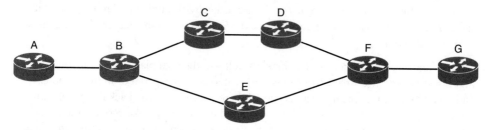

Figure 14-5 *Fast Convergence Trade-offs*

Assume the following:

- The best path from Router A to Router G is through (A,B,E,F,G).

- The path (A,B,C,D,F,G) is a loop-free path, but the cost is high enough that it is not considered a loop-free alternative or an EIGRP feasible successor.

To use the loop-free path through (A,B,C,D,F,G), the network administrator could do one of the following:

- Configure some form of FRR that will create a tunnel between Routers F and B to use the second path.

- Modify the metrics on the segment (B,C,D,F) so the second path is considered a loop-free alternate or EIGRP feasible successor.

What additional state would be required to configure some form of FRR? First, and most obvious, is the additional configuration required on at least Routers B and F. The actual configuration might be simple, just a couple of lines, but it's still an added bit of complexity in creating and managing this complexity. Beyond this is the additional state in the control plane—some amount of additional routing information is needed to find the alternate route and build the correct routing table entries to forward traffic around network failures. This state would normally take the form of additional entries in the local database.

What additional state would be required to configure the metrics? There's no immediately apparent state, but the metrics of every interface along the alternate path must be managed with a view toward keeping the alternate path available for fast recovery if the (B,E,F) path fails. These configurations are not directly connected to the primary path, or to the origin or destination of the traffic, so they must be documented, and considered, when changes to the network are being put in place to meet other requirements. In this

case, the complexity comes out on the human side of the equation, rather than in the control plane.

Security is another area that needs to be explored in the case of fast reroute mechanisms; most of these mechanisms require traffic to be forwarded through dynamically created tunnels in the network. What type of security hole will you be opening by allowing any device in the network to terminate a tunnel without any prior tunnel configuration? For networks that often work with MPLS tunnels, where dynamic tunnels are the rule rather than the exception, this might just be another part of the risk factor to be as "normal operation." But in a world where networks are "crunchy through and through," and internal traffic can pose as much of a threat as external, this is a point that needs to be taken into consideration.

There is another area of complexity here, as well—in the data plane. For FRR solutions, additional forwarding table entries must be created and managed. For both solutions, care must be taken to ensure there is enough bandwidth along the backup link, and any necessary per hop behaviors must be created and managed to make certain end-to-end quality of service guarantees are met. If the reroute takes place across a router with local destinations attached, service to the locally attached destinations can be disrupted by the increase in transit traffic across the device.

Detecting failures quickly adds its own set of challenges. Fast hellos must be managed properly; additional care must be taken to ensure processor and link utilization aren't adversely affected by fast hello mechanisms. False positives must be handled, as well.

A Single Complexity Number?

The ultimate goal of all complexity research is a "single number" describing the overall complexity of the network—a unified theorem of network complexity, like the Shanon theorem of information. This goal, most likely, will never be reached. Why? Because network complexity interacts with design in very strong ways—and math does a very poor job of describing intent. In *Science and Complexity* (1948), Warren Weaver argues there is a huge difference between disorganized complexity and organized complexity. Disorganized complexity is aptly described through statistical methods, such as predicting the path of a billiard ball out of a group of billiard balls moving randomly on a pool table.

To consider organized complexity, imagine a pool table where all the balls have been lined up in a neat row along the edges of the bumpers. The balls are somehow moved along the bumpers, each ball moving such that it never contacts another ball, but the entire set of balls rotates around the table. How can you measure the complexity of such an organized system? In observable rules, the system is quite simple—but clearly there is some intent to the movement of the balls, and this intent, or teleology, is outside the realm of clear and simple measurement.

By definition, organized complexity, particularly in the field of network architecture, interacts with the intent of the designer, which in turn relates to the difficulty of the problem being solved. Because these intentions are, effectively, outside the realm of measurement, there isn't likely ever going to be a way to say, "A network of complexity X

is sufficient to meet the demands of problem set Y." It's very difficult to set down "Y" in this example.

What is likely is that there is a solid set of heuristics, or ways of thinking about a problem, that will provide a pretty good guess about what is too complex and what is not. We can use such heuristics as a framework through which we can understand complexity in networked systems to better understand when we need to add complexity and when we don't.

A single number? No. A way of thinking about complexity as a problem set that can prove useful in real-world network architecture? Yes.

Managing Complexity Trade-offs

Defining complexity is difficult, but we can generally break the problem into several simpler pieces:

- The amount of information carried in the control plane, and how often it changes

- The depth and dispersion of control plane configuration

- The depth and dispersion of data plane configuration

Each of these elements will trade off against the optimal flow of traffic through the network, either in terms of the actual path chosen to reach any given destination, or in the treatment of packets and flows on a per hop basis. There aren't any definitive measures for many of the elements we encounter in the area of complexity; because some of these elements are subjective, there probably won't ever be any way to measure them with any degree of accuracy.

But even with all of this, network architects, designers, and engineers can't afford to ignore the problem of complexity. A network that's too complex will

- Converge more slowly because of data plane overload, positive feedback loops, and other phenomena—see Chapter 8 for more information about these.

- Be more difficult to manage and plan around because each piece of policy distributed throughout the network must be considered when a new policy is deployed, when the network is modified to increase or decrease capacity, or, generally, whenever the network is "touched." Networks tend to "ossify" over time, building up layers of policy and configuration, becoming brittle without thought. In their brittle state, a network can fail (unexpectedly!) for apparently no reason at all—though the real reason is hidden in layers of overlapping systemic complexity.

- Be more difficult to troubleshoot, impacting MTTR and, therefore, the services the network provides to the company.

Is complexity a bad thing? Clearly the answer must be no. On the other hand, network architects need to be realistic in assessing the amount of complexity being added to the

operation and maintenance of a network to attain specific goals. Some important questions to ask:

- Have I looked for, and found, the trade-off? If you've not found it, you've not looked hard enough.

- Is this change really necessary to meet specific requirements?

- Is fulfilling this requirement worth the trade-off?

- Have I thought of other ways to solve this problem, and whether or not they might add less complexity?

- Have I thought about the future of this change, the systemic dependencies?

Remember: *There is no such thing as a free lunch.*

Network in Motion

People just can't sit still any longer. Looking for users at their desks? Forget about it. They're probably out in the yard, sitting at a table at the local café, or maybe even sitting on the beach using a tablet to access services on your network. Or they're driving their car (don't text and drive!), or... What's a network architect to do with all these people moving around?

Design mobility into the network, of course. If you can't beat 'em, join 'em.

Fair warning, however: mobility isn't an easy problem to solve. In fact, among all the problems to solve on a modern network, mobility is probably one of the hardest you'll encounter. It might be neat to be able to check your email from the porch of a mountain getaway while watching a sports game in the background, but it's not easy.

We turn to the business case first—why is mobility such an important part of network design today? After considering some of the good things mobility can bring to a network, we then dive into a bit of the complexity that pushes back, making the delivery of mobility difficult. What are the realistic bounds of mobility within a network?

To understand the complexity introduced by mobility, we'll consider some hard and fast realities about device mobility, primarily focused on how and where to hold the state needed to make mobility work. Following this, we'll consider some specific IP-centric mobility technologies—Identifier-Locator Network Protocol (ILNP), Location Identifier Separation Protocol (LISP), Mobile IP, host routing, Mobile Ad Hoc Networks (MANET), and dynamic DNS (DDNS).

Finally, we'll look at some of the problems involved in providing remote access through the Internet or some other large public network for remote users.

So—stand up and get mobile. Don't even try to read this chapter sitting down.

The Business Case for Mobility

The case for mobility isn't difficult to make, but let's work through a few examples to get a feel for the space.

A Campus Bus Service

In large campus environments, particularly where hundreds of thousands, or millions, of people pass through the campus in a given day, an internal transportation system can be vital to effective operations. Let's use a large theme park spread out over a wide area as an example. The most cost-effective solution to managing traffic flow between the various venues (or even independent parks), local hotels, eating establishments, and other entertainment options might be a widespread bus service. A city bus service might do just as well, but the demands of a large theme park operator might require a more interesting array of services.

The first problem the business will encounter is handling safety and maintenance issues. Should every bus be brought in for service on a periodic basis? This is easy to plan for, but it might mean buying and running more buses than are necessary. Some system that marks a particular bus for maintenance on a per mileage basis, rather than periodically, might be better—but this produces the overhead of actually recording the mileage on a daily basis.

A mobility solution can bring a higher degree of efficiency to the problem. Rather than manually reading the odometer on a regular basis, a small host can be installed in each bus to read vital information and feed it back through the network to a central maintenance system. Not only can the odometer be read in this way, but any maintenance information provided by the electronics installed in the bus already can be remotely cataloged—brake pressure, tire inflation, engine temperature, fuel mileage, and so on. All this data can be fed through data analytics to optimize the maintenance of each vehicle to reduce cost while maximizing safety and operational tempo.

A second problem the park operator encounters is the optimal routing and operation of these buses. Should each driver always take the same route at the same time intervals? How is a crowd at one particular stop handled efficiently? Again, a mobile network can contribute significantly to solutions. Bus stops could be equipped with some form of monitor that allows operators to see how large a group is waiting at any particular location. Routing algorithms can be deployed to dynamically modify the flow of buses in particular places to alleviate crowding, and optimize service by reducing the average wait time per customer to a minimum.

Finally, there is the bus experience itself. A patron who is leaving the sensory rich environment of a theme park might feel a little let down on entering the plain gray interior of a bus in the middle of the day. Best to keep the patrons excited, drawing them back to the experience when they're done with lunch. At night, on the other hand, a quiet, more subdued atmosphere might fit better with a group of tired patrons who just want to get back to their rooms and rest up for the next day's activities. The morning presents

a different challenge entirely—pump the riders up, encourage them to visit less-often used venues (to spread load through the park more evenly), and encourage impulse buys throughout the day ahead. People with tight schedules (like most engineers!) might like being able to check their work email while they're riding to the park, as well—and their kids might like to play an interactive game with people already in the park, or on the same bus.

How can the bus operator achieve different effects at different times of the day? Again, network mobility can provide some critical pieces of a solution. Large video screens installed along the sides of the bus (perhaps even projected onto or between the windows) could play different content at different times of the day. The network could be used to push media in real time, providing up-to-the-minute information; if one venue is already overwhelmed (or even down for unplanned maintenance), take it out of the advertising round in the vehicles in real time.

The business case for a mobile network is clear, but the challenges are clear, as well—what appears to be a simple problem can be solved only with a complex set of network capabilities. Any host installed in the bus needs to be able to connect to a wide array of systems on board, including video, audio, on board navigation, and the various electromechanical systems. The host on board must be able to receive multicast and send and receive unicast, interacting with a variety of services connected to the fixed network. If the geographical ground is large enough, streaming video and other content must be pulled from the nearest server, rather than the "only" server.

A Mobile Retail Analysis Team

Large retail environments cope with their own sets of problems for which mobility can provide a key resource. Take, for instance, the case of a large retailer with hundreds of large footprint stores scattered across a wide geographical area, possibly even on several continents. Although the store normally arranges each retail location in roughly the same way—for instance, higher-priced items that lend themselves to impulse buys greet the customer coming through the door, women's clothing is always to the right, men's to the left, and electronics straight back—they've decided to provide more flexibility to the use of floor space in each region, and possibly even in particular stores, to improve sales numbers. But how should the stores decide on the right layout? And how should the company decide how much flexibility is good for business, and over which line they are harming business by reducing the consistency customers might expect across several regions within the same brand?

There is, in fact, an entire branch of analysis that works around these types of questions. How do you position merchandise, how long should a customer be in the store before being approached by a salesperson, what colors should be prominent at eye level, and where should the cash registers be located? These are all questions that can be investigated and answered by analyzing video recordings, buying patterns, and other information that comes out of the store itself. Suppose that, to provide the necessary information to make intelligent decisions, the retailer decides to build a small team of business analysts who travel to stores and carry out the necessary investigation.

But how can the network support this team? The team will clearly need to be mobile, so some form of mobile solution is called for. How much bandwidth will the team need? Will they carry the necessary processing power with them, or rely on services within the corporate data center—or even a cloud-based service? This team will clearly need corporate services and support while they are on location, including human resources, payroll, benefits, email, video conferencing, audio conferencing (and its old fashioned counterpart, the telephone!), and everything else an employee might expect.

The business case is clear: A dramatic increase in per store sales can easily pay for the team and necessary modifications to the network required to support the team. But the challenges are clear, as well. Team members must be able to communicate as if they were sitting at their normal desk, and yet have access to some powerful processing, along with the requisite data transfers.

Shifting Load

This final use case is based around services that move, rather than hosts that move—an important, and ever growing, part of the network mobility problem space. A typical situation here is a single service—for instance, one that allows a user in an auto parts store to look up the part number for the alternator in a 1969 Willis Jeep with a four cylinder flat head engine, and then determine where such a part might be found (or ordered). Let's look at two specific problems with such a service that require a mobility solution.

The first is that the information being accessed might need to be housed in multiple places to allow for the best possible search response times. For instance, a user in Atlanta doesn't want to wait the network round-trip times required to access a database located in London, even over a fast network. The business probably doesn't want to pay for hauling the lookup and response across the Atlantic Ocean, as well. Thus, the user needs to access one of many instances of the service in question.

The second is that the service itself might need to move throughout the day for various reasons. Common reasons here are for service resilience (being able to move the service onto a different physical device in the case of server failure), power management (moving the service to a physical device that is drawing off peak hours power), load balancing (moving the service to a more lightly loaded physical device), or one of many other reasons.

Service mobility, like the other two use cases discussed to this point, has clear business value. Again, however, there are challenges in providing this type of mobility that rise above the ordinary complexity a network engineer faces. How much complexity is it worth injecting to achieve specific types or instances of service mobility? Assuming the return on investment has been computed and found sufficient to provide service mobility, where is the best place to inject the required complexity into the system?

Pinning the Hard Problems into Place

Each of these use cases appears to present a completely different set of problems and requires a completely different set of solutions. But backing up a little (and squinting

hard!) makes it possible to see a common set of problems, in turn suggesting a common set of trade-offs. Let's see if we can pin down these hard problems and their associated trade-offs.

Mobility Requires State

If a host or service is going to move, some system, some table, or some protocol must know where the host or service is and how to get to that location in order for the host or service to be reachable (and therefore useful). This might seem like such a simple idea that it doesn't even need to be said, but it's surprising how many times mobility systems are designed without a fully thought-out idea of the amount of state required, or how to handle the state involved. All too often, people will say, "Well, I can use a default route to get to the service no matter where I connect my host," and never think through the problem of the service getting back to the host that has moved its physical location in the network.

Or mobility systems will be designed where the state is simply pushed into the routing protocol, or into another mapping table, or some other new construct—and the engineer smiles and says, "See, I fixed it." Pushing state into another layer, another system, or another location doesn't make the state go away.

You can reduce the amount of state through caching or gathering it "on demand" through a reactive control plane, but each of these is going to have an impact on the speed of mobility in the system and the complexity of the control plane.

Mobility Requires Speed

It's increasingly common for the network to be required to react in near real time. How close to real time? Consider these two points of reference:

- Routing Information Protocol (RIP) converges on network topology changes, with default timers and in its original deployed form, in around 3 minutes. Today, Fast Reroute systems count the number of packets lost in the convergence process, rather than the number of millisecond lost.

- Millions of dollars can be gained or lost in milliseconds on a financial trading floor, and a few milliseconds can be the difference between life and death on the operating table.

Not all applications will need "near real time," of course; an application that measures the health of a bus in a fleet pool, for instance, may only need to converge in minutes, rather than milliseconds. On the other hand, the trend is always faster, so we should prepare ourselves for that trend now. We build networks, essentially, because humans are impatient; there is no (apparent) lower bound on the speed of human impatience.

The "reality checks" on speed will always be complexity and cost. Mobility that spreads state between the host and the control plane is going to provide the fastest reaction times—but it's also going to add the most state to the network, and therefore cost the most to deploy.

State Must Be Topologically Located

The state required to provide mobility must be present in a database on some set of physical devices in the network; the more dispersed the state is, the more optimal traffic flows will be through the network. You can think of this as another instance of "state verses stretch," discussed in Chapter 6, "Principles of Modularity."

There are two extremes:

- If all the state is held in individual hosts, traffic flows will be optimal, and the network control plane will be minimally simple. At the same time, the hosts will need to deploy complex discovery and routing systems to find and route to other hosts to which they are trying to communicate.

- If all the state is held in a centralized (or even somewhat centralized) set of devices within the network, then all the traffic passing between, to, or from mobile devices must be taken to where the state is located. Hence, traffic must be backhauled to the point where the state resides, resulting in "trombone routing," or other highly inefficient traffic flow patterns.

Between these two extremes are a number of options. State can be distributed to some specific modular edge within the network, or some state can be distributed to the hosts while other state is retained at a more central location, and so on.

There is one caveat: if caching or some form of reactive control plane is used to manage the amount of state, the topological location of the state becomes a matter of application performance in a larger sense, and not just suboptimal traffic patterns. Let's use Figure 15-1 to examine this class of problems.

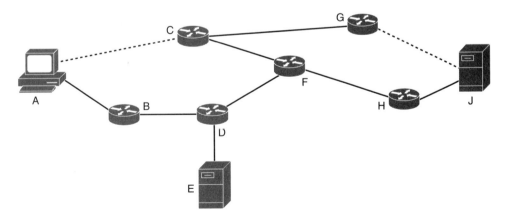

Figure 15-1   *Example of State in Network Mobility*

Assume that Host A currently connects to Router B, but could move its connection to Router C at any moment. Server J (where the service resides that Host A is accessing) could also move its connection point from Router H to Router G at any moment. Server E is a "fixed location server," useful for mapping services. Without diving into specific

protocols, assume we want to reduce the state to the minimal possible across all nodes on the network, while still maintaining the ability to modify the connection point at Host A and Server J. When A wants to open a session to J

- It sends a packet toward J's address. Router B uses a proactive control plane to discover a route to Server J, installing state throughout the network. In this case, if J moves its connection point, there is no way for Router B to know that Server J has moved, so the next few packets in the flow from A to J will be lost, or otherwise misrouted, until the state at B times out, and the discovery process takes place again.

- It sends a packet toward J's address. Router B queries a database at Server E (which is in a fixed location) and uses the information obtained to either build a tunnel to Server J (ending at Router H) or to build some other state that allows it to reach Server J. If Server J moves, Router B must be notified, and this state must be rebuilt.

In either of these two cases, the host itself—Host A—doesn't know about the disruption in the network or the flow of traffic. Moving all state off the host simplifies host development and deployment.

Or does it? From the perspective of Host A (and Server J), the network is simply unstable. There is no telling when a packet might be delivered in a few milliseconds, or a few seconds. Because mobility events are outside the control of the host, and hence unpredictable, mobility appears to be a very unstable network. To make matters worse, in both of these cases the information about how to build a path is cached. If the cache times out anywhere along the path while a flow is being transmitted, the entire flow path must be rebuilt—again, this would appear to the host to be an unstable network.

Anyone who has ever developed host-side software knows that unstable connectivity is probably one of the most difficult problems to deal with. What do you do if you're transferring a real transaction, and the network apparently "goes dead?" You don't know if you've lost connectivity entirely, or just for a few moments. What should you do about jitter in real-time communications, or how much buffer do you need for each streaming media application to prevent jumps and skips? As long as the host has no knowledge of the actual network state, there's no clear answer to any of these questions.

The decision of where and how to cache, or where and how to distribute the state necessary to build a successful mobility environment, isn't as cut and dry as it first appears. Distributing state all the way to the hosts creates one set of problems, while keeping all the state in the network creates another set of problems. Centralizing the state needed to support mobility creates one set of problems, while distributing the state all the way to individual hosts creates another set of problems.

There aren't a lot of "good answers" to a lot of these problems—just trade-offs.

State and the Network Layers

Finally, the state required to support mobility in a network must be carried, or held, in a specific layer—or it must cross layer boundaries in some way. Like the other areas we've

examined, this choice isn't so clear cut as it seems at first; there are trade-offs that need to be considered for each option.

It might seem simple to have the application interact with the routing protocol directly to resolve state issues in the network. But there are dragons down this path. Network protocols are designed in layers for a specific set of reasons; opaque APIs hinder in some ways, but provide great freedom in others. Some specific (and probably controversial) examples of layering violations causing a lot of heartache include the use of IP addresses as identifiers rather than locators. How did the networking world reach the place where the location of a device became an identifier for the device itself? There are several lines of reasoning involved:

■ Routing is fast, DNS is slow. We want fast mobility, so mobility must be handled in the routing system. The routing system deals with IP addresses, so we must base mobility on IP addresses.

■ IP addresses are guaranteed to be configured correctly; a working network is proof that the addressing, at least, is correct. DNS naming, however, is often sloppy, a secondary concern in the building and managing of networks. The IP address, therefore, is more stable and more certain to uniquely identify a device on the network, so we should embed IP addresses into applications.

How have these types of assumptions caused heartache? Three words: *Network Address Translation (NAT)*. Close to 100% of the problems accounted to NAT are actually the result of layering violations on the part of applications; specifically, misusing the IP address as an identifier rather than a locator.

Note   This is also an example of how pushing the problem to another system doesn't really solve it—and can quite often make the problem worse than it was in the first place. Had application developers pushed network operators to correctly configure and use DNS, much of the complexity involved in network mobility could have been resolved years ago.

Layering violations are attractive solutions when you're in a corner, but they almost always come back to cause more problems than they solve in the long run.

IP-Centric Mobility Solutions

Let's look at some of the various solutions that are currently deployed. Our interest in examining each of these is, of course, to gain a general idea of how each works, but also to consider each solution in terms of how it manages the state required to provide mobility, and where complexity is added. Understanding these things will not only help you determine the best solution for any given problem, it will also help you understand the cost/benefit trade-off from a business perspective. Ultimately, the question must come down to this: Does the added productivity and flexibility of deploying any particular

mobility solution, or mobility in a specific situation, outweigh the cost in terms of complexity and added state?

Identifier-Locator Network Protocol (ILNP)

ILNP is based on a simple idea: rather than treat the entire IP address space as a single location, split the space into two pieces, a locator and an identifier. A simple way to look at this solution is to consider the host part of the IP address an identifier, while the network part (including any aggregation) becomes the locator. As the host moves through the network, the lower bits of the IP address do not change, so the host remains uniquely identifiable no matter where it is actually connected. The network portion of the IP address, however, changes, so other devices can direct traffic to the right location within the network to reach any specific host.

In more specific terms, ILNP divides the IPv6 address space into two 8 octet fields. The upper 8 octets (a /64) are called the locator and are determined through the normal process of numbering networks at the interface and link level. The lower 8 octets (the lower /64) are called the identifier and are assigned using local methods that (attempt to) ensure global uniqueness, generally using the Extended Unique Identifier 64 bit (EUI-64) address taken from a local Media Access Control (MAC) address.

Note   ILNP works with IPv4 as well as IPv6, but it is primarily designed around, and standardized, for IPv6.

Figure 15-2 illustrates ILNP operation.

1. A process on Host A generates a packet destined to a process on Server J.

2. The DNS client on Host A sends a DNS resolution request for the hostname (or process name).

3. The DNS server returns a DNS record; this reply has an ILNP extension field that returns the current location of J (the upper 8 bits) as well as the identifier (the lower 8 bits).

4. Host A builds a destination address by combining the locator and identifier portions of the address, and transmits the packet normally.

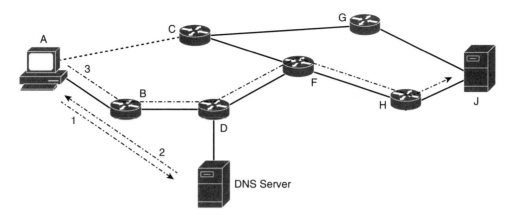

Figure 15-2 *ILNP Operation*

If the location of Host A changes, it will notify a DNS server, which will then propagate a new locator through the DNS system. There is also a mechanism within ILNP by which Host A can notify the process on Server J that it is about to change locations, or that it has changed locations, so the communicating process needn't do a DNS query or wait on a transmission timeout to discover location changes. Of course, if both the endpoints move at the same time, they can both query for a new location through the DNS system to rebuild or continue the connection.

ILNP, then, has the following characteristics:

■ The DNS system acts as a set of fixed services that are used to find the information needed to build an initial connection. This is no different from DNS usage today, other than the requirement to bring the DNS cache timers in line with the expected mobility rate. Because each device can set its own cache timer, only those with high expected mobility rates need to have shorter cache timeouts.

■ The identifier is essentially bound to the name of the device in DNS terms. One identifier can be matched to any number of DNS names, and one DNS name can be matched to any number of identifiers.

■ The additional control plane state required to provide mobility is shared between the DNS system and the end hosts between which communications are taking place. Each local host must have a cache of mappings on which it can build packet headers, and the DNS system must be extended to include an initial "reach me here" location.

■ Although there is some delay in setup, and there can be delays introduced through the movement of a device from one topological location to another, the host itself is aware of these delays and can react accordingly.

■ The location stored in the DNS system may not actually be the location of the device in the network. It may, instead, be an intermediary device that knows how to reach the correct location. As a proxy, such intermediary devices can redirect the first few packets in a flow while using ILNP mechanisms to provide the correct location within the network.

Locator Identifier Separation Protocol (LISP)

LISP, originally designed to counter the continued growth in the size of the default-free zone in the Internet at large, has been reshaped into a mobility solution (as well as a proposed solution for a number of other problems). This protocol is also based on the idea of separating the location of a device from an identifier, but the LISP control plane, its interaction with existing control plane protocols, and its interaction with individual hosts, are all completely different from ILNP.

> **Note** LISP, over the years, has developed into a set of protocols and ideas. In the current world of LISP, some slight changes to ILNP, discussed in the last section, would allow ILNP to be called LISP. The data plane piece of LISP is often called "LISP," even when it's combined with other control planes, and there are several different control planes that are all called "LISP." This section describes the original operation of LISP, treating the control and data planes as one "thing."

Figure 15-3 illustrates the operation of LISP.

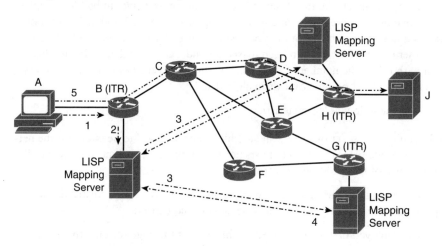

Figure 15-3 *LISP Operation*

1. Some process on Host A generates a packet (or a stream of packets) destined to a service running on J. The packet, as generated by Host A, has an IP address that is designated as an identifier, rather than a location; this address is unroutable from the routing protocol's perspective.

2. The Ingress Tunnel Router (ITR), generally the first hop router, on attempting to forward this packet, finds it has no forwarding table entry toward this destination. The ITR sends a query to a local mapping server to find the correct mapping between the destination identifier and the destination location.

3. The LISP mapping server (which could be a service running on the local ITR, rather than an off-board server, as shown here), sends a query to each of the other ITRs

in the local network, asking for information about the location of the service or host indicated by the identifier contained in the destination address of the packet received from Host A. Note that after the first query for a particular destination, this information could be cached at a master server (MS) to reduce latency.

4. Each of the ITRs that receive this query respond with any information they have about this specific destination identifier. In this case, G will return an indication that it does not have access to the service indicated, and H will return a locator through which this service can be reached. The LISP mapping server uses this information to build a mapping entry, which is then passed to Router B (the ITR). A local forwarding table entry is built (cached) at Router B.

5. Packets generated by Host A toward this identifier are encapsulated (tunneled) at Router B (the ITR) to the egress ITR closest to the actual service or host being accessed.

There are a number of variations on the general theme. Specifically, LISP extensions for DNS have been proposed that would allow the DNS server to return the correct mapping on the initial query (much like ILNP), and there are proactive schemes to build a complete view of the mappings at every mapping server to eliminate steps 2, 3, and 4. The idea of implementing LISP on end hosts, or in hypervisor software, instead of on the first hop (or some other edge) router has also been tossed around, again bringing LISP into closer alignment with ILNP. The number of variations on this basic scheme are almost limitless; it would take an entire book to cover them all in detail.

LISP, then, has the following characteristics:

■ LISP requires a new set of servers and a "shim control plane," to be built into the network. The trade-off is that neither hosts nor the routing protocols need to be modified because of this additional control plane.

■ Packets are tunneled through the network from ITR to ETR, which creates the attendant packet size, security, and other issues you would expect.

■ If LISP is deployed on the network edge, the hosts at the edge see only the impact of LISP on traffic flow, and not the operation of the protocol itself.

■ LISP controls the amount of control plane state injected into the network (particularly at the ITRs) by creating control plane caches in the network itself, outside the scope of the routing system or the end hosts (given that LISP isn't implemented *on* the hosts). This may raise scaling and speed of operation issues (depending on your view of caching control plane information in this way).

Mobile IP

Mobile IP, documented in RFC5944 (for IPv4) and RFC6275 (for IPv6), is one of the oldest, and most seasoned, mechanisms developed to provide IP-centric mobility. Figure 15-4 illustrates the operation of Mobile IP.

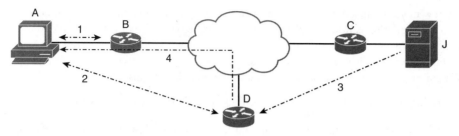

Figure 15-4 *Mobile IP Operation*

Each mobile host has two addresses:

■ A *home* address, which is the address it is assigned when it is connected to its "default," or "home," network.

■ A *care of* address, which is the address it receives when it is attached to a remote, or foreign, network.

A (somewhat simplified) operational overview is as follows:

1. Host A attaches a network; it uses protocols defined in the Mobile IP specifications to determine if this is its home network or a foreign network. For this example, assume this is a foreign network.

2. Host A registers with its home agent, Router D in this case, providing the home agent with its current care of address. The home agent is, essentially, the fixed location server E in Figure 15-1. When Router D receives this registration, it (essentially) builds forwarding information that will tunnel traffic received for Host A toward Host A's current care of address.

3. Server J attempts to open a stream to Host A. The last address Server J has for Host A is its home address, so it sends the traffic toward this destination.

4. When the traffic reaches Router D, which is Host A's home agent, it is tunneled to Host A at its care of address.

Mobile IP is widely deployed in carrier mobile networks to provide IP connectivity to handheld devices.

Host Routing

This is the simplest, and probably the oldest, method used in routed control planes to handle host mobility. Some older hosts implemented RIP (in part) so they could inject a host route into the RIP domain, and hence they could be moved without risking loss of reachability. IS-IS was originally designed with Level 1 domains being essentially host routed, as well, with summarization occurring only on the Level 1/Level 2 flooding domain boundary.

Very few modern implementations of host routing to provide host mobility exist, however. One exception is Route Health Injection, which allows a router (or a server load-balancing appliance/device) to inject a host route on behalf of a host connected to a particular port. This is primarily used to fail over between two different hosts, or two different interfaces on the same host—a rather limited view of host mobility.

The primary challenges when using host routing for mobility are the following:

■ In IPv4, the host needs to participate in the routed control plane to ensure reachability for full mobility.

■ In IPv6, the Neighbor Discovery (ND) process can be used to determine where a host is attached to the network, but there are few implementations that tie ND to routing advertisements.

■ Scaling can quickly become an issue when using host routes for mobility. There are two specific areas of concern: the rate of change in the control plane and the breaking down of barriers required to provide mobility over a large topological area within the network.

Mobile Ad-Hoc Networks (MANET)

MANETs are a rather specialized slice of the mobility arena. The genesis of the MANET idea was a military operation, where a number of vehicles and people might be air dropped into an area and have a need for immediate, configuration-free communications among themselves. As such, MANET protocols are generally designed around several principles:

■ Low power consumption, because the devices used in a MANET network are often battery powered

■ Low overhead, because the links used to interconnect devices are often lower-speed wireless links

■ High mobility rates, because the devices tend to move a good bit "on the ground"

■ Restricted topological use, because the highly mobile environments tend to be short lived, or to separate and then rejoin larger groups where more standardized networking protocols are used

■ Host routing, to support the speed and flexibility required in these environments

A number of MANET protocols have been proposed over the years, along with modifications to existing protocols to support MANET requirements. To illustrate the type of work done in this space, we'll use Figure 15-5 to examine modifications made to the OSPF flooding mechanism, documented in RFC5820, designed to support MANET.

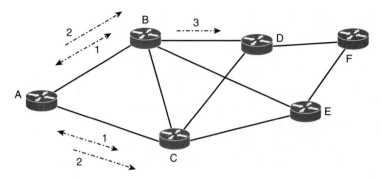

Figure 15-5   *OSPF Overlapping Relay Operation*

Each router in this network is also a host; every host, in other words, supports both local traffic generation and the capability to route traffic through to other hosts connected to the network.

1. Each of the routers in this network uses a somewhat modified mechanism to discover its OSPF neighbors.

   a. Neighbors on the same link are included in only enough hello packets to build the neighbor adjacency; after the adjacency is built, a sequence is included rather than a neighbor list to reduce the size of the OSPF hello packets.

   b. Router A not only discovers that Router B is a connected neighbor, it also discovers that Router B's neighbors are Router C, D, and E. Each OSPF hello carries not only the connected neighbors, but also the "two hop neighbors" to facilitate discovering the "two hop neighborhood."

   c. After these first hop neighbor adjacencies are built, Router A determines the minimal set of first hop neighbors that can be used to reach all the routers in its two hop neighborhood. In this case, Routers B and C have the same two hop neighborhood—each other, Router D, and Router E.

   d. Router A will determine which of these two neighbors should be marked as the "overlapping relay," or rather the router which will reflood any LSAs Router A itself floods into the network. Assume Router A chooses Router B as its overlapping relay.

   e. Router A notifies the other routers—the routers which are not the overlapping relay—that they should delay reflooding any LSAs Router A sends for a few tens or hundreds of milliseconds.

2. When a change to the topology occurs, Router A floods an LSA containing the change to both of its neighbors, Routers B and C.

3. Router B refloods this LSA immediately, and Router C delays.

   a. Router C sets a "reflood timer"; when this timer wakes up, it will reflood the LSA it just received from Router A.

b. Routers D and E, on receiving the LSA flooded by Router B, send an acknowledgement to each of their neighbors.

c. When Router C receives this acknowledgement, it resets the reflood timer so it does not wake up, preventing it from reflooding the LSA.

The added complexity here is typical of the additional protocol level work required to reduce on-the-wire packet usage. As with all things, there is a trade-off between control plane state, complexity, and efficiency.

Although MANET networks aren't widely deployed, many of the ideas developed for MANET environments can be directly applied to large-scale link state protocol deployments, such as data centers.

Dynamic DNS

Dynamic DNS (DDNS) is similar to ILNP in relying on the DNS system as a "fixed resource" (Server E in Figure 15-1) through which mobility events can be tracked, but it's different in that it doesn't provide the signaling and other processes required to make mobility truly "mobile." DDNS is really designed for "slow mobility," or for situations where a system disconnects and receives a new IP address when reconnected (such as a home gateway into a high-speed Internet access system). Figure 15-6 illustrates the operation of DDNS.

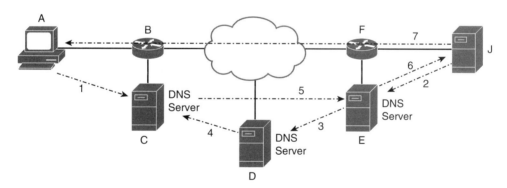

Figure 15-6 *DDNS Operation*

In this illustration:

1. Host A connects to a local network, receiving an IP address from Router B. On connection, Host A connects to a DDNS server (C), notifying the server of its current address. The IP address for this server can either be manually coded at Host A or provided by Router B while Host A is acquiring an IP address. Host A's DNS name must be manually coded for this signaling to work properly. The DDNS server (C) builds or modifies its DNS entry based on the information received from Host A.

2. Server J attempts to send a packet to Host A. At the operating system level, Server J realizes it has only a domain name for Host A (not an IP address), so it queries a local DNS server to find the correct IP address information for this domain name.

3. The local DNS server (E) discovers its local cached copy of the DNS information for Host A has timed out (more on this in a moment), so it queries through the DNS system as needed (in this case to a recursive, or perhaps authoritative server), to find the correct IP address.

4. The DNS query eventually recurses through to Host A's local DNS server (C).

5. A reply is sent back to the DNS server Server J originally queried (E).

6. This response is transmitted to J, which builds the correct local DNS to IP address mapping.

7. Server J now builds and transmits the packet originally destined to Host A.

The key point in the operation of DDNS is the amount of time each DNS server in the system—here Servers D and E—will keep the DNS to IP address mapping cached for future use. Normally, to reduce load, DNS servers will cache these mappings for some relatively long period of time, on the order of 24 hours. In the case of DDNS, the cache needs to (generally) be set low so that changes in the IP address of the mobile host are accurately reflected in the DNS system as soon as possible. Most of the time, DNS entries for DDNS are cached for a very short period of time, on the order of seconds, or they are not cached at all.

Final Thoughts on Mobility Solutions

To reemphasize a point made in the introduction, notice that each of these mobility solutions adds additional state someplace in the network. This might be said to be a more specific instance of the state versus stretch rule discussed in Chapter 14, "Considering Complexity"—and it's also a solid lesson in the concept of mobility in general. Every new mobility technology must perform the same actions in some way, and each of these actions require state of some sort to be stored someplace. It's important to ask where this state is stored, and how it's managed.

Given the available options, which one should you deploy? The answer depends on a fairly simple set of questions:

- Which one is available on the platforms and devices you'll be deploying?

- Which one stores state in a way that makes sense for your application and network? If a mobility system requires state to be carried in the control plane across your network core, it's probably not going to scale in the long term (unless you have a tightly controlled set of conditions under which new devices can be added to the mobility solution).

- Which one meets the requirements of your application? If you need fast convergence, you'll probably need to find a way to support the required state, regardless of whether it's optimal for your network design.

- What is the scope of the mobility solution in the network? If the entire mobility solution can be contained in a small topological region of the network, you can

control the spread of state in a way that effectively counters otherwise difficult scaling issues.

Remote Access Solutions

Mobility within a network is only one part of the problem facing network architects today—another entire realm of mobility is providing connectivity for hosts attached from the outside, such as through a mobile phone network or the Internet. The challenges in this space are far different from those designers face in the data center, network edge, or network core.

Remote access solutions span the scope from virtual desktop (VDI) to web-based access to some specific resources (through secure sockets, or SSL), to virtual private networks (VPN) that allow access to any resource anyplace on the network. Which of these is the right solution? It all depends on the needs of your users when they are out of the office.

The following sections cover several areas network architects need to take into account when designing for, or around, remote access solutions.

Separate Network Access from Application Access

Providing access to remote users doesn't always mean providing access to the network—it can mean providing access to just a handful of applications resident on the network. The first point to consider, then, when building a remote access solution, is to separate network access from application access.

Many designers start by assuming users need access to the network, including every application, remote access to file services—that users need to be able to access the network outside work in the same way they would inside work. This is a false assumption; most users don't want access to the network, but rather a specific set of applications residing on the network.

So the first step in determining how to best provide for remote access is to divide the concept of network access from the concept of application access. By focusing on application access, network designers can focus their efforts on providing what 80% of the users need for their day-to-day work, and then solve the remaining 20% using more complex solutions.

Email, most file shares, and many corporate applications could be made available through a web-based interface that is accessible through an SSL interface that doesn't force the user to dedicate the entire machine to the VPN process. If the application is running remotely, there is no reason to restrict access to local printers, ports, storage, or other resources, making the user experience much more seamless. These interfaces may not provide the full "at work" experience, but they often allow users to blend their personal lives with work in a way that reflects in the overall experience of the employee, raising productivity and loyalty.

When should you consider a full-on VPN solution? Two specific situations suggest full VPN connectivity.

The first is applications that simply can't be remotely accessed through a web or remote-friendly interface—or applications where it makes no sense, from a data flow perspective, to do so. The sheer size of the data transferred in order to replicate a remote environment locally can easily be larger than the data being manipulated.

The second is when the number of individual application access methods becomes more complex than the single network access method. If every employee must access 10 or 15 applications in the course of the employee's daily work, and each of these applications requires a different remote access process at the application level, it may quickly become cheaper and easier to manage a single network-level remote access system than a wide array of applications, each with its own remote access.

Consider Cloud-Based Solutions

A second point to consider in the world of remote access is the growing prevalence of cloud-based solutions to specific applications. Offloading an application to a cloud-based service allows you to separate the application from the network entirely, allowing partners and roaming employees to access the application without any VPN access at all, whether application or network level. There are, of course, trade-offs to be considered when moving an application to a cloud-based provider. (See Chapter 16, "On Psychologists, Unicorns, and Clouds," for a more detailed look.) Two crucial questions are

- How can the identity of a user be unified between the cloud-based service and internal network access? Resetting or changing the password on the internal network should somehow carry over to the cloud-based service; otherwise, you and your users must manage a menagerie of usernames and passwords. One possible solution to this problem is to build or take advantage of interfaces that allow credentials to be dynamically shared between different systems. An example of this type of interface is the Learning Tools Interoperability (LTI) project, which allows an external tool (such as Big Blue Button) to access the username and password credentials contained in a learning management tool (such as Moodle).

- How can corporate information be kept private in the cloud? Architects should be concerned about protecting corporate information in any cloud-based environment, from physical security through holes in the cloud-based authentication system, access by employees of the cloud provider, and many other issues.

It might seem like removing the VPN interface between the user and an application is a step down in security, but this isn't necessarily so—placing an application that needs to be accessed by employees and partners into the cloud might simplify security in many ways, and simplify network operation.

Keep Flexibility as a Goal

One of the major obstacles facing network architects in the space of remote access is the specificity of each possible solution. A remote access system designed for one email system might need to be completely scrapped when that email system is replaced with another. A VPN solution that's running well might need to be completely replaced when the hardware supporting it is moved to end of life status, or the company changes primary vendors.

A major consideration in remote access, then, must be flexibility in the face of change. Even if the entire backend must change, the user experience should stay as close to the same as possible. In many situations, this will mean not being able to solve every possible problem, or making the user experience all it might be, but rather balancing between the ability to migrate easily and current functionality.

If the application environment is changing constantly, a network-level VPN service might be best. On the other hand, if the network is always changing, individual application-level access might be best.

Virtual Desktop Solutions

One common solution in the remote access space is Virtual Desktop Interface (VDI); Figure 15-7 illustrates.

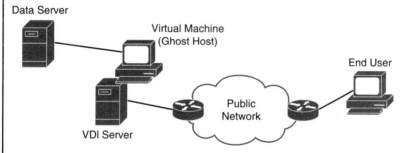

Figure 15-7 *Virtual Desktop Interface Solution*

A VDI system works in this way:

- The end user logs in to a server that kicks off a virtual machine. This virtual machine often loads a set of user-specific configurations and opens as a desktop within the user's desktop (a desktop within a desktop).

- The user opens applications, such as word processing and web browsers, that are displayed on this remote virtual desktop.

- As the user modifies the desktop, opening and editing files, opening web pages, and so on, the modifications to the screen on the virtual machine are transmitted over the network to the end user's machine, where they are displayed in the desktop within a desktop.

- The user's keystrokes and mouse movements are also transmitted over the network, so they appear to be local actions on the virtual machine.

In this way, the end user can manipulate data stored on the data server without having any actual access to the data from the end user's computer. Because data is not stored locally on the user's machine, it cannot (in theory) be downloaded, so there is no local information that can be stolen or otherwise compromised. This is an attractive solution for highly secure environments—or when the network managers want to provide remote access without worrying about the security or software installed on the end user's computer. Remote VDI provides a solid solution to the use of personal equipment in a corporate environment. But there are trade-offs and problems, as always.

The first point to consider is the amount of data being transmitted to the virtual machine versus the amount of data being transmitted to the end user's desktop within a desktop. For instance, consider the case of a user editing a word processing document stored on the data server. The information transmitted between the data server and the virtual machine is mostly just text, along with some embedded images. The information transmitted between the virtual machine and the end user's desktop within a desktop, however, is each screen modification, each keystroke, and each mouse movement. Essentially, we've converted text data into a video stream with near real-time feedback— so the bandwidth requirements for editing a text file suddenly become the same as watching a video. It's important to consider this as a trade-off when considering remote access through a VDI solution.

The second point to consider is how this relaying of information impacts quality of service—and application performance in a more general sense. For instance, assume the user opens a video conferencing package on the virtual machine and starts a video call. The video between the virtual machine and the data server serving the call is probably highly compressed, and the quality of service within the network configured to provide the right service level to the video traffic. Once this video stream is displayed on the virtual machine, it is suddenly placed inside a virtual desktop data stream, which will look just like the data stream of a user doing word processing. If you give the VDI data stream the same quality of service parameters as a video stream, you could well be eating a lot of queue space for word processing. If you give the VDI data stream the same quality of service parameters as a word processing application, carrying video from the remote virtual desktop to the user's actual desktop might not work so well. And then there's that public network in the middle. How can you control the user's experience across the Internet? Not very well.

Increased bandwidth consumption, quality of service, compressed data that becomes uncompressed, and controlling the user experience—are these good trade-offs to make against data and network protection? Because every situation is different, it's hard to give a general answer. But network architects should be aware of these issues and design their network around them.

Consider Total Cost

It's often easy to overlook the cost of creating and supporting remote access solutions. How much, for instance, does a single call into your technical assistance center cost? How many calls will be generated in a remote access system by issues that cannot be controlled by your network operations folks, such as dropped traffic across the Internet, local computer problems, and so on? How much will it cost in lost employee time when the remote user's access to the solution is unavailable?

Other hidden costs you should consider include the following:

- The cost of transporting desktop screenshots across a network (see the previous sidebar on VDI solutions).

- The added complexity of quality of service configuration and management (see the previous sidebar on VDI solutions).

- The trade-off between removing local access and loss of productivity. Many companies block employee access to local resources, such as printers and network attached storage, when the user is "dialed in" to a VPN service at the network level. Some companies even block access to all personal email, or all email services outside the corporate network, when the user is "dialed in." There are (sometimes) good reasons for doing this, specifically around the capability of a user's session being hijacked and used as a back door into the corporate network. There are, however, costs in terms of productivity. Each time the user wants to print out a document, the user must sign out, print, and then sign back in—a process that's not only disruptive to work flow, but also to online presence and availability.

Total cost not only needs to include the easier-to-measure budgetary impacts, but also costs to productivity, network operations, bandwidth requirements, and so on.

Consider Making Remote Access the Norm

One option in the remote access space is to unify all network and application access, no matter how the user is connected, through the remote access system. Although this might seem like a daunting task at first, or even possibly a nonsensical idea, it's actually a fairly realistic option in many situations. Making users access internal resources and applications through the same system, no matter where they are physically located, results in the following:

- It unifies user access across the enterprise. By making remote access the norm, you can force all authentication through a smaller, and more uniform, set of systems. Physical security onsite, when it comes to open Ethernet ports and wireless access, becomes less of an issue. This separation of the physical from the logical can sometimes pay huge dividends in simplification.

- It focuses access on a smaller set of systems, hence decreasing the attack surface of the enterprise. By focusing access on a few gateways into applications or the network

at large, you can actually decrease the overall attack surface of the enterprise at large, allowing you to focus on a smaller set of problems and deploy a smaller set of solutions.

- It unifies user experience across the enterprise. By unifying all access through systems that would normally be used for remote access, you inject a level of discipline into network operations and design that brings the experience of remote users into sharper focus, forcing the design to deal with remote access more fully. This, in turn, puts systems in place that allow more flexibility in siting and managing the workforce, with all the attendant benefits from a hiring, staffing, and quality of life perspective that brings.

In the end, it's worth considering unifying all application access through what would traditionally be considered remote access solutions for at least some large part of the enterprise users. Consistency can breed flexibility in these areas.

What Solution Should You Deliver?

Should you deliver remote access through SSL, IPsec, VDI, by transferring some applications to a cloud provider, or what? The bottom line is to consider each application separately. Provide 80% of your users' needs through application level access, using federated identity solutions to provide seamless credentials. Provide the rest of the requirements through a tightly controlled network level VPN service.

On Psychologists, Unicorns, and Clouds

There is an old joke that runs something like this: What is the difference between a neurotic, a psychotic, and a psychologist? Neurotics build castles in the sky, while psychotics live in them. Psychologists collect the rent. In networking terms, then, business managers dream of clouds that will resolve all their network problems, network engineers actually build these clouds, and service providers collect the rent.

At press time, it certainly does look like "the cloud" is taking over. Personal computer sales are collapsing, while the sales of mobile devices are reaching new highs. Companies are looking to "the cloud" to simplify their information technology infrastructures everywhere from networking to applications. Just dream up an application you need, build it, put it on a server someplace in the Internet (or private cloud), and you're done.

Sounds simple, right? Perhaps it's a little too simple—from unicorns to clouds, a general rule is: *if it sounds too good to be true, it is.*

The bottom line is that cloud is good for some things and not so good for others.

So networking professionals, from engineering to architecture, shouldn't panic. What goes around comes around. As an example, consider the case of the collapsing computer sales. The underlying reality is that there have always been more consumers of data than creators. One person makes a movie and thousands (or millions) watch it.

Precloud, there wasn't much difference between devices that could create content and devices that could consume it. The hardware needed for creating a movie wasn't that much different from the hardware needed for watching one—and the personal computer was, in fact, the smallest and most practical form factor that could do both.

The "mobile revolution," in partnership with "the cloud," has effectively split the creators from the consumers, in terms of hardware. Creators need local processing, local storage, and wide open software that allows the creation and modification of a wide variety of mixed media. Think of the photographer who does in-depth photo retouching to bring out a unique style or the absolute best results on an individual basis, or a movie creator

who builds unique and interesting environments from scratch, combining recorded video, computer generated graphics, and other elements.

Content consumers download video, compressed and optimized for a particular device, or a book that has been marked up and managed to prevent sharing, or some other digital content. Even the quick snapshot—the phone picture type of content creation—falls into the realm of content consumption. The user takes a quick picture, and then uses software that will run across a predefined space of options to modify the image. The user is consuming the software, rather than creating in the larger sense.

So now the creators—and the creative piece of our lives—have been split from the consumers—or the consuming part of our lives. The dream of replacing local storage and local processing with "the cloud," is just that, a dream, so long as we value creativity and creation in the larger sense. Getting rid of a laptop in favor of a tablet might work for a CEO, who mostly creates through relationships rather than through content, but it will never be an option for authoring a book that's different from anything that went before, or laying out a coffee table book full of images that doesn't fall into one of the various "standard layouts" offered through a service.

Pendulums swing, and to prove the point, we'll start our examination of cloud computing with a look back through the history of information technology, so we can put it all in context.

A Cloudy History

In the beginning, there were mainframes. Network engineers were primarily folks who installed TN3270 cards in Z100 (and later Z250s!), strung 4-wire telephone cables to each workstation, and set up modems, multiplexers, and reverse multiplexers. Computers were big boxes that sat in special rooms; terminals were what you had on the desktop, and all computing, from processing to storage, happened in these rooms. Often these rooms had glass windows so "normal" people could walk by and envy the computer geeks working on all that massive—and massively interesting—equipment. Most information technology people loved this environment because IT was firmly in control of the entire computing environment. Terminals were too expensive for ordinary folks to buy—and what would you connect a terminal to if you had one anyway?

In a way, this was the original cloud computing environment.

Over time, personal computers replaced terminals. It wasn't an easy transition—personal computers were purchased out of departmental budgets and hidden in closets so no one would know about them. Lotus 123 was installed, and data copied from the mainframe terminal into these spreadsheets so financial figures could be run. People bought and ran TRS-80s at home to play text-based games loaded into memory from cassette drives. IT didn't like the spread of information into devices they couldn't control—so, eventually, the IT department moved in and took over the management and control of all those personal computers.

The computing world entered the first phase of distributed computing, where data is stored and processed close to the user, rather than in a central location. We built Xerox Star networks on Thicknet, dropping heavy cables through vertical plenums in buildings that were never designed for this type of cabling, tapping the cable to run Thinnet to individual workstations. Or we would install ARCnet over the exiting 4-wire telephone lines using equipment that would need to be replaced after every lightning storm.

When John needed to share a file, or a set of files for a project, with Jane, we added file servers—and from file servers came database servers, middleware, SQL, and an entire world of centralized databases. The IT world moved all the data back into central data stores, and the computing world began its second centralization phase. Minicomputers and mainframes were back in style, only accessed through middleware. We were going to "right size" data processing at last, putting the right processing and the right data in the right places all the time.

But then mobility took off. Laptops replaced desktops, and personal data assistants came in alongside mobile phones (at least until the mobile phones took over). Wireless networks extended the range of high-speed local networks, and the Internet drove content "online," making things easier to find from anywhere. Software and data returned to local storage, and the computing industry entered its second decentralization phase.

Today, mobility has taken the driver's seat in computing; people want their data all the time, anywhere they are. But the devices we want this data on don't have the computing power to store and process all that information. So we return to the mainframe again—only this time we call it "the cloud." Figure 16-1 illustrates this swing between centralized and decentralized through the history of computing.

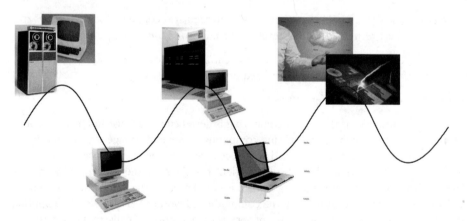

Figure 16-1   *Cycles of Centralization and Decentralization*

What's the point of this history? To point out that we've been through all this before. We've centralized because computing power was expensive and data was easier to control. We've decentralized because computing power was cheap, and local data facilitates more creative uses of data, more personal ownership, and faster processing. Now we're centralizing because, once again, computing power in the sizes of devices we prefer is

expensive, and because centralized control of data is better for various commercial interests (content creators, in this case).

Centralization is going to protect our data, decentralization is going to give us productivity. Centralization is going to make computing cheaper, decentralization is going to make computing ubiquitous. The pendulum swings back and forth—and it's not going to stop swinging on this pass through the arc anymore than it has in the past.

Maybe it's time for the computing world to look at the problem a little differently. It's fun to chase the fashion world's changing hem lines and tie widths; it's not so much fun to chase our data into and out of distributed systems.

What is the right answer?

How many balloons fit in a bag?

It depends.

To begin our investigation into cloud computing, let's start by trying to understand how it's different from all the past attempts to centralize computing.

This Time It's Different

For a thousand years, people have been trying to discover a process that will convert lead to gold—and it's never worked. *But this time it's different.*

For two hundred years, people have been trying to invent a perpetual motion machine—and it's never worked. *But this time it's different.*

For hundreds of years, people have been trying to regulate economies "scientifically" to produce the "best results"—and it's never worked. *But this time it's different.*

For twenty years, people have been trying to centralize processing and storage—and every time we've gone back to decentralized processing and storage.

Shouldn't we ask why it's different this time?

The primary difference is that cloud computing is designed to package and manage computing services as a commodity. Treating computing power and storage as a commodity allows services to be narrowly focused and priced based on volume and usage patterns, rather than on the customized needs of a particular business. In the customized world of IT we live in today, software and data storage is built based on the requirements of a particular business (or business unit). In the commoditized world of IT that cloud computing represents, it's up to you to find the set of services from those available that will best fulfill your needs. It's the difference between buying a car that's been completely customized for your tastes and purposes and buying a car from among the models available on the lots of local dealerships right now.

Commoditization isn't, in and of itself, a bad thing. IT projects have a long and storied history of running over their budget and schedule—most of the time because the requirements are inevitably a moving target—much like building a car for someone who keeps

discovering more things his car must be able to do. IT projects always start with a simple goal—I want to commute from home to work while using the smallest amount of gas possible. Then the buyer remembers he needs to be able to carry his kids to soccer games, adding four more people and a lot of equipment to the load. When the car is half built, he suddenly remembers the boat he was just about to buy, so the car has to be hastily refitted with a hitch and a new engine.

Commoditization short circuits this process, enforcing discipline on the buyer. Various kinds of cars are available today—right now—at various dealers. The buyer needs to make a list of requirements, compare and contrast the available models against this list of requirements, determine which trade-offs make sense, and then make a purchasing decision.

But commoditization also represents a trade-off. As commoditization sets in, choices narrow—and as choices narrow, the ability to differentiate your products and services, based on the data you manage and use on a daily basis as a part of your business processes, declines. One of the challenges, moving into a cloud-centric world, is going to be balancing between taking advantage of commoditization while holding on to the differentiation that makes your business unique.

Don't be fooled, at this point, by the old line, "We don't sell information, we sell widgets." No, you don't sell widgets. Anyone can make widgets anyplace in the world and sell them anyplace else in the world. "Make a better mouse trap and the world will beat a path to your door," is true only if you can actually build the better mouse trap (based on intellectual property), and the world can find out about your mouse trap. Information is integral to this process—and commoditizing information carries with it the risk of making your mouse trap that much less unique (in fact, as we'll discuss in the section "What Are the Risks?", you might be handing the information that makes your mouse trap unique to someone else along the way).

So what's the solution to this conundrum? The solution is to choose the right solution for each problem. The section "What's It Good For?" covers some of the different types of cloud services, and where they might fit best.

For the moment, let's turn to the cost of cloud, to get a better grasp on how much commoditization is really going to save you. Or, perhaps, cost you.

What Does It Cost?

Do you know how much it would cost to move from an internal service to a cloud-based service for all your data processing needs? Do you really know the cost, or are you just guessing? Is cloud really cheaper? Let's think through some of the costs to get a better handle on the things you need to look for when considering moving to a cloud-based service.

First, remember that the network still isn't free. Delivering data from a remote hard drive to local memory and computing power requires hardware, power, skills, management—everything you think of when you think about running a network. Outsourcing data processing to a cloud puts all this work into a black box, so it doesn't look complex—but

don't be fooled into thinking all that work still doesn't need to be done. Someone has to pay for the network between you and your data. And that someone is going to be you, no matter how you slice it.

Second, remember that you can't outsource all the complexity in your network. Data is separated through virtualization to support different access policies and varying quality of service requirements in your network today. Access is controlled through AAA mechanisms, traffic flows are analyzed, intrusion detection systems are deployed to detect and shut down attacks and virus incursions, and a thousand other things need to be done. Outsourcing your data to a cloud provider isn't going to change any of these things.

Third, remember that outsourcing data and processing is always a trade-off. Sometimes that trade-off results in a win/win, sometimes a win/lose, and sometimes a lose/lose. There are costs associated with pushing data and processing to a cloud that might not be apparent or easy to account for. Managing SLAs and relationships are not cost-free or simple activities.

By outsourcing IT services, you are reducing complexity in one place at the cost of increased complexity elsewhere. These things aren't easy to measure and quantify, but they are important to consider.

What Are the Risks?

The primary risks you need to think through when moving to a cloud environment are security and accessibility. Much has been made of the security issue within the cloud environment, but it's far from a solved problem. Should data that's stored offsite in a cloud provider's network be encrypted? Should you turn off your engine before you start filling your car with gas?

But making certain data stored in a cloud is encrypted isn't enough—what type of encryption is in use, and who has the key? A general rule, in terms of encrypted data, is that if you don't have the key, the data might as well not be encrypted. Whoever owns the key, in essence, owns the data. In practical terms, this means that you need to make certain applications you use that store data on the cloud store that data in an encrypted format.

Why is this important? Consider what happens when a cloud provider swaps the physical media they use to store data in their server. Are the old hard drives (or other media) properly handled to ensure your data isn't exposed or compromised? What about if a tornado comes through and knocks the walls out of the provider's building, leaving hard drives scattered all over parking lots. Can someone pick a hard drive up and reconstruct the information on which you base your business? The only way to be certain of the answers to these questions is to encrypt your data before you hand it over to a cloud services provider to store it.

Encryption is important for data being carried to and from the cloud service, as well; data that would normally be protected by ensuring it only crosses links and devices you control should now be encrypted as it passes to and from a cloud service.

There is a flip side to this equation, of course—while centralized data is easier to attack, it's also easier to defend. Remember that villages built castles in the Middle Ages for a reason. By gathering together in a single place behind well-fortified walls, they could reduce their defensive perimeter, making defense much easier than offense. Information stored in a cloud system might be easier to find and attack, but it may also be defended by a set of services and controls that you can't afford to build into your local network. Both sides of this coin need to be considered to make an intelligent decision.

Another security issue that's often overlooked is how the provider will treat, or use, your data. One way to reduce the costs of providing an application or service is to mine the data stored in your service to create value that can then be sold. For instance, if you outsource your email services to a cloud provider, one question you should ask is whether the provider plans to mine the emails passing through the provider to discover information that can be sold to a third party. The capability of data analysis algorithms to find trends and facts you, yourself, aren't aware of could pose a risk of leaking information about business plans, supplier issues, and other material.

If the service is free, you are the product. If the service costs less than it should (in relation to the actual infrastructure and management required to provide the service), the provider must be offsetting that cost in some way—probably through selling information gleaned from examining your data as it passes across the provider's network.

Risks in the cloud space don't end with security concerns—anytime you outsource any service, you're going to need to deal with the problems associated with the friction between two different organizations with two different sets of goals. If the service provided through the cloud is simple, more akin to providing coffee to break rooms than the complex contracts associated with information technology outsourcing, then moving information into the cloud can externalize political issues, making them simpler to resolve. If the services being placed into the cloud are complex, however, contracting out the development of a new internal software system might end up looking simple in the end.

The key is to determine the right level of care and feeding a particular cloud service is going to need. Don't assume that cloud computing, because it represents a commodity model of purchasing storage, data processing, or even application services, will let you off the hook of doing the work normally associated with outsourcing some part of your network or IT infrastructure.

In short—there ain't no such thing as a free lunch (TANSTAAFL—with a bow to Robert Heinlein)!

What Problems Can Cloud Solve Well?

To understand what problems cloud is good at solving, we need to consider some specific aspects of the way cloud services interact with existing infrastructures and business processes.

First, because cloud is designed to be a commodity service, cloud is going to be good at cutting costs for those pieces of your business that don't really provide competitive

differentiation. For instance, if you sell books, there are only so many ways that books can be distributed to buyers—the scope of the problem is limited by the delivery systems to which your customers are connected and by the software and operating systems your customers have available to them. Cloud services of various types can simplify the distribution of your books (unless distribution is really a competitive differentiator in your line of business), cutting distribution costs to a minimal level while reaching the broadest possible audience.

To extend the advantages cloud gains through being a commodity service—cloud separates your business operations from the risks and complexity of managing low-level systems by converting them into a service. This means you don't need to think about how much storage capacity you'll need in a year, for instance; that problem is abstracted behind the commodity interface of a cloud service. You can think of a cloud service as an abstracted "black box," separate from the failure domains and complexity of your network.

Second, for services that interact with individual mobile devices, it's important to keep in mind that most of the networks mobile devices connect to are designed to download data, rather than upload it. In the mobile world, cloud services are going to be better at distributing data than they are at collecting it. The type of data is going to matter, of course—small files, simple responses on forms, and the like are perfectly suited to a cloud environment. An application that uploads large amounts of high-quality video probably isn't as well suited for cloud services.

Finally, data that's put into the cloud—at least in the case of public cloud services—is available (in theory), anywhere and anytime. Again, this points to public cloud services being very useful for data distribution or low overhead data collection services. On the other hand, if the data is available anytime from anywhere, you suddenly have a huge attack surface to manage—this probably isn't a good thing. We'll say more about how cloud services interact with attack surfaces in the section "Cloud Deployment."

Now let's move from what cloud services are good at to what they are good for.

What Services Is Cloud Good at Providing?

There's not, of course, a single answer to this question—so we're going to give you a bunch of different answers. Most of these answers revolve around the way the cloud is built, or a generic "class of service," that the cloud provider offers. It's more interesting to think of cloud services as quasi-commodity; like buying a car, or a new set of clothes, there are varying degrees of customization, service levels, and price ranges available. In the following sections, we consider several situations where cloud services might be useful.

Storage

Storage is already common enough on the cloud that there's little to be said about it—from backup to synchronized drives to cold storage, there's little that isn't available in the

realm of storage in the world of cloud computing. The attractive qualities of cloud-based storage solutions are these:

- The data stored in a cloud service is accessible from anywhere, so cloud services are often an easy way to provide for widely diversified data replication.

- The data stored in a cloud service is generally backed up and well managed.

There are downsides, of course, including these:

- The cost of cloud-based data storage can still be very high compared to buying the hardware to support the same storage requirements on local drives.

- The cost of the network must be factored in, particularly in areas where network providers charge per unit of data transferred. Even when they don't, transferring large amounts of data into a cloud-based storage solution can be painful, taking up many hours (or days).

- Delays in transferring data may cause backup solutions to be so far behind in their scheduling that the user still loses a large amount of data if local storage fails. A lot of solutions aren't very transparent about how much of your local data is backed up, or how quickly backups can be made.

- Your data is essentially unsecure, no matter what the provider promises. If you don't hold the key to the encryption process, your data is at risk—no matter how much encryption is provided elsewhere.

For an enterprise (or small business), cloud-based storage solutions can provide effective access to files collected for projects; combined with a solid versioning and check in/check out system, cloud-based storage can provide universal access to documents that need to be shared in near real time. So long as the security aspects are handled correctly, cloud-based storage can be an effective solution for a wide array of problems.

Content Distribution

Cloud tends to be a really good distribution channel because most service provider networks are designed to provide a lot more download bandwidth than upload. Movies, music, and books are increasingly placed on cloud-based services for distribution to a wide array of end customers (or consumers). A less well-known area of cloud content distribution is software; a number of companies are distributing software on a subscription basis, keeping applications installed on local devices updated, and managing the transfer of small amounts of data (such as highlights in a book) across multiple platforms.

For an enterprise, this type of service might be ideal to manage the applications installed on thousands of devices scattered across a wide geographical area. The downside of this type of installation is the loss of control over environment and content an enterprise might encounter.

Database Services

Storage and distribution can morph into database storage with some additional intelligence. Like other data stored on a cloud provider connected to the public Internet, a database, and the logic embedded in the database, can be accessed from applications installed and managed on a wide array of devices scattered all over the globe. The security considerations discussed in regard to cloud storage solutions will apply to cloud-based database solutions, as well—think about who holds the encryption key and what the trust model looks like.

An example would be a database system that's accessible over the global Internet. Application creators might use this service to store high scores in a shared gaming environment, or the locations of every coffee shop in the United States for a mapping software package, or some other data. The developer builds an application (or app) that retrieves information from this globally available database, allowing the information to be stored once and retrieved many times.

Application Services

An example of an application service provided over a public cloud might be an email system that offers a web-based interface instead of (or in addition to) an interface that local email clients would use to send and receive messages. Application services often work best when the flow of data is more download than upload, because edge networks are often optimized to provide optimal download services. Application services rely on the cloud for processing power as well as storage. Public application services can be used to support applications and processing that isn't unique, or can be easily commoditized— where one or two sizes fit all.

An example of a private application service might be a custom application to support technicians who travel around the world working on a specific type of computer system. This application might include data, such as diagrams, specifications, and spare parts information, but also an interactive troubleshooting and repair system.

Network Services

Network services are an old, but new, entry in the field of cloud. A VPN concentrator that allows users from all over the world to connect to a cloud service, and then tunnel into a corporate network, is one example. Another example of network service provided over a private cloud might be DDoS mitigation; traffic is redirected into the service, "scrubbed" to remove attack traffic, and then carried over the Internet or through a private peering point back to the original destination.

The key selling point for these types of services is the relatively high concentration of specialized equipment and expertise required to deal with the problem at hand. Hard problems that require specialized equipment and deep expertise are likely candidates for transitioning to this type of service.

Security is a primary consideration in deploying cloud-based networking services. Who gets to look at your traffic, and what do they do with the information they find? Management is another issue; what is the impact on your ability to accurately measure traffic flow and trends if you're pushing your inbound traffic through a DDoS mitigation service?

Deploying Cloud

One of the key points vendors will make in selling a cloud service is the ease with which cloud services can be deployed and managed—but it's important to keep telling yourself, "There is no such thing as a free lunch." Let's think through some of the issues you need to consider when deploying an application or service in the cloud.

How Hard Is Undoing the Deployment?

Data mobility is a concern for both Software as a Service (SaaS) and Infrastructure as a Service (IaaS) cloud services—after you get your data in, how easy is it to get your data out? If you build up a lot of information about customers, suppliers, products, and leads in a cloud-based sales management application, for instance, what happens to all that data when you decide it's time to switch?

- How long does it take to get the data out?

- How much does it cost to get the data out?

- Will referential integrity be maintained between related tables or information?

- What happens to binary and custom data fields when the data is pulled out?

- What happens to customized business logic if the data is pulled out? How can this be captured?

- When considering outsourcing, consider the service's ability to export data. What formats does the service support? How long does it take to export the data? How much does it cost?

How Will the Service Connect to My Network?

"Well, you're connected to the Internet, right? Then you're connected to the cloud service!" It might sound that simple, but it rarely is that simple—particularly for platform as a service (PaaS) and infrastructure as a service (IaaS) services. Databases must be built, applications written, and other "stuff" uploaded. If the application you're building is "internal only," designed to be built on a private cloud only for users connected to your network, how will your network connect to the private cloud service?

Not only is security an issue here, but also simple things, such as IP addresses. Will the cloud provider address its resources within your private numbering plan? Does the provider use public address space, and how will that interact with your routing and network policy?

These are areas where complexity can sneak up on you, so pay particular attention to connectivity issues before making a final decision on using (or moving to) a cloud service.

How Does Security Work?

Network architectures often rely on "defense in depth," where policy is implemented in multiple places through the network. Defense in depth provides resilience in network security; the attacker who must move through multiple security points, each using a different type of security, is going to move more slowly.

But defense in depth relies on the depth of the network to provide those policy implementation points. Moving to a cloud service, particularly in the case of public cloud services, means the security edge moves from your network to someone else's—the only security mechanisms you have left are those built into the application.

Don't forget about traffic monitoring and attack detection, either. Normally, the depth of the network allows you to monitor traffic going to and coming from a service at some distance from the service itself, allowing you to put devices on which you can implement reactive security measures in front of the service itself. How will this work with a cloud-based service? Can you place virtual routers, switches, firewalls, or other devices in front of your virtual server? Will any of them do any good against attacks that eat the bandwidth between the rack and the physical server your service is running on?

Systemic Interactions

Finally, moving a single system or application to the cloud might be simple—but what happens when another service moves to another cloud provider, and a third to a third cloud provider, and...? What will happen when you have a lot of different outsourced pieces that need to be managed—and what happens when a previously unthought of connection suddenly becomes obvious? After you've outsourced the service, how quickly can you really reconfigure it, or rebuild it on a different service? And how can the various services you're putting into the cloud interconnect?

Abstracting complexity out of your network is generally a good thing—until the abstraction ends up causing more complexity than it removes. It's often hard to see these situations after you get trapped in the routine of dealing with it on a day-to-day basis, so you need to think this through as much as possible before building or moving services into the cloud.

Flying Through the Cloud

Now that we've looked at the cloud as an abstraction—a set of services with attendant advantages, disadvantages, and risks—let's lift the hood a little and try to understand just what a cloud service looks like. While the way in which a cloud service is built is as individual as the service provided by the cloud, there is a set of common themes running through storage, database, and application cloud services. Each of these services is generally built

like a large multiprocessor system, with an operating system, a hardware interface, a set of interfaces, and a set of applications running on top. Figure 16-2 illustrates.

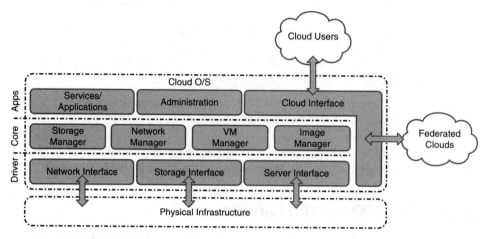

Figure 16-2   *Cloud Components*

Components

Each of the components in the application layer does pretty much what you would expect: running the actual applications sited on the cloud, providing a provisioning and management interface, and providing a public (or external) interface to users. The core is more interesting, containing the following:

■ The *storage manager* controls the location of data on physical storage units, which are connected to the processors across a network or fabric. The fabric used to connect storage and processors could be dedicated, or shared with network management and user access. Storage is normally divided from processing to allow more flexibility in placing workload on available processors, and to break storage and processor scaling into two different problems. Even in the cloud, failure domain separation is a solid design principle.

■ The *network manager* manages available bandwidth, connections, and quality of service to meet the needs of the cloud service. This service might be skinny, in the case where the distributed control plane within the network handles most of the control plane functions. In an SDN (see Chapter 17, "Software-Defined Networks," for more information on SDNs), the network manager could be tightly integrated with the rest of the cloud operating system.

■ The *virtual machine* (VM) manager controls the VMs needed for applications and services running on the cloud. This includes the placement of these VMs (which physical processor or core the VM is placed on), the VM's connection to storage, the amount of memory the VM may use, and other factors.

■ The *image manager* provides a library of images that can be loaded on a VM after it is spun up. An image may contain a base operating system, a set of applications,

a set of mappings to a particular storage location, and other configuration elements stored as a part of each image. Images may be classified as publicly accessible, private, tied to a particular application or service, generic, or in other ways.

These four elements, combined with the federated cloud interface, make up the core of the cloud operating system. In the operating system running on a desktop computer, these services might be implemented through a series of Dynamically Linked Libraries (DLLs) the operating system calls to perform certain functions.

A *scheduler* is often included in a cloud operating system (although it may be contained within the VM manager). The scheduler may be considered part of the core or an application, depending on the specific cloud operating system deployed. As workload is placed on the cloud, the scheduler interacts with the storage, network, VM, and image managers to determine when and where the application or other load can be run.

Looking Back Over the Clouds

Centralized computing and distributed computing—the information technology world has been shifting back and forth ever since the first screen of data was "scraped" off a terminal window to be processed with a spreadsheet running on a computer locked in a closet. Will we ever find the right answer?

No, probably not.

But asking the right questions can go a long way toward knowing which type of computing power is right for each specific problem at hand. Be open minded, think carefully about the costs, and don't get crushed under the next swing of the pendulum.

Software-Defined Networks

As networks have become both more crucial to business operations and more complex to operate, they have also become expensive to build and manage. This combination of realities has led the network world to seek solutions beyond the network management and protocol realms, specifically in a concept called the Software-Defined Network (SDN). In this chapter, we'll begin with a discussion of what an SDN is, and present one specific taxonomy, or method of classifying SDNs. After this, we'll discuss some business cases for SDNs.

Understanding SDNs

What, precisely, is an SDN? What sort of framework can we use to understand how an SDN works and what it does? This section is one set of answers to these two fundamental questions—a number of other answers to these questions are available, as well, but the definitions here are attuned to the interaction between design, business, and the network.

A Proposed Definition

An SDN can be defined as a network where there is an application programming interface (API) into the network that allows applications to both understand and react to the state of the network in near real time. Isn't this the job of network management? Three specific points separate network management from SDNs:

- SDNs are an interface into the *network* rather than *individual network components.*

- SDNs interact directly with some level of the data plane (or the forwarding table) rather than primarily the configuration and current state.

- SDNs focus on the forwarding of traffic through the network, or the control plane, rather than on "whole box health."

Although it's difficult to precisely define what an SDN is, it's even more difficult to classify SDNs, or to determine what is "in" the SDN world and what is "out." Are implementations that centralize all control, taking the role of distributed control planes over completely, the only "real" SDNs? What about applications that modify traffic forwarding by installing static routes through the command-line interface?

A Proposed Framework

The framework presented here isn't designed to replace all other possible taxonomies, but rather to provide one view of the SDN world that might prove to be useful, particularly to network designers and architects. Rather than focusing on the bits and bytes of how each proposed solution works, this model attempts to expose how any particular solution interacts with applications and other network elements.

This framework is based on two points:

- Where the SDN injects information into routers and switches (forwarding devices)

- How the information injected by the SDN interacts with other control planes

Figure 17-1 provides the background for a discussion about where information is injected into forwarding devices.

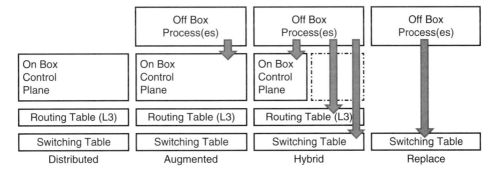

Figure 17-1   *Software-Defined Networking Frameworks*

Four models are presented here:

- The *Distributed* model ties the forwarding hardware to a fully distributed control plane.

- The *Augmented* model uses a fully onboard control plane that is augmented, or managed, in some way by off-device processes.

- The *Hybrid* model uses on and off box processes in parallel.

- The *Replace* model moves the control plane completely off the forwarding devices and into off-box processes.

Each of these models is described in more detail in the following sections.

The Distributed Model

The *Distributed* model within this framework isn't really considered a form of SDN because it doesn't meet the core tests. There is no API into the control plane that is designed to provide a tight loop between applications and the forwarding of traffic through the network. The lack of such an interface means there is no way to distribute policy at the forwarding level either at the routing protocol, routing table, or forwarding table in any or all devices in the network. Examining this model in some detail will help us understand the remaining models, however.

Although we tend to think of a router or switch as a hardware/software combination that all works as one unit, the reality is far different. Within most modern routers and switches there is a clear separation between the control and data planes. Figure 17-2 provides an overview of the architecture of most modern routers and switches.

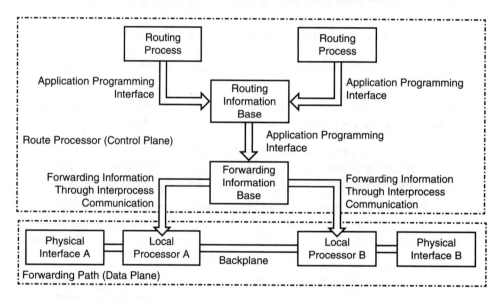

Figure 17-2   *Model of Router Operation*

To follow a single packet as it is switched through the device illustrated in Figure 17-2:

1. The packet enters at Physical Interface A, which is responsible for reading the packet off the media into local memory (normally this memory is located on a line card).

2. Physical Interface A then sends a software signal (an interrupt) to Local Processor A noting that a new packet is available for processing.

3. Local Processor A looks in a local table to determine the correct outbound interface and line card. If this information isn't available in a local table (if the local table happens to be a cache), then the packet (or information about the packet) must be punted to the Route Processor to create the correct entries in the local table; this is called a *punt*. Most modern routers do not punt packets.

4. Local Processor A replaces the current packet header with a new one appropriate for the outbound physical link (this is called the *MAC header rewrite*).

5. The packet is placed on the backplane so it can be transported to Local Processor B, where it is read off the backplane into memory local to the line card.

6. Local Processor B performs any additional processing required, and places the packet onto the correct queue for output.

7. Physical Interface B reads the packet from memory and onto the physical media.

The route processor, the actual set of processes on which the distributed control plane protocols (such as EIGRP and OSPF) run, doesn't normally participate in the switching of packets from one interface to another, but it does run on hardware that is "just across the bus" from where packet switching is done. This tight coupling between the control plane and data plane hardware provides some advantages, including very short delays between the control and data plane, allowing the control plane to interact with the data plane in near real time. The distribution of network state throughout the network also makes it possible for the control plane to react to changes in the network topology in near real time.

The negative impacts of tightly coupling the control plane and the data plane and distributing control plane data across the entire network are the following:

■ A single view of the network—end-to-end, application to transport—doesn't exist on any single device anywhere in a distributed control plane, making it difficult to understand and adjust network conditions as a whole on a near real-time basis.

■ Policy, or rather exceptions to the normal routing rules, must follow the distributed control plane throughout the network in the form of configuration on individual routes and switches. There is no single place or "control point" where policy can be injected so it is applied in the right places, at the right time.

The first step in moving from a fully distributed model to some form of SDN is to move some part of the control plane out of the physical device where packets are switched—to break the tight coupling between the data and control planes. The amount and type of separation imposed by any given SDN model will vary, but an SDN will always have more distance between the control and data planes than a fully distributed model.

The Augmented Model

The *Augmented* model provides an outside element of visibility and control to a limited part of the network (typically one, or a handful, of routers), using a disparate set of tools. Normally, distributed routing is augmented by modifying the configuration of policy on individual devices, which then impacts the operation of the distributed control plane in some way.

Consider, for example, devices that react to inbound Denial of Service (DoS) attacks by injecting information in the routing protocol to block the attack traffic at all inbound

edges simultaneously. Such a device would run a routing protocol, like BGP, solely for the purpose of injecting policy information into the routing system, not to provide reachability information. Another example would be a device that monitors several available links for performance, cost, and other factors, and then uses various means to configure static routing information on a device to modify the path chosen.

Cisco's Performance Routing (PfR), for instance, is a second example, although PfR moves closer to the SDN realm than modifying route policies through filtering, or the injection of black hole routers. PfR uses a dedicated API to interact directly with the router. This dedicated API can be used to examine a narrow set of states within the router, such as specific routes or interface information, and to inject routes into the routing table (RIB) by creating static routes.

Because of its low impact on existing network control planes, and the narrow nature of its solution set, Augmented models are widely deployed in many networks. But is the Augmented model truly an SDN? While the lines have begun to blur, the narrowness of the feedback loop—it's held to single applications in small sections of the network— would lead most engineers in the network world to conclude augmented control planes are not, in fact, a form of SDN.

What we do see in the Augmented model is the idea of near real-time imposition of policy in near real time by devices that do not (fully) participate in the distributed control plane. This is the second step in moving from a distributed control plane implementation to some form of an SDN.

The Hybrid Model

The goal of the *Hybrid* model is to allow distributed routing to do the major work of building a loop-free topology and providing forwarding information for the majority of traffic, while allowing policy (exceptions to the loop-free topology for specific applications), to be managed in a more centralized manner.

The Hybrid model combines the two steps we've covered thus far—moving at least some of the control plane into off-box processes with near real-time policy—so that applications can interact with the network directly. This is the first "real" SDN model with what can be classified as an API into the network, including a feedback loop and the availability of near real-time information on end-to-end conditions in the network.

The Hybrid model opens an API into the RIB (and potentially the forwarding engine) directly, providing off-box processes the capability to interact with the routing table in the same way as distributed routing processes. The off-box process essentially acts like another routing process, interacting with the RIB and other routing processes running on the device as a routing process. In this case, the API between the RIB and the routing processes is opened into, in effect, a Remote Procedure Call (RPC), so processes not located on the device can interact with the RIB directly.

Direct RIB interaction not only allows the remote process to install routes in the routing table as a local process would, it also allows the remote process to redistribute routes to

and from other routing processes through the RIB, and to discover each device's view of the network topology from a local perspective.

Interface to the Routing System (I2RS)

One example of the Hybrid model is the RIB interface of the IETF's Interface to the Routing System (I2RS).

Note   I2RS is actually a superset of an Augmented model. Other interfaces include the ability to modify policy (or configuration, depending on your perspective), and route import/export.

I2RS' RIB interface includes:

- Route preference, so the RIB can decide which route among those offered by different routing protocols to install

- Route metric, so multiple routes within the off-box routing process can be properly managed (including backup paths for fast reroute)

- Route process identifiers, which makes it possible to redistribute between various on- and off-box routing processes

- Interaction with route import and export

- Interaction with VLANs, VRFs, and the like

- Call backs for route installation, removal, and other events

From the RIB's perspective, the I2RS off-box process behaves precisely like an on-box process. The off-box process might be anything from a routing policy engine to a specialized implementation of BGP.

Depending on any particular vendor's implementation, it's possible for the I2RS off-box process to have a local database of routes, like the BGP table, a link state LSDB, or an EIGRP topology table. This sort of local table would facilitate faster callbacks, installation of backup routes, redistribution events, and other interactions with the RIB, as well as providing a local source for the off-box's RIB independent table for troubleshooting and management purposes.

Cisco OnePK

Another example of the Hybrid model is the Cisco's OnePK interface (although OnePK could also be considered a superset of an SDN, rather than a pure example of one). The OnePK API is essentially a set of libraries a developer can pull into either a C compiler or a Java virtual machine environment that allows direct access to a number of data structures on a Cisco router. The data structures include the following:

- The Routing Information Base (RIB)

- Interface statistics and other information

- Netflow information

- Routing policy

OnePK also allows for the interception of flows so the packets themselves can be modified. For instance, it's possible to build a small application that intercepts the Telnet traffic passing through a router to make trivial changes, such as encrypting their contents.

The pieces of OnePK that are most interesting from an SDN perspective are those that overlap with I2RS' interaction with the routing table, above—specifically, the capability to install routes in the routing table, examine the contents of the routing table, modify control plane policy, and other similar capabilities.

Hybrid Mode and the Rope Problem

The main drawback to hybrid mode is that it does, in fact, act just like an off-box routing protocol—at least from the dynamic control plane's perspective. Just like all other routing processes, then, any off-box hybrid mode controller must take into account existing routing conditions before injecting routes, or modifications to routes, into the local RIB.

The simplest way to think of this is two routing protocols running as "ships in the night," where the combined effect of the two protocols is to produce a permanent loop in the control plane routing information. Static routes are a prominent example; hybrid mode SDNs must avoid the "static effect" by being careful to interact with the routing table in near real time, rather than simply injecting routing information without regard to the existing state of the network.

The Replace Model

The *Replace* model is what most network engineers think of when they think of SDNs— moving the entire control plane from the individual routers and switches to a centralized control system. The control system might be a single controller, or it might be a distributed system of controllers spread throughout the network that run protocols among themselves to distribute policy and forwarding information as needed. The Replace model opens the API between the FIB and the hardware controllers, or the RIB and the FIB, in effect allowing the controller to program the individual entries in the switching devices themselves. The IETF FORCES working group and OpenFlow are examples of replacing the entire in-box control plane with an off-box system of controllers distributed throughout the network.

Replace model SDNs can be deployed in a variety of ways, some of which are similar to traditional networking models, and others of which are completely foreign to traditional networking.

Offline Routing/Online Reaction

Traditional networking models put the control plane in-band, which means control plane packets are carried over the same links as data traffic. This allows the control plane to react to changes in the network topology by recalculating the best path to reach a given destination in near real time—when a link or node fails, a routing protocol discovers the failure, propagates information about the failure, and finally calculates a new set of paths through the network that routes around the failure.

Proponents of the Offline Routing/Online Reaction (OR/OR) operational model argue that the Distributed model of network control is fundamentally broken. A control plane that reacts to changes in the network topology can never react fast enough to prevent major packet loss without building in a lot of complexity that makes the network difficult to design, deploy, and manage. Very specialized timer tuning, along with complex additions to the routing system, are required to react to network topology changes in near real time.

OR/OR resolves this problem by calculating all control plane information offline, including a set of backup paths that can be used in the case of the failure of the best path for any given traffic flow. This is much like an MPLS-TE network with fast reroute, where the primary path to any destination is calculated, and then a backup path is calculated. Both paths are installed in the forwarding table of every device through the network proactively at the time they are calculated.

If the primary path fails at any point in the network, the device that detects the failure can immediately switch traffic to the backup path and then notify the control plane that an alternate path needs to be calculated for this particular destination. This is, in a broad way, identical to the calculation of alternate paths in a traditional routing protocol. EIGRP, for instance, can discover alternate loop-free paths (*Feasible Successors*), and install those backup paths into the routing table for immediate use when the primary path fails.

The apparent simplicity of precalculating routes isn't, however, as simple as it appears at first blush. Figure 17-3 illustrates some of the complexity involved in precalculating backup paths.

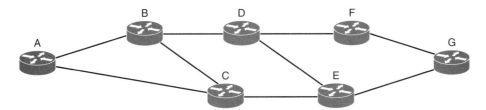

Figure 17-3 *Example of Precalculation Complexity*

Assume an offline controller determines the best route between A and G is along the path (A,B,D,F,G), so it installs the correct forwarding state in each device along the path. The controller software also determines a good backup route is along the path (A,C,E,G), so

it installs alternate forwarding information in each of these routers to provide a backup path for this traffic.

This apparently simple solution presents three separate problems:

- First, the state in the network has just doubled. Simply calculating routes for every source/destination pair is bad enough—traditional networks only calculate the path to every destination, so that forwarding state is naturally aggregated as you move closer to the actual destination. But not only must every source/destination pair be calculated in this solution, and forwarding information installed for every source/destination pair, backup path information for each source/destination pair must also be installed in every device along the backup path. Router C, then, now holds a path for (A,G), a path it would not have held in a traditional network.

- Second, how should Router C treat this forwarding information? There were once two states in the routing and forwarding tables in every device—a path is in use, or it is a backup for another path that is locally in use. Router C, however, doesn't have a local path for (A,G) at all, so it will need a separate state to indicate the installed path is a backup path for a path that doesn't locally exist.

- Third, how should we deal with nonlocal failures along the primary path? In the scenario proposed, if the link between Routers A and B fails, A can simply reroute traffic along the alternate path, through Router C. But what if the link between Routers B and D fails? How can A know to reroute this traffic? There are only two available solutions to this problem.

Router B can examine its local forwarding table and send some sort of signal along to each source that is using Router B as a transit device. This would mean the addition of a signaling protocol to provide this "crank back" function throughout the network. Cranking back a path in this way is clearly going to take some time—in fact, the same amount of time it would take for a traditional routing protocol to detect and flood information about the same topology change. A crank-back signal is not only complex, it will most likely result in convergence times roughly equivalent to in-band control planes.

Another option is for Router B to notify the out-of-band controller of the link failure. The controller can then signal Router A that it should switch to the alternate path for this traffic. But the primary determinant in switching between links in this case is going to be the signal path from Router B to the controller and back to Router A—not the amount of time it takes for the controller to calculate and install an alternate path. If this is true, why bother with calculating and installing the secondary path? Can't the secondary path be just as easily computed and installed in real time, like a traditional in-band routing protocol?

It's also possible for the controller to compute not one, but two, alternate paths through the network. The alternate path for Router A could be (A,C,F,G), and the alternate path for the same flow at B would be (A,B,F,G). Now if the link between Routers B and D fails, any traffic can be rerouted by B directly—at the cost of a lot more state in the network, however.

Finally, there is the question of what happens to the traffic "on the wire" when a failure occurs. If the link between Routers F and G fails, and Router F must either "crank back" the path by signaling Router A, or must notify the controller, which must then tell Router A to switch to its backup path, what happens to any packets sitting in the memory of Routers B and D? Are these packets simply discarded?

Dynamic routing protocols resolve all these problems by allowing each node in the network to compute an alternate local path for each destination. IP fast reroute mechanisms can be designed to add little or no state to the network, and to react quickly enough to reduce convergence times so that only packets in flight (physically being transmitted on the wire) at the time of the link failure, or packets physically residing in the memory of a failed node, will be lost in the event of a failure.

Although this argument of the right network model—traditional routing versus OR/OR— is likely to continue forever, there is little doubt it's a matter of trade-offs and current technologies, rather than a case of one model winning absolutely over the other on technical grounds.

OpenFlow

OpenFlow defines a set of interactions between a switch (really a forwarding plane with no control plane) and an off-box controller. These interactions are modeled as a set of states in the switch's forwarding path, a set of protocols on the connection between the controller and the switch, and as a set of objects on the controller. Manipulating objects in the controller's data model causes OpenFlow messages to be sent from the controller to the switch, which then results in a state change in the switch's forwarding plane.

These interactions are based around individual flows (or microflows) of data, defined by a set of tuples, such as the traditional five-tuple flow description (source IP address, destination IP address, protocol number, source port, destination port). The number of tuples used to identify a flow is variable, with some implementations supporting up to 12 tuples (including the Layer 2 MAC address, protocol numbers, port numbers, and so on). A group of flows can be indicated by placing wildcards into the various tuples; all the traffic between 192.0.2.1 and 198.51.100.1 can be described using the five tuple: (192.0.2.1, 198.51.100.1,*,*,*).

Each flow (or group of flows) is assigned an end-to-end path by the off-box controller using a global view of the network. The controller must ensure that traffic does not loop between various nodes in the network by using some form of a path calculation algorithm (SPF, as used in OSPF and IS-IS, is one such algorithm). If a link or device fails, traffic must be dropped until the controller discovers the link failure and responds by finding and installing a new path through the network.

OpenFlow Operation

In terms of forwarding information, OpenFlow can operate in either proactive or reactive modes.

In the proactive mode, the forwarding table is populated based on network topology information held at the controller before any packets are received in the network devices themselves. Because this mode is similar to the traditional routing model most architects are familiar with, we won't spend any time on it; instead, we'll move directly to the reactive model, which is less familiar.

In the reactive mode, the forwarding plane is populated as new flows are started by hosts attached to the network, rather than attempting to describe the full range of reachability information at any given time. Figure 17-4 shows the reactive process of building a flow in an OpenFlow network.

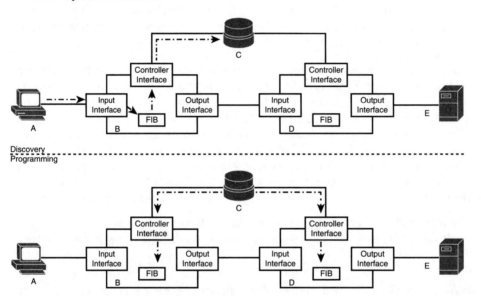

Figure 17-4   *Reactive OpenFlow Operation*

OpenFlow operation is broken into the same two basic parts any reactive control plane is composed of: discovery and programming. To begin the process, Host A sends a packet toward Server E. Switch B receives this packet and checks the local forwarding table (FIB) for information about this particular flow. Assume for this example that no such flow record (or forwarding table entry) exists in the local FIB.

Note   The forwarding table entry doesn't need to match all five tuples of this new flow to be used to forward traffic towards Server E—a forwarding table entry can contain wildcards that allow all traffic destined to Server E to take a single path through the network, or follow a specific tree towards this server.

On receiving a packet for a flow with no forwarding information, the OpenFlow switch, B, encapsulates the entire packet and sends it through a controller backchannel interface to the controller, C, for further processing. At this point, the controller has two options:

■ First, the controller could simply process the packet, including placing any information needed to forward the packet on toward its final destination, and send the packet back to Switch B for further processing. Switch B would receive this packet, discover the information needed to forward the packet in the OpenFlow headers attached by Controller C, and forward the packet according to those instructions.

■ Second, the controller could process the packet and send it back to Switch B for forwarding, and then program a forwarding table entry at every switch along the path through the backchannel interface, as shown in the programming phase in Figure 17-4. In this way, the second packet Host A sends to Server E will be forwarded along the path through Switches B and D using hardware-based processing. This flow path, built by the controller dynamically in response to the first packet in a flow, can be thought of as an end-to-end policy route for this specific flow.

This flow path is retained until some policy local to the network or the individual switches deployed throughout the network removes it. The removal process would normally rely on a simple timer (if a flow label hasn't been used to switch a packet in a given number of seconds, remove the label), or it might be based on a more sophisticated mechanism, such as watching for well-known protocol stream endings. For instance, a switch might be configured to forward traffic that falls within a specific stream, but also to replicate any TCP packets with specific bits or control messages up to the controller as well. This would allow the controller to monitor the state and health of each TCP connection and remove the flow entry for TCP sessions that have either timed out or been terminated.

The entire SDN network, from OpenFlow edge to OpenFlow edge, is considered a single Layer 2 domain from the routing perspective, much like a single spanning tree or TRILL domain.

Note   Engineers who work in the OpenFlow space argue that it is neither Layer 3 nor Layer 2, and that there are no "broadcast domains," in the traditional sense, in an OpenFlow network. Since the flow tables are built around all 12 tuples of the header, potentially all the way into the port number (for situations where this much specificity is required), packets can be switched at "any layer" within the network. Hence OpenFlow really isn't "Layer 2 switching," any more (or less) than "Layer 3 switching." This is one of the reasons the framework presented here doesn't rely on layers to differentiate SDN systems, but rather on the point in the switching device that the SDN solution touches.

Objections and Considerations

Most of the objections to SDNs revolve around scaling, complexity, separation of the data and control planes, and the reactive nature of the control plane as discussed in the sections that follow.

Scaling

The most common objection to SDNs is that it won't scale. This is a catch-all objection to virtually every technology in the network engineering space, so we really need to dive into this objection a bit to both understand it and to understand the answers to it. What do we mean when we say it won't scale? Generally, this means the protocol or system in question won't be able to handle large numbers of users or hosts because of protocol overhead or operation.

In the case of SDNs, there are three specific charges in terms of scaling.

The first objection in the space of scaling is we simply can't build hardware that will support hundreds of thousands of flows or microflows. At the time of this writing, OpenFlow-capable switches can support only hundreds or thousands of forwarding table entries; it seems difficult to see how we're going to find the processing power needed to build and quickly find entries in a table with millions of 5- to 12-tuple entries.

If we look back in the history of networking, we find that this concern over scaling has been faced—and overcome—many times. Ten years ago, a 5,000 entry routing table would have been considered excessive outside the Internet core, and the 100,000 route Internet core was considered absolutely huge. Today, routers support over a million routes in the routing table, with corresponding forwarding tables of the same size. What happened?

Hardware vendors, protocol designers, and network designers learned how to tweak their hardware, protocols, software, and network designs to build and manage networks. It has not been an easy road at times, but packet-based networks are scaling beyond anything someone 10 or 15 years ago would have imagined.

As the demand rose, engineers learned how to build what was demanded. SDNs are likely to answer this scaling problem in the same way—as the demand arises, hardware vendors will learn how to build large-scale forwarding planes optimized to SDN requirements. Algorithms, hardware, and other components will be shaped around the requirements at hand, and the scaling problems that appear so daunting today will be but a memory.

The second scaling objection is that an SDN network effectively represents one huge flat domain—that hierarchy, and the lessons of hierarchy, are being thrown out the window for SDNs. Unlike the first scaling objection, this is a structural issue. Only time will tell if a shift in design philosophy can overcome this objection. Network engineers might find SDNs are limited in scope to a single data center, or a single campus, and "interSDN routing" must be handled like BGP handles interdomain routing today. There's simply no way to know at this point in the development of SDN.

To put this into context, the issue at hand is the full mesh problem taken to the host level. If every host in a network can connect to every other host in the network directly through the network, then there will need to be n(n-1)/2 connections in the network. At the level at which OpenFlow addresses the network, this problem isn't per host pair, but per socket pair—so the formula needs to be applied to every process, or rather every flow through the entire network. Full-mesh scaling simply doesn't hold up in the long run. It's not a

matter of number of entries in a given table, nor a matter of handling the control plane flow, but simply the problems inherent in any-to-any full-mesh environments.

This problem will, in the end, need to be solved in the same way it's solved in more traditional networks—by aggregating control plane information. The only real question that needs to be answered is this: How will this aggregation take place? There appears to be at least three options.

- Areas of the network where Replacement model SDNs have been deployed can be treated as a single Layer 2 domain within the network, just as a spanning-tree domain is in traditional IP network design. This would limit the size of the SDN domain, breaking up multiple failure domains with IP routed interconnection points. For this type of design to work, the SDN controllers must run a routing protocol and inject reachability information into the routed control plane at the SDN domain edge.

- Multiple layers of replacement SDNs could be deployed in a network, with some form of "edge node" acting as a host on a higher level, or overlay, SDN network. Figure 17-5 illustrates this concept.\

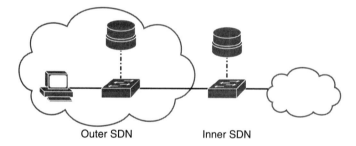

Outer SDN   Inner SDN

Figure 17-5 *Hierarchical Replacement Model SDNs*

In Figure 17-5, the outer SDN appears to be a single device to the Inner SDN, even though the Outer SDN may represent thousands of devices. This type of hierarchy is familiar to engineers who have deployed L3VPN, L2VPN, or other "over the top" virtualization services.

- SDN control planes could be modified to aggregate information just as routing protocols do in more traditional networks. The use of wildcard bits could be expanded, for instance, to include the concept of a subnet mask, so that information about groups of reachable destinations could be advertised and installed, rather than each individual destination. This type of control plane aggregation is already well understood, and would therefore be fairly easy to deploy and manage in large scale Replacement model SDNs.

Which of these three will ultimately be deployed? If experience is any guide, all three of them—and many more. In the end, it will be up to network architects and vendors to decide how to address the scaling issues inherent in a full-mesh topology.

Complexity

The complexity problem in SDNs can be summed up in two points:

- Software engineers look at networks and think, "Wow, this is really complex; think of how simple this would be if I could just write a few lines of code to manage all this stuff."

- Network engineers look at software and think, "Wow, this is really complex; all those lines of code, all those software interactions, and all those bugs and security vulner-abilities, and... Network implementations are much cleaner and simpler. SDNs will just be replacing my nice clean design with spaghetti code!"

The problem is—they're both right.

In both cases, the engineers are comparing a rather simplified view of the problem they face against the apparently complex problem they see in some other space. The software engineer sees a large, complicated network with hundreds of different types of devices, hundreds of different protocols all interacting with one another, hundreds of different versions of code, hardware revisions, and the like, and thinks, "This is so much harder to manage than a quicksort." The network engineer looks at a complete computer, with all the different pieces of software, all interacting (with often ill effects), and thinks, "This is so much harder to manage than OSPF."

The reality is that both network systems and software systems are complex because the problems they address are complex. The key question to ask when considering the complexity of an SDN (or any other) solution is: complex compared to what? Is a 5,000 VLAN deployment really more complex than an SDN deployment? Is a distributed rout-ing protocol really more complex than the code required to calculate loop-free and opti-mal paths in a controller?

There aren't any easy answers to these questions.

Separation of Data and Control Planes

Two objections fall under this heading. The first of these is the problem of fast conver-gence in the case of network failure. This was covered previously in the "Offline Routing/Online Reaction." We won't repeat that discussion here.

The second objection is the concern over failures in the connection between the data plane in one device and a control plane located in another box. Is it possible to build protocols that can control and manage, in real time, millions of flows across an off-box connection? It's well known that network interfaces and devices drop packets when heav-ily loaded; what happens when the controller sends a message that is dropped someplace along the path to the switch? Worse, what happens when the connection between the forwarding device and the controller fails entirely?

Part of this objection comes from our perception of traditional routers and switches as "one box." In reality, they are not one box, but a collection of processors, each running

different processes, connected through an internal bus system. Very few network engineers have ever had to deal with communication failures along those internal bus systems because hardware and software designers have learned how to make these internal bus systems robust enough to handle the workload and to fail as gracefully as possible.

This objection, like the first, is a matter of learning to correctly design the hardware, software, and architecture to make a Replacement model SDN work. To return to experience in the realm of traditional control planes, link state routing protocols are designed to flush and reflood their link state information on a regular basis. EIGRP, likewise, was originally designed with the "stuck in active" concept as a short leash on the state of the network. These measures were designed into routing protocols to account not only for common link and device failures, but also to account for corner cases. Link state protocols are now often operated with these flush and refresh timers set to the maximum possible, or simply turned off, and EIGRP's stuck in active process has been rewritten to take advantage of newer networks and their capabilities.

This is another area where we can expect SDN hardware, software, and protocol designers to learn and grow over time, eventually minimizing or eliminating this problem.

Reactive Control Planes

A number of structural objections that can be raised against reactive control planes can be applied to SDNs operating in a reactive mode. The primary objection, and most difficult to overcome, is that caching in the data plane always counts on specific patterns of traffic flow. Caching counts on a relatively small number of all possible end hosts opening flows to one another at any particular point in time. If traffic falls outside these specific patterns in large enough amounts, caching fails—and it fails dramatically.

As an example, consider a cache that can hold 10 entries. In normal operation, it is safe to keep four or five slots filled in the cache; if the cache reaches 80% full (8 entries), older entries need to be timed out more quickly to prevent connections through the network from being refused because of lack of cache space.

In the case where the flow count overflows the cache, the cache will attempt to dump older connections, even though they might still be in use, to build new connections. Older connections that continue sending traffic after they are removed from the cache are treated as new connections, causing another older connection to be removed, which then becomes a new connection in the next round. The cache will churn constantly, allowing apparently random connections for apparently random periods of time.

This type of cache failure has caused a number of complete network failures, particularly when control plane traffic (including link status polling) is transmitted in line with transported data. Cisco redesigned its entire forwarding plane infrastructure, moving from the fast cache to Cisco Express Forwarding, to resolve widespread caching problems of just this type. While a number of possible solutions have been proposed to resolve this type of problem, there is a deep reluctance in the routing community to move back toward a cached forwarding table.

Conclusion

SDNs hold out great promise for helping reduce the complexity of distributed network models while providing a road for the growth of networking technologies into the future. Although there's no clear answer to the question of which model is best, or whether SDNs will eventually "take over the world," understanding the different ideas in play, and how they do or could fit together, is crucial to seeing the landscape and making clear decisions. Hopefully, the framework of models presented here can provide you with another view of the world of SDNs and how they relate to more traditional distributed networking systems.

Software-Defined Network Use Cases

Whether you should consider deploying SDNs is a matter of business drivers, rather than technological ones. The best way to decide is to consider the positive and negative aspects of the technology in specific situations, determine which problems the technology might be able to resolve, carefully consider as many side effects and consequences as possible, and then decide if, where, and how to deploy it.

In the case of SDNs, the strengths and weaknesses of the technology should provide a good idea of where different versions of SDNs will be useful and where they might not. Here we will consider two specific areas in the network where an SDN deployment might prove useful. The first example is from a data center; the second is from a core wide-area network.

SDNs in a Data Center

Data center environments have been a focused area of research and development over the past several years. Data center specific protocols and technologies have proliferated to handle the massive scaling and management needs of large scale deployments (tens to hundreds of thousands of devices in a single building). Deployments this large bring several complex control plane problems into the world of network design, including managing large scale virtualization, managing policy, and managing the configuration of the large numbers of networking devices required. As an example, let's consider how deploying OpenFlow could resolve some of these problems, and then consider the flip side— what challenges does OpenFlow cause?

What OpenFlow Brings to the Table

Large scale data centers are often designed for multiple tenants, such as multiple business units within a single company, multiple companies within a holding company, or a single company selling data center (cloud) services to other companies. This multitenancy problem is presented to the network architect as a data separation problem. Each tenant's data must somehow be kept separate from every other tenant's, even as data is moved around within the network to optimize resources and traffic flow.

Normally, this separation of traffic is handled by provisioning a VLAN per tenant or, in more recent deployments, by provisioning each tenant with either an L3VPN or L2VPN using MPLS transport through the data center. Both of these solutions, however, are difficult to deploy and manage. How could an SDN based on OpenFlow resolve these problems? A centralized control plane would be very useful in dynamically managing the flow of traffic to and from various locations in a data center network designed around multitenancy, as shown in Figure 17-6.

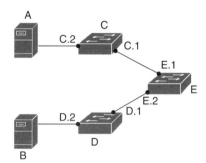

Figure 17-6   *Moving a Flow in a Data Center*

When a service is moved from some server in Rack A to some server in Rack B, the switch ports E.1, C.1, and C.2 must be reconfigured to remove them from the VLAN this service resides in, and switch ports E.2, D.1, and D.2 must be configured to insert them into the VLAN this service resides in. To prevent huge amounts of reconfiguration in a traditional network, every VLAN is channeled to every rack (or a large subset of racks in which the service is allowed to be placed). Keeping all the VLANs, services, and the various possible combinations of these two straight is a big job from the network management perspective.

In an OpenFlow deployment, however, the service move would be done through a centralized system that not only moved the correct processes from one server to another, but would also move the various ports into the corresponding VLANs—or, more simply, move the appropriate flows from one set of ports to another. This would greatly simplify the management of the network and the network design.

Other difficult problems that could be more easily resolved in an SDN data center environment include the following:

- Forwarding unknown flows, or flows that have been marked as being a security threat, through hardware designed to scrub out viruses and mitigate DDoS attacks

- Building forwarding state in conjunction with authorization and authentication systems, so that users only have forwarding paths to servers they are allowed to access

Challenges to the OpenFlow Solution

SDNs in the data center, like all technologies, present the network architect with trade-offs; there are negative aspects as well as positive ones. Defects in the algorithms that tie various systems together could cause a positive feedback loop, allowing a failure in one system to leak over into another, or even cause a general network failure. Resiliency isn't just about having multiple controllers; it's also about isolation of failure domains. Replacement model SDNs, with their centralized control planes, present challenges in the area of true failure domain separation.

Another issue is that the SDN's controllers themselves must now be secured. Any attack against the SDN's controllers represents a far worse threat than attacking and overcoming a single router. Distributed control planes are highly resilient to single node and link failures because every node in the network plays a relatively equal role in the running of the network itself.

The capital expense savings many network managers seem to expect when moving to an SDN solution probably won't materialize in the long run, either. Hardware that supports the number of flows required to deploy a large-scale data center with the potential for millions of flows isn't likely to be any less expensive than the standard routing and switching platforms we're used to today.

SDNs in a Wide-Area Core

Although Replace model SDNs show the most promise in data centers, campuses, and other environments where they fit into a specific set of requirements, Parallel model SDNs show the most promise in wide-area and network-core applications.

At edges where traffic exits along two possible paths, it is often desirable to choose a path based on more information than BGP provides. For instance, a network operator may want to take into account the cost of using a link per unit of data, which might include time of day restrictions (peak hour rate increases or surcharges), additional costs per unit of data over a base unit, or even the cost of sending traffic to one specific destination. The cost of using a link might need to be weighed against the financial gain represented by using the link, including faster reaction to market conditions during specific time periods.

Inputs to such a system could include the following:

- Cost per unit of data sent
- Time of day
- Urgency of data traffic or flow
- Exit point performance, including historical jitter, delay, and available bandwidth, possibly on a per destination basis
- Availability of a specific destination through a given link at the per destination basis (more specific than the routing protocol provides)

Metrics could be added to BGP, or any other routing protocol, to provide this additional information. Fine-tuned algorithms could be developed and deployed within routing protocol implementations themselves, but that would involve making massive changes to the way routing protocols work in an attempt to account for every possible set of parameters a network might want to consider for what is likely a small set of use cases. This is both impractical and detrimental to protocol scaling.

A problem of this type, with multiple independent variables, is best resolved by collecting the data in an out-of-band device or appliance, and then feeding the resulting routing decisions back into the routing system. Out-of-band devices providing this type of processing normally discover topology information by querying every edge device through SNMP or some other mechanism, or they hook directly into the routing system by peering with each of the edge devices. To inject path information back into the routing system, peering into the routing system is sometimes used, or direct injection of information into the edge devices' routing tables through screen scraping, SNMP, or some other technique.

All these solutions, however, have a number of drawbacks:

■ Discovering topology through direct interaction with the routing system often results in an incomplete or poorly developed view of the network. The out-of-band controller, in this case, cannot re-create the same view of the network as the edge devices, so the controller's view of the network will necessarily produce routing decisions that are not always optimal at all edge devices. For instance, SNMP cannot report multiple equal cost paths from the routing table, so a controller relying on SNMP would never be able to truly get a complete view of the network topology and the routing table changes during the process of being read.

■ Mechanisms that inject routing information through screen scraping, proprietary means, SNMP, or other systems do not allow the injected route to interact with routes installed by the onboard routing systems in a natural way. For instance, static routes injected through any means must, by their nature, change the configuration of the device, which can be problematic when network operators are trying to understand the operation of the network, or troubleshoot current problems. Routes installed through the static subsystem are also difficult to redistribute into other protocols to draw traffic to a specific exit point, and it can be difficult to fine-tune how these injected routes interact with routes learned through other routing processes.

■ Mechanisms that attempt to influence the routing of traffic by modifying routes in the routing system itself often cannot provide the weight of influence necessary; routing works by drawing traffic to the device advertising the destination, it is difficult for a third party to move traffic between two links to which it is not connected.

With I2RS, the best path could be calculated using any number of custom written mechanisms, and the routes injected into the right places in the network to effect the most efficient drawing of traffic to the best exit point. Changes in the network environment could quickly cause traffic to be shifted to alternate exit points when circumstances dictate.

Final Thoughts on SDNs

SDNs are so difficult to define because they're not really "one thing," but rather a collection of technologies that interact with or possibly replace existing control plane systems. SDN control planes can operate in every mode distributed control planes operate in, as well.

> SDNs are, in essence, a different way of looking at or solving the control plane problem in large scale networks.

Network architects and businesses should look to SDNs to resolve specific problems in a way that reduces the overhead cost of deploying and managing a network. Hardware (CAPEX) costs aren't likely to be the major cost savings point in SDN deployments. Human error will always be a factor in network operations; SDNs are no different in this area from any other control plane.

Overall, SDNs present unique opportunities and challenges to the networking industry and businesses that use networks, no matter what their scale. They have the potential to disrupt network engineering as we know it from the perspective of protocols and network management, but will probably do little to modify the tried-and-true models, theories, and design paradigms (such as separation of failure domains) that make solid network engineering tick.

Data Center Design

"I've completely revolutionized our network by converting it all to a set of cloud services."

"Wow, that's really interesting. How did you get it all done so quickly?"

"Everywhere on our network diagrams there was a data center, I changed the symbol to a cloud and replaced the data center label with a private cloud label. The CIO is really happy now because we moved our entire network to the cloud so quickly!"

As funny as this little story might be (and it's a story from real life), and as much as cloud-centered folks might object, there is some truth in the switch. Cloud services still need to be backed up with physical storage, physical processing power, physical switches, and physical wires. The guts of a cloud don't, in essence, look much different from the guts of a data center from a physical perspective.

So although it might seem a little old fashioned, in this chapter we're going to discuss the ins and outs of data center design, focusing on the control plane and topology. Although there are a lot of hard problems in cooling and power, those pieces won't be covered here. Nor will specific tunneling technologies—this chapter is designed to give you a solid theoretical understanding of the problems onto which you can lay specific solutions.

Data Center Spine and Leaf Fabrics

The place to begin in data center design is not with the physical cabling, or cooling, or power, but with the concept of a fabric. Across the years, in talking to a lot of network engineers, one of the most difficult things to get across in the area of data center design is the idea of a fabric, in contrast to an aggregation layer. The key difference is *fabrics don't aggregate traffic.*

Understanding Spine and Leaf

What does "fabrics don't aggregate traffic" mean? Let's begin with Figure 18-1 in our exploration of this concept.

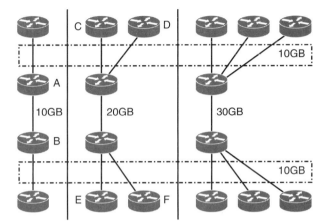

Figure 18-1   *Traditional Aggregation Topology*

In Figure 18-1, if we want to provide enough bandwidth for every edge router to send 10GB to every other edge router connected through the two central routers, we must add bandwidth between Routers A and B as we add edge routers. If we have one pair of edge routers, we can connect the two center routers with a single 10GB link. Doubling the number of edge routers means we must double the bandwidth of the link between the two center routers.

Why? If Router E sends a 10GB stream to Router C, and at the same time Router F sends a 10GB stream to Router D, but there is only one 10GB link between Routers A and B, one of these two streams must be blocked in circuit switched terms. In packet terms, packets from both streams must be interleaved onto the oversubscribed link so that both senders get an equal amount of bandwidth. Both blocking and oversubscription cause delay and jitter in the network, which can adversely affect applications running over the links. Data center applications tend to be very sensitive to delay and jitter, so we need to find some way to provide a full bandwidth path between every pair of edge devices (or rather, between each pair of edge ports).

The simple solution to this problem is to increase the bandwidth between the core, or central, routers—Routers A and B in this network. Up to a certain point, this is possible (in fact, a fat tree spine and leaf design uses just this sort of aggregation to a fixed point, as we will see later). But there is some point where higher-bandwidth links aren't available, or the expense of building a higher-bandwidth link increases dramatically. The cost of infrastructure changes can make it less expensive to install ten 10GB links than one 100GB link. These observations lead us to the design shown in Figure 18-2.

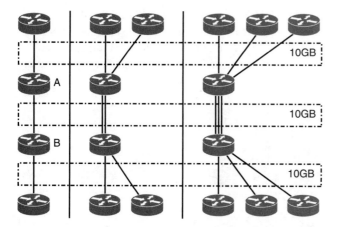

Figure 18-2   *Increasing Bandwidth Through Additional Links*

It is possible to increase the number of links between Routers A and B so that for each pair of edge routers, we have a link equal to the edge connection link in the center of the network. This is again a feasible design, although it does have two drawbacks:

■ The design adds two ports on both Routers A and B for each pair of edge devices.

■ As the port count requirements for Routers A and B increase, the size, complexity, and cost of these two devices increase as well.

As with link costs, the cost of a single large device can be much greater than a number of smaller devices that, combined, produce the same amount of capacity. This observation leads to the network design shown in Figure 18-3, where the core devices are divided, effectively exposing the internal fabric within the network design and spreading that fabric across multiple devices.

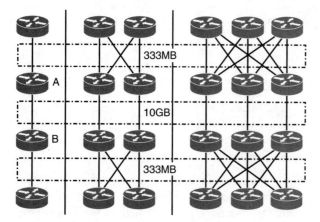

Figure 18-3   *Next Step to a Fabric*

This design effectively trades core ports for edge ports, allowing the central devices to be similar (or identical) to the edge devices. Now we observe that the links between the central devices are, essentially, worthless—they do nothing but forward traffic between two identical routers. If, instead, we merge the central devices into one device, we end up with a spine and leaf design, as shown in Figure 18-4.

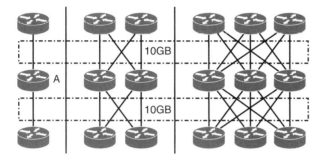

Figure 18-4 *Spine and Leaf*

The result is a *fabric where each edge device has the full bandwidth of the fabric available to every other edge device*. You've seen this image before, back in our discussion of Clos fabrics in Chapter 11, "The Floor Plan," but it bears repeating here to illustrate the traffic flows in such a fabric (see Figure 18-5).

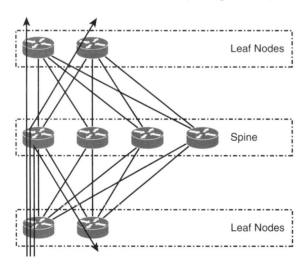

Figure 18-5 *Traffic Flow in a Spine and Leaf Fabric*

It is still true that a set of edge devices (or leaves) can send more traffic toward any other single edge device (or leaf), causing an oversubscription or blocking situation, but there is no real way around this problem other than some sort of asymmetrical link bandwidth, with smaller links inbound from each leaf than what is available back out to the leaves.

A spine and leaf design pushes traffic along multiple parallel paths to handle the required bandwidth, while providing enough cross-connects to allow any node to reach any other node—effectively placing multiple traffic streams in parallel. Traditional designs aggregate traffic by stacking multiple streams onto a single link and cross-connecting all the devices within a single device—or carrying the streams serially, rather than in parallel.

The Border Leaf

How does the rest of the network connect to this fabric? In the same way any other service or resource does—through a leaf. It is tempting to connect directly to the spine in a spine and leaf design, but this isn't a good idea. If you connect the outside network to just some of the spine devices, you end up creating a "hot spot" in the spine along those devices. Traffic flowing through the spine switch that is connected to the rest of the network will be forced to pass through one of several oversubscribed switches, reducing application performance.

If, on the other hand, you connect the outside network to every spine, you've effectively created a leaf node anyway—in which case there is no reason not to treat these connections to the rest of the network as if they were a leaf.

Beyond connecting to the rest of the network, the border leaf also normally contains compute and storage resources set aside for managing the fabric, as well as any network level services that need to be accessed by all the VLANs running through the fabric.

Sizing a Spine and Leaf Fabric

What does this mean for the capability of a spine and leaf fabric to carry traffic? The natural inclination in network design is to stack traffic through aggregation; if a network needs to support 10 video streams of 1GB each, the network needs to have 10GB links. This isn't the way spine and leaf fabrics work, however. There are three numbers network designers need to be concerned about when dealing with spine and leaf fabrics:

- The speed (or bandwidth) of the fabric

- The number of edge ports

- The total fabric bandwidth

Speed of the Fabric

The first bullet point, *speed of the fabric*, is not the total carrying capacity between every pair of leaves in the fabric; it is the total bandwidth between each leaf and all the spine switches. For example:

- If there are four spine switches, and each leaf switch has one 40GB link to each spine, the result is a 160GB fabric.

- If there are four spine switches, and each leaf switch has one 100GB link to each spine, the result is a 400GB fabric.

- If there are six spine switches, and each leaf has one 40GB link to each spine, the result is a 240GB fabric.

The speed of the fabric needs to be matched to the flows being put onto the fabric itself, or the number and size of devices connected behind a leaf switch, rather than the aggregate of all the flows across the entire fabric. For instance, if a single leaf device is going to have 24 10GB ports into which blade servers can be connected, the fabric needs to support 24×10GB, or 240GB of bandwidth. We discuss modularity more in a later section, "Modularity and the Data Center," but essentially the speed of the fabric needs to be sized to the largest amount of traffic any single leaf node could send.

Increasing the fabric speed can be accomplished in one of two ways:

- Increase the speed of each individual link between the leaves and the spine.

- Increase the number of spine switches, which increases the number of links between each leaf and the spine.

Note the first idea, increasing the bandwidth of each link, results in what is called a *fat tree* fabric, where link bandwidths increase as you move closer to the center of the fabric and decrease as you move toward the edge of the fabric. To create a nonblocking design, it's important that the total bandwidth not change from layer to layer. Only the bandwidth of individual links should change. For instance, each set of four 10GB links along the edge of the fabric should be matched with a single 40GB link from leaf to spine. If the link bandwidth stays the same edge-to-edge, the fabric is called a *skinny tree*.

Number of Edge Ports

The second number network engineers need to be concerned about when building a spine and leaf fabric is the number of edge ports. This, essentially, is directly related to the number of leaf nodes in the fabric. If each leaf node provides ten 10GB ports (10×10GB), then each additional leaf the fabric supports will provide another set of ports, increasing the total port count along the edge of the fabric. To increase the number of edge ports in a spine and leaf fabric, increase the number of ports available on each spine switch.

Combining the fabric speed with the edge port count creates a chart of possible fabric sizes, as shown in Table 18-1 (assuming all links and ports are 10GB).

Table 18-1   *Spine and Leaf Fabric Sizes*

			Spine Switches			
			2	4	6	8
Spine Ports per Switch	6	Leaves	6	6	6	6
		Bandwidth	20GB	40GB	60GB	80GB
		Edge Ports	12	24	36	48
	8	Leaves	8	8	8	8
		Bandwidth	20GB	40GB	60GB	80GB
		Edge Ports	16	32	48	64
	10	Leaves	10	10	10	10
		Bandwidth	20GB	40GB	60GB	80GB
		Edge Ports	20	40	60	80
	12	Leaves	12	12	12	12
		Bandwidth	20GB	40GB	60GB	80GB
		Edge Ports	24	48	72	96
	14	Leaves	14	14	14	14
		Bandwidth	20GB	40GB	60GB	80GB
		Edge Ports	28	56	84	112
	16	Leaves	16	16	16	16
		Bandwidth	20GB	40GB	60GB	80GB
		Edge Ports	32	64	96	128

A typical fat tree fabric might use 40GB links between the leaves and eight spine switches, with each spine switch supporting twenty-four 40GB ports, for a total of 320GB bandwidth and 768×10GB ports along the fabric edge. Because most devices will be connected to two 10GB ports at the edge, this type of configuration will support 384 fully redundant devices, including servers, service devices, and storage.

Total Fabric Bandwidth

Finally, the total bandwidth across the entire fabric can be calculated by multiplying the number of edge ports by the speed of those ports, or the number of spine ports by the speed of those ports (if the fabric is not oversubscribed, these two numbers should be

the same). The smallest fabric in Table 18-1 has 480GB of aggregate bandwidth, and the largest has 1280GB of aggregate bandwidth. The typical fat tree fabric discussed here would have 7680GB of aggregate bandwidth.

Why No Oversubscription?

Oversubscription is a normal part of network design—100GB Ethernet feeds into a 10GB metro link, which feeds into a 1GB wide-area link. Oversubscription in a data center fabric, however, needs to be kept to as few places as possible—preferably, no more than one, generally at the point where traffic is taken into the edge of the leaf nodes (often called the Top of Rack [ToR], regardless of where it is physically located). It might seem like a waste to throw a lot of bandwidth at what appears to be a small amount of traffic, but several points need to be taken into consideration.

First, spine and leaf fabrics are supposed to be nonblocking; oversubscription, while not true blocking, is a form of blocking that can severely impact application performance. Halving an application's bandwidth to a remote resource doesn't just cut its performance in half—the impact is much more severe.

Second, most data center designs don't run Layer 2 or Layer 3 directly on the fabric. Instead, the fabric runs as an underlying media over which a set of virtual topologies is built. As traffic is encapsulated into tunnels to build such an overlay, fine-grained quality of service controls are often lost. Some transfer is often possible, but it's difficult to carry or act on all the quality of service information available in the original packets in highly virtualized environments. The result of oversubscription, then, on application performance is even worse in a virtualized environment than one where traffic is placed directly on the underlying network.

Finally, if there are multiple points at which traffic can be dropped when crossing the network from source to destination, there are also multiple points where you're going to need to spend time monitoring and troubleshooting in the case of an application performance issue. If oversubscription is limited to the edge, you have a single place to start when working on performance problems—and that single place is the most likely place for performance problems to originate.

If you find your data center fabric very underutilized, you can take comfort in knowing that traffic grows in almost every network over time, so that capacity will likely be used eventually. Rather than seeing this as a negative, spin it as a positive—you planned for the future. Or you can rethink and fine-tune your ideas about the load offered by various applications for the next design.

The Control Plane Conundrum

Building a fabric that can carry the traffic required for a data center is actually the simplest part of the data center design; dealing with the various control plane issues generally presents a far more complex set of problems. In this section we'll start at Layer 2 and work our way up, looking at various problems (and some potential solutions) in the data center control plane.

Why Not Layer 2 Alone?

The first, and most obvious, question is: why not just connect everything in the data center into one large Layer 2 broadcast domain and go home for the night? The most likely reason is that your hours at home will probably be far fewer and less restful than you might imagine if you do this. There are a number of scaling issues in large Layer 2 networks, including the following:

■ Network discovery traffic, such as the Address Resolution Protocol (ARP), broadcast, and others. Although a single host might not generate a lot of this type of traffic, connecting several thousand hosts to a single broadcast domain can amplify discovery to the point of causing a network collapse.

■ The scope and rate of change in the control plane. In our discussion on network complexity in Chapter 14, we noted that there is a trade-off between the amount of information carried in the control plane, the speed at which that information changes, and the stability of the network. Connecting several thousand hosts to a single broadcast domain will create large tables of forwarding information; because hosts are likely to be attached and removed from the network on a regular basis, it will also create a high rate of change.

■ Traffic separation between different tenants or organizations within a data center is a common requirement, as is the capability to share a common set of services among a group of tenants, or to provide communication between the various tenants for specific processes and applications. The most natural way to separate traffic among various tenants is to place each tenant in a different broadcast domain—but two hosts connected to two different broadcast domains cannot communicate without some sort of router to interconnect the two Layer 2 domains.

It is possible, of course, to create an all Layer 2 data center with multiple tenants if the tenants never need to communicate with one another. Shared services can be handled by virtualizing all services and spinning up a new instance of any required service within the tenant's Layer 2 broadcast domain. This solution, however, hits a scaling limit when the network must actually be managed; each service instance within each tenant's Layer 2 broadcast domain must be configured with the right set of policies, and these configurations must be updated and managed as policies change over time. Here the network architect runs into the policy dispersion versus manageability trade-off in the network complexity space.

Where Should Layer 3 Go?

If a simple Layer 2 control plane won't resolve all the problems we face when building large-scale data centers, the designer is pushed to consider Layer 3 solutions. The first, and most pressing, problem when deploying Layer 3 in a data center is where precisely to deploy it. There are three different places you can put a routed edge in a spine and leaf design:

- In a border leaf node where all the Layer 2 flooding domains terminate
- At the spine
- At the outside edge of the leaves.

Figure 18-6 illustrates.

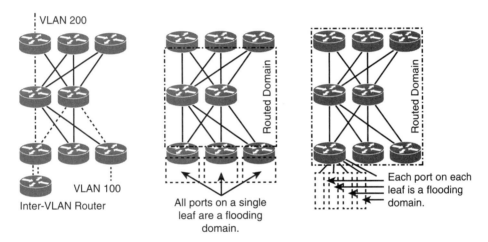

Figure 18-6 *Layer 3 Edge Options on a Spine and Leaf Topology*

Most designers only consider pushing Layer 3 to the ToR, or keeping all Layer 3 functionality within the border leaf node. Why would a network designer choose one option over the other? The trade-off is primarily between Virtual Machine (VM) mobility versus optimal traffic flow through the fabric and reduced failure domain sizes. Specifically:

- **VM Mobility:**
    - If interVLAN routing is performed at the border leaf node, VMs can be moved at Layer 2 to any compute resource available in the entire data center. When a VM is moved, the VLAN to which the VM is attached must be configured at the correct ToR switch.
    - If interVLAN routing is performed at the ToR, VMs can only be moved at Layer 2 within the flooding domain behind a single ToR switch port. This restricts VM movement to within a single compute domain, or removes the option of moving VMs within the data at Layer 2 altogether.

- **Broadcast, Discovery, and Control Plan Scaling:**

  - If interVLAN routing is performed at the border leaf node, broadcasts (such as ARP and other discovery mechanisms) must be carried to the top of rack switch at every leaf on which the VLAN into which the broadcast is sent touches. The control plane at each ToR must discover and maintain switching state for hosts attached to every other ToR on a per-VLAN basis.

  - If interVLAN routing is performed at the ToR, each individual port is a VLAN, so broadcast discovery packets are not carried outside the leaf node. The control plane must learn IP reachability to all the hosts within the data center, but the spine switches are spared learning and holding any Layer 2 forwarding information. This aggregation of Layer 2 forwarding information into the Layer 3 table improves scaling and reduces the scope of the failure domains.

- **Optimal Traffic Flow:**

  - If interVLAN routing is performed at the border leaf node, all interVLAN traffic must be carried across the fabric to the border leaf node, where it is routed, and then carried back to the destination. This is true even if the source and destination are both attached to the same ToR, as shown in Figure 18-7.

  - If interVLAN routing is performed at the ToR, all interVLAN traffic is routed at the ToR directly, allowing optimal traffic flow to every destination attached to the fabric.

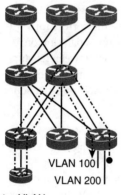

VLAN 100
VLAN 200

Inter-VLAN
Router

Figure 18-7   *Suboptimal Traffic Flow Through the Border Leaf Node*

Which of these is the "best" design? The answer to that question depends on the nature of the load for which the data center fabric is being designed. If the load is going to require a good deal of interVLAN routing, so services can be chained, or information shared between processes running on different VLANs, then placing the routing at the ToR is probably going to be the better design solution. The problem with configuring routing on the ToR is the lack of VM mobility at Layer 2. If your applications or

virtualization solutions are able to handle Layer 3 mobility, rather than Layer 2, configuring routing at the ToR will always produce better scale and more stability.

On the other hand, if it's important to be able to move VMs within the data center at Layer 2 (without changing their IP address), then the only real option is to configure interVLAN routing at the border leaf node. This will have a negative impact on link utilization, and therefore possibly application performance—application mobility often trumps these concerns.

Note   There are solutions, such as Cisco Dynamic Fabric Automation (DFA), which offer both Layer 2 switching and Layer 3 routing at the ToR. These technologies provide Layer 2 mobility throughout the data center while also providing optimal traffic flow using Layer 3 routing. These solutions are beyond the scope of this book, but the reader is encouraged to consider them as options in the long history of resolutions to the problem of deciding whether optimal traffic flow or a high degree of Layer 2 mobility is more desirable.

Software-Defined Networks as a Potential Solution

One potential solution to the trade-off between control plane scaling, Layer 2 VM mobility, and optimal traffic flow through the fabric is the Software-Defined Network (SDN). Although SDNs are covered in more detail in Chapter 17, "Software-Defined Networks," it's useful to spend a moment considering the positive and negative aspects of using an SDN in a data center environment.

An SDN such as OpenFlow allows the network operator to choose the correct forwarding information on a per flow basis. This means there need not be any separation on a VLAN level within a data center in order to enforce traffic separation between tenants. Instead, the controller would have a set of policies that only allow the traffic from within one "VLAN" to be forwarded to other devices within that same "VLAN" on a per source/destination (or flow) basis.

To forward traffic across an interVLAN boundary, the forwarding information programmed by OpenFlow would simply include a MAC header rewrite string that carries any specific packet from a source in one "VLAN" to a destination in another. For switching traffic within a "VLAN," OpenFlow simply programs the switches in the path of the flow to move the traffic from one port to another without any MAC header being rewritten.

Hence, traffic can either be switched within a flooding domain, or interVLAN routed between flooding domains, at any device in the fabric. This has huge advantages from a simplicity of management and design perspective.

At the same time, this also means that information must be kept in the forwarding tables of every device in the fabric for each and every flow that is currently active in the network. This is a formidable task, because flow states change much more rapidly than Layer 3 forwarding table changes, VM state change, or anything else in the network that the

control plane needs to keep track of. The first challenge for SDN-based solutions to the problems described here is scaling; vendors will need to build switches that rise to the challenge of managing tens or hundreds of thousands of flow.

SDN solutions must also find a way to carry broadcast discovery protocols throughout the network, as these SDN solutions are attempting to make a subset of hosts believe they are all connected to a single physical wire, with no intervening switches.

Network Virtualization in the Data Center

Network virtualization plays a large role in the design of data centers, especially data centers specifically designed for use in the cloud space. There is not enough space here to survey every virtualization solution proposed or deployed (such as VXLAN, nvGRE, MPLS, and many others); a general outline of why network virtualization is important will be considered in this section.

The primary point of these technologies is to move control plane state from the core of the network toward the edges. For instance, VXLAN allows Layer 2 broadcast domains to be built across a simple Layer 3 fabric. The spine switches, in this case, know only a handful of addresses (or maybe even one address) for each ToR, reducing the state carried in the IP routing control plane to an absolute minimum.

The first crucial question relating to these technologies and their use in the data center is what impact tunneling will have on visibility to quality of service and other traffic segregation mechanisms within the spine, or the data center core. Tunneling traffic edge-to-edge does offer a major reduction in the state held at the spine switches (and maybe even the ToR switches), but this could come at the cost of fine-grained control over the way in which packets are handled as they pass through the fabric.

The second crucial question is: where should these tunnels be terminated? If they are terminated in software running on compute resources within the data center itself (such as in a user VM space, or in the software control, or hypervisor, space), this can make for some rather exciting traffic flow patterns across the fabric, as traffic threads its way from VLAN to VLAN through various software tunnel end points and virtual routing devices. If, on the other hand, these tunnels terminate on either the ToR or some device in the border leaf node, traffic patterns can still be a concern, as well as the problem of maintaining and managing hardware designed to provide the necessary services.

No matter the answer to these questions, the control plane conundrums described here remain. Traffic must still be drawn into these tunnels, across interVLAN switch points, through the right services, and back out into the customer network.

Thoughts on Storage

Network designers don't like to spend a lot of time thinking about storage within the data center environment—"Isn't this a topic best left to experts in that field?" Radical changes are taking place in the storage space, however, that are likely to dump the problems of

connecting, managing, and transporting storage directly in the designer's lap. Two trends are worth noting here.

Unified fabrics are the first. Fibre Channel over Ethernet (FCoE), Network File System (NFS), and iSCSI are examples of mechanisms specifically designed to transport storage across a single fabric shared by user data, the control plane, and storage.

As its name implies, FCoE is designed to carry storage over an Ethernet network—but not just any Ethernet network will do. Every switch along the path of the data carried over FCoE must be able to understand and support FCoE switching. Zoning, or the ability to allow specific compute resources to access only specific blocks of storage data, is often a requirement in order to break up failure domains and provide security; some FCoE switches don't support zoning, throwing another monkey wrench into the idea of a unified fabric.

NFS and iSCSI, on the other hand, carry storage information directly in IP. The underlying IP network isn't necessarily aware—or rather doesn't need to be aware—of the type of traffic these specific IP packets are carrying. Storage packets are treated like any other IP traffic on the network. But treating storage traffic just like "any other traffic" might not be such a good thing. A process's access to storage can dramatically impact performance; jitter, delay, and reliability are major requirements when carrying any sort of storage traffic across a unified fabric.

The second major trend worth noting, from a network architecture perspective, is the potential collapse of Ethernet and IP directly into the interfaces of disc drives themselves. Old timers in the computer industry can probably still remember the "MFM versus RLL wars," where geeks took to ink and paper to argue over the relative merits of these two drive access technologies. One performed better, the other used platter space more efficiently. These wars lasted until the drive manufacturers moved the file access logic into the drives themselves, standardizing on what is essentially a networking standard to connect the drive directly to a wide array of computer buses.

The "MFM versus RLL wars" can be directly related to the FCoE, NFS, iSCSI, and Fibre Channel wars raging in the storage industry today. Some drive makers are already offering an Ethernet port directly on drives (with a standardized connector for general industry use). It may only be a matter of time before all storage is directly connected to the network, cutting out the controller that connects Ethernet, IP, and other standard networking protocols to the drive interface protocols.

Modularity and the Data Center

There are, in reality, two ways to approach modularity in data center design.

The first is to build each leaf (or pod, or "rack") as a complete unit. Each of these pods contains the storage, processing, and other services required to perform all the tasks related to one specific set of services. For instance, a single pod might be designed to provide Hadoop database processing and storage, or another to provide an entire human resources system, or perhaps a build environment for some application.

Using this style of modularity allows the network designer to interchange the different types of pod in a way that is fairly independent of other pods and services offered in the network. The fabric becomes a "black box" to which services are connected (or from which services are disconnected) as needed. This is a very flexible model for enterprises and other data center users whose needs change rapidly.

The second is to modularize based on the type of resources offered in specific pods. For instance, block storage pods, file storage pods, virtualized compute, and bare metal compute might be housed in different pods. This allows the network operator to upgrade one type of resource en masse, with little impact on the operation of any particular service running in the data center. This is more suited for organizations that can virtualize most of their services onto standard hardware and want to be able to manage the hardware life cycle separately from the software life cycle.

A mixture of these two options is possible, of course. A set of data protection pods might provide backup services for all the other pods, which are then organized according to the services running on them, rather than the type of resources they provide. Or a resource based modularization plan might be interrupted by the occasional service running on bare metal servers, rather than virtual servers. In these cases, it's important to understand what's connected to the fabric where, and what can be moved to optimize traffic levels versus what can't.

Summary

Data center design is the subject of much discussion, innovation, and change, driven by the need for changing functionality. Some of these innovations, such as SDN, may change the way we do networking in general. Although it would be impossible to define exactly which technologies and designs will be widely adopted, it is safe to say that data centers—and networks—of the future will look very different from just a few years ago. As you evaluate the developing technologies and designs, remember that you work at the intersection of business and technology. Keep in mind the fundamental concepts of letting your business requirements drive your technology choices, while understanding that your technology choices will drive your future business capabilities.

And remember the questions.

Asking the right questions will get you the information you need so that your network provides a foundation for business while transforming business and provides boundaries for information and people while still enabling collaboration. This is the key to fitting new—or old—technologies with your specific business problems, bringing you into the artistic world of network architecture.

Index

D

E

I

J-K-L

M

N

Q

S

W-X-Y-Z

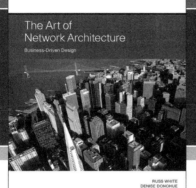

FREE
Online Edition

Your purchase of **The Art of Network Architecture** includes access to a free online edition for 45 days through the **Safari Books Online** subscription service. Nearly every Cisco Press book is available online through **Safari Books Online**, along with thousands of books and videos from publishers such as Addison-Wesley Professional, Exam Cram, IBM Press, O'Reilly Media, Prentice Hall, Que, Sams, and VMware Press.

Safari Books Online is a digital library providing searchable, on-demand access to thousands of technology, digital media, and professional development books and videos from leading publishers. With one monthly or yearly subscription price, you get unlimited access to learning tools and information on topics including mobile app and software development, tips and tricks on using your favorite gadgets, networking, project management, graphic design, and much more.

Activate your FREE Online Edition at
informit.com/safarifree

STEP 1:   Enter the coupon code: SPXQSZG.

STEP 2:   New Safari users, complete the brief registration form.
Safari subscribers, just log in.

If you have difficulty registering on Safari or accessing the online edition,
please e-mail customer-service@safaribooksonline.com